THE SMUGGLER'S PROMISE

RUFUS HYLTON

THE SMUGGLER'S PROMISE

First Edition, 2015
Published by Rufus Hylton

ISBN 978-1515024644

www.RufusHylton.com

This book is dedicated to Kaydden, who encouraged me to continue when I got weary of writing and wanted to quit, so he could finish reading the book.

And to my wife, Diana, who endured the whole process with love, support, and much patience.

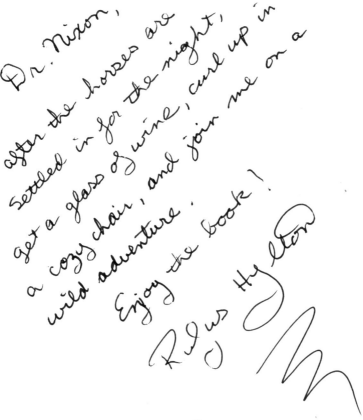

Dr. Nixon,

after the horses are settled in for the night, get a glass of wine, curl up in a cozy chair, and join me on a wild adventure.

Enjoy the book!

Rufus Hylton

LIST OF CHARACTERS

Ryan O'Dair ……….....……….…..…..……..…… Main Character
Angela Blackman …………......………… Colombian Boss Lady
Beth …………………………………………..……….. Judy's Sister
Bill Bell ……………………………………………… Charter Pilot
Billy …………………….....……..……… Ryan's Youngest Son
Bobby ………………….…..….…......… Bryan's Miami connection
Bridgett Hargrave ……… The Bahamas' Fuel Company Owner
Bryan Morgan ………......…...…..… Drug Dealer and Smuggler
Captain Ron White ……….....…..….……....…..……….… Pilot
Corey …………....……………..……….… Colombian Rancher
Danny ………....…….…..… Pilot and Daryl's Money Collector
Darius Lewis ……………………….…....…….....….. The Salty Dog
Daryl Kirby ……………………...…...………….…… Smuggler
Jason …..…………..………………....…... Beverage Truck Driver
Jeremy ……...…....….…......……… Bryan's Chicago Connection
Jimmy ……...…….…...…..…....…… One of Bryan's Workers
John Taylor ……………....….…… Bryan's Partner and Smuggler
Judy Foster …….………….…......…...…...…..……… Ryan's Wife
Keith …………………….....…..…….…..…... Ryan's Oldest Son
Marc ………………………....…... One of Bryan's Workers
Marcos Aguilara ...…......…………....…..……… Cuban Smuggler
Mauricio ……......……………….……..… Colombian Connection
Pepito ……………………...….…..….…… Colombian Orphan
Randy Parrish …………..….…...…..………….… Drug Dealer
Ray Foley ………………....…...…….……… Airplane Dealer
Renee Thompson …………....…...………..… Bryan's Wife
Sandi ………………………………...….……….…… Ryan's Sister
Santino …………………..…....…...…....…… Colombian Native
Scott Jones …………………....…..…...………….… DEA Agent
Stephen ……………………...…....…… Undercover DEA Informant
Striker …………………..…....….......…… One of Bryan's Workers
Tom Cleveland …....……………..…...… Great Inagua Contact
Vicente …………....………....…...…….....…… Colombian Attorney
Zeke …………....…..…......…..….… Drug Thief Working with DEA

iv

PREFACE

I ALWAYS SAID THAT IF MY story was ever published, it would have this disclaimer:

This story is based on true events but the names, dates, and places have been changed to protect the guilty.

However, I think that enough time has passed that the guilty would no longer be in any danger anyway. They have either died or have already been convicted.

There are a few instances in this story where I was not present to acquire firsthand knowledge of the events that took place. In those cases I recreated accounts of those events as they were told to me, or had to make some assumptions. In either case, I portrayed those events as I believe they must have happened.

I know what is true.

You, on the other hand, will have to decide what you want to believe.

Ryan O'Dair

CENTRAL AMERICA AND THE CARIBBEAN

PROLOGUE

Spring 1981 – Southern Colombia

THE PLAN WAS TO PICK UP 20,000 pounds of Colombian pot that was waiting for us on a grass airstrip by a river in the jungles of southern Colombia. We had departed from Great Inagua in a four-engine DC-6 that morning. There were three of us onboard: the pilot . . . Captain Ron White, a Colombian native . . . Santino, and me . . . Ryan O'Dair.

We searched up and down the jungle river but the torrential rain made it impossible to spot the airstrip from our altitude. The captain took the plane lower and lower so we could see better, but the rain and approaching darkness still cloaked the elusive airstrip.

Time was running out. We needed to land because the fuel gauges were on empty. Then, our situation became even more dire . . . the first engine quit!

Oh, God! We're out of fuel! I panicked.

Captain Ron quickly feathered the prop to cut down the drag but that didn't help because seconds later engine 2 sputtered to a stop, quickly followed by engines 3 and 4.

"Tighten your seat belts . . . we're going to crash!" the captain yelled as he pitched the nose down to keep our airspeed up and prevent the huge plane from stalling in the air and falling like a rock.

It became eerily quiet when only the wind noise replaced the powerful roar of the four 2,400 horsepower Pratt & Whitney R-2800-CB-17 engines.

"Don't hit the trees! Don't hit the trees!" I screamed, as if the captain had any choice. My eyes became as big as saucers as the ground raced up to meet us, and my life flashed before my eyes.

Leaves and branches thrashed the windshield as the plane sheared off the tops of several trees.

The impact into the river ripped the starboard wing off the plane and I watched it cartwheel through the air as the plane began sinking, nose first, into the dark water.

CHAPTER 1

Summer 1975 – Daryl & The Van

IT WAS A HOT AND HUMID day in the Florida Keys and the tropical breeze blowing across Summerland Key didn't do much to cool things off. Sweat dripped down Daryl's face as he worked on a car in the shop behind his house. He rented the house because it had a shop that was large enough for him to work on cars that he bought at the used car auctions up in Miami. He'd trailer them down to his shop, tune them up, do a little bodywork, give them a cheap paint job, and sell them on his used car lot in Key West. They weren't quality cars, and they wouldn't be very reliable, but they would run for a while, and they'd look good when he sold them.

His latest purchase had an engine knock and really needed an overhaul. But some STP should make the knock less noticeable . . . at least long enough to get it sold to some unsuspecting buyer.

As Daryl was pouring the thick oil into the engine, he heard a crash outside and the lights in his shop went out. The sound made him jump and he spilled the oil all over the engine.

"What was that?" he yelled as he ran outside to see what had happened.

A white van had run into the electric pole in front of his house and the transformer atop the pole was showering sparks onto the grass below.

"You idiot!" Daryl shouted at the Cuban that was coming out of the van on the driver's side. "Don't you know how to drive? You knocked the power out to my shop and caused me to spill oil all over my car. And those sparks are probably going to catch my yard on fire. I'm going to go turn the water on…you grab that hose and spray the grass so it doesn't catch fire."

The Cuban sprayed the grass quickly while he spoke rapidly

in Spanish.

"Speak English!" Daryl yelled. "I don't understand what you're saying."

"I'm in trouble," the Cuban said. "The cops are looking for this van and they'll probably be down this road any minute. I need to hide the van so they won't find it."

"I hope they do come . . . and arrest you for all the trouble you've caused me," Daryl yelled.

"No, man, no," the Cuban pleaded. "Look in the back of my van," he said as he opened the cargo doors. The van was loaded with boxes . . . and from the aroma coming from inside the van it was obvious that the boxes were full of pot. "If the cops find these bales, I will be in a lot of trouble. Can you help me?"

Being a used car salesman, Daryl could smell opportunity. "See if the van will start," he said quickly while looking down the road to see if anyone else had seen what happened. There was no one else in sight.

Steam was spewing out from under the hood of the van, but the Cuban jumped in and tried the key. "Nothing!" he yelled. "It's dead!"

"Quick," Daryl insisted, "let's push it into my driveway." Working together, they managed to push the van away from the pole and up the driveway. "Now let's push that car out of my shop and push the van inside to get it out of sight."

Just as they closed the shop doors, Daryl could see a cop car turn the corner down the street and head their way.

"Get in the shop and stay inside," Daryl told the Cuban. "I'll take care of the cop."

Daryl walked out to the road and stood by the damaged power pole while he waited for the cop. The cop car stopped and the officer got out of the cruiser.

"I'm looking for an old white Ford van," the cop said to Daryl. "Have you seen one come down this road?"

"Yeah, I did," Daryl answered. "It ran into this power pole and knocked out my electric. I came running outside but the driver took off before I could stop him. The last I saw of him he was turning left at the end of street. I don't know why you're looking for him but if you catch him, arrest him for hitting my power pole. By the way, can you get someone out here to fix this?"

"You'll have to call the power company yourself for that," the cop answered. "And, if you see that van around again, call the police department right away. The guy driving it is dangerous."

"Sure thing, officer," Daryl replied. "Hope you catch him." Daryl watched until he saw the cop turn left at the end of the street.

CHAPTER 2

The Cuban

MARCOS AGUILARA WAS NEVER ALONE. TODAY there were four other Cuban men with him in the posh residence in Key West. He was waiting for Miguel to arrive with the American.

One of the men was on the front porch sitting in a rocker with a magazine in his hands. To anyone who saw him, he looked like he was just another native of Cuban descent enjoying a beautiful day in the Keys. But he was keenly aware of his surroundings. The bulge of the .38 automatic tucked into his waistband was hidden by the tropical shirt he was wearing. He was the first line of defense for those inside the house.

There was another Cuban in the back yard by the pool. He was lying on a lounge chair. Wearing sunglasses and swimming shorts, he looked like he was working on his tan . . . and he was . . . but the weapon hidden under the towel within easy reach told of his primary purpose. He was there for protection.

Inside the house, Marcos was sitting in an overstuffed easy chair and was nursing a rum and coke. The two Cubans inside with him were those he trusted the most. They were always by his side . . . and they were always armed. Their only purpose in life was to keep Marcos safe.

A tap on the wall from the front porch was the signal that someone was coming.

It was Miguel. He had told Marcos of the accident with the van and how the American, Daryl Kirby, had helped him hide the van full of pot in his shop . . . and how Daryl had covered for him when the police officer had pulled up by the damaged power pole. Marcos had instructed Miguel to bring the American here so Marcos could meet him.

"Fix Mr. Kirby a drink," Marcos said to one of his henchmen, never taking his eyes off the American. "Miguel

4

tells me that you covered for him and protected my cargo from the police yesterday. Why did you do this?"

Daryl hoped he didn't appear as nervous as he felt. Obviously this Cuban was a man of importance and he wanted to impress him. "This is America and it was founded on free enterprise," Daryl answered. "It appeared to me that the police officer wanted to interfere with Miguel's right to do a little free enterprise and make a living. And, I would rather help the rightful owner of that pot sell it than for it to be confiscated by the police and let them sell or destroy it."

"How would you be able to help the rightful owner sell that pot?" Marcos asked.

"I am a businessman," Daryl said, "and I know a few people who sell a little pot from time to time but they can never get enough. They can only get 50 pounds or so at a time. If I had access to a steady supply, I could be their connection."

"I trust very few people," Marcos said. "I don't like people to know who I am or what I do. It's too dangerous. The cops want to bust you, and everyone else wants to steal from you. Is my merchandise still in your shop?"

"Yes," Daryl answered. "And I have someone guarding it to keep it safe for you."

"You appear to be someone I can trust," Marcos said. "If I gave you my permission to sell that pot to some of your connections, how long would it take you?" he asked. "Bear in mind, you would be permitted to sell only to one or two wholesalers…no street dealers."

"I think I could move that much pot in 3 weeks," Daryl replied.

"If you can't move that little bit of pot in a week's time," Marcos said, "then this is probably way out of your league. I think maybe I should just have Miguel go pick it up and I'll give you $5,000 for your trouble."

"Please don't do that," Daryl begged. "I know I could move the pot in a week, but I'd need a few weeks to pay you in full for it."

Marcos thought for a moment before he answered,

"Because of what you did yesterday, I am going to give you one chance at the opportunity of your lifetime . . . if you think you can do it. If you don't think you can do it, tell me now and we'll part ways. There were 15 bales of pot in that van, about 900 pounds. At $150 a pound wholesale, that's $135,000. I will give you one week to get it sold and get half the money back to me. The balance will be due one week after that. But, I want to know who you are dealing with."

"You want names?" Daryl asked. "These guys don't like to have their names passed around."

"Yes," Marcos answered, "I want their names. If I'm going to trust you with that much of my money, I want to know the names of who you are dealing with and I want to know where they live. I will hold you personally responsible for the entire debt even if they don't pay you. If you don't satisfy the debt in full, my men will pay you and your dealers a rather unpleasant visit. No one has ever *not* paid me in full. Do you understand what I am saying?"

"You are being crystal clear, and I understand completely," Daryl replied. "The two dealers I will work with are Bryan Morgan and Randy Parrish. Bryan lives just north of here on Big Pine Key, and Randy lives in Tallahassee."

"Very good, Daryl, I will see you here one week from today. Bring me $67,500 when you come. Do not be late and do not disappoint me. My men do not like to see me disappointed. I get angry and take it out on them."

"Thank you," Daryl said. "I'll see you in a week, and you won't be disappointed." He hoped he could pull this off. He also hoped that Marcos didn't see the small trickle of sweat that he could feel dripping down his face. "By the way, what is your name?"

"My name is Marcos Aguilara."

CHAPTER 3

It's Colombian

DARYL WASTED NO TIME. HE STOPPED at a pay phone on the way home and called Randy. Randy said he could leave for the keys in a few hours. Then, Daryl called Bryan. He told Bryan to meet him at his house within an hour.

When Bryan arrived, Daryl took him out to the shop to see the bales of pot that were still in the van. They spread some plastic on the floor and lifted one of the bales out of the van and set it on the plastic. Using a knife, Daryl slit open the box so they could see the contents.

"Wow!" Bryan said. "This looks like good stuff."

Bryan reached into his pocket and pulled out a pack of rolling papers. He peeled a paper out of the pack and with his other hand he took a healthy size pinch of pot out of the bale. After he sprinkled the pot into the rolling paper, he took the time to remove a few seeds from the joint. He used his thumbs and first two fingers to roll the paper around the pot starting in the middle and working out towards the ends. He licked the edge of the paper and rolled it between his fingers one more time to seal the joint. Then he placed the joint between his lips, flicked a Bic lighter to the end, and inhaled.

"Wow . . . this is awesome pot . . . and it's definitely Colombian," Bryan said, coughing as he passed the joint to Daryl. "This will be easy to get rid of. How did you get so much?"

"That's not important right now," Daryl answered. "The important thing is that it has to be moved quickly. How much can you sell right now?"

"I want to sell it all," Bryan answered, "but it'll take a few weeks."

"We don't have that long," Daryl said. "It has to be paid for in a week if we ever want to get more. I'm going to let you and

Randy sell it. He's on his way down here now. Get in touch with your connections and get them down here. Your price is $200 a pound. I can front you the pot but you have to pay for it within a week. Let's see what you can do."

Bryan knew that Daryl was going to have the same talk with Randy when he arrived. He didn't want Randy to get more of the pot than him. He stopped by the Winn Dixie to get a couple rolls of quarters after he left Daryl's house. He was going to need those quarters for the pay phone. He wouldn't make business calls like this from his house.

CHAPTER 4

The Coded Numbers

BRYAN'S FIRST CALL WAS TO CHICAGO. It was a very short call.

"Jeremy? It's Bryan. Go out to a pay phone and call me back at this number. I'll be waiting."

Then he made a quick call to Miami.

"Bobby? It's Bryan. Go out to a pay phone and call me back at this number. I'll wait here for your call so hurry."

Bryan had parked his car in front of the pay phone at the convenience store. He waited in the car for the phone to ring. It took 7 minutes.

"Bryan? It's Jeremy. What's up?"

"I've got some product for you." Bryan said. "It's from down south and it is high quality. It's more weight than you are used to doing, but this is the connection we have been waiting for. If you can move it quickly we may have an unlimited supply in the future. Send down a car with 2 drivers so they can drive straight through. Time is of the essence so they need to be on the road within a couple of hours. Then gather as much cash as you can today and catch a flight to Key West in the morning. After you check into a motel, call my house and ask for Jimmy. I'll tell you Jimmy isn't here and you'll ask me to give him a message to call Louie at a number for a pay phone near your motel. Add or subtract '5' to each digit in the pay phone's number. So if the number is 785-0649, you would tell me the number is 230-5194. Got it?"

"OK, I got it. I'll see what I can do and I'll call you when I get there in the morning," Jeremy said before he disconnected.

The call from Bobby came just a couple of minutes later.

"Hey, Bryan . . . it's Bobby. What's the urgency?"

"You need to get as much money as you can get your hands on in the next hour or so and get down here to see me tonight," Bryan said. "Come straight to my house. I'll be waiting on you. This is the opportunity we have been waiting for and time is of the essence. I'll explain everything when you get here."

"OK," Bobby said. "I'll see you in a few hours."

Now all Bryan could do was wait and hope Jeremy and Bobby could make it happen before Randy got the lion's share of Daryl's pot.

CHAPTER 5

The Ground Rules

RING . . . RING . . . RING . . .

Bryan didn't hear his house phone ringing. He was too deep in thought, How much cash would Jeremy and Bobby bring? When would their drivers arrive? How fast could they move the pot? Did Daryl really have a contact with an unlimited supply of marijuana? If he used his other contacts in Cleveland, Seattle, and Denver, how much would he be able to move every month?

Just thinking about the potential profits was staggering. Five wholesalers; each doing 1000 pounds a month; say 6 months a year; $50 a pound profit; that's a profit of $1.5 million a year!

RING . . . RING . . . RING . . .

The ringing finally jolted Bryan back to reality and he grabbed up the receiver. "Hello," he said.

"Can I speak to Jimmy?" the caller asked.

"Jimmy isn't here," Bryan responded.

"Can you give him a message to call Louie at 708-9468 when you see him?" the caller asked.

"Sure," Bryan said, as he wrote down the coded number. "I'll give him the message." He hung up and then deciphered the code. The number he needed to call was 253-4913.

* * *

It only took Bryan 3 minutes to walk to the pay phone in front of the bar on Big Pine Key. He dialed the pay phone number and Jeremy picked up on the second ring.

"Hello," Jeremy answered.

"It's me," Bryan said, "which motel are you checked into?"

"I'm at the Sunset Motel," Jeremy answered, "room 201."

"I'll meet you there within an hour," Bryan said before he hung up.

* * *

Jeremy had been getting pot from Bryan for more than a year, but only 20 to 50 pounds at a time. The price had been $275 to $300 a pound and it always had to be paid for up front. Jeremy was anxious to find out about the deal that Bryan seemed so excited about.

Bryan was in Jeremy's motel room in 30 minutes.

"How much cash did you bring with you?" Bryan asked.

"I was able to round up $15k," Jeremy answered.

"How much pot can you move in a couple of days," asked Bryan, "if your price is $250 a pound and you get a week to pay the balance?"

"I have never been able to get enough," Jeremy said. "My customers have to buy from a couple other suppliers to get enough to meet their demand. I usually give them a better deal so they prefer to buy from me but they won't front me the money in advance. That's why I have only been able to do a maximum of 50 pounds at a time. But if I could get pot at that price and get a week to pay for it, I think I could sell 500 pounds in a week's time."

"Ok. Here's the deal," Bryan said. "I'll take the $15k you brought today. When your drivers get here, call me at home and have Louie leave a message for Jimmy . . . just like you did before. When I call you back on the pay phone, I'll tell you where I'll meet your drivers. They will give me their car keys and I'll take their car to the stash house and load 4 bales in the trunk. I'll weigh the pot before I load it into their car. You can check the weight when they get to Chicago. These bales weigh about 60 pounds each. So, you'll be getting about 240 pounds. At $250 a pound, that's $60k. You gave me $15k today, so you will owe me $45k for this load. You'll need to catch a flight back to Chicago today and get your buyers lined up so they can pay you cash as soon as your drivers get the pot up there. Once your buyers see the pot, tell them there is more available but it will be gone quickly. Get the cash for this load and any extra you can gather up and then get on a flight back down here. There are only 15 bales available right now, and you are not the only buyer. It's first come, first served, so time is of the essence."

"Okay," Jeremy said, "that all sounds doable."

"Here are the ground rules for our business," Bryan continued. "We will talk business only on pay phones. And don't use the same one all the time. You will always meet me in a motel room like this to give me money. You and your drivers will never be allowed to go to the stash house. We will never have the money and the pot together. It's not illegal to be walking around with a briefcase full of money. If we get caught with the pot, we can only be charged with possession. But if we get caught with the pot and the money together, it's a whole other ball game. That would result in a charge of possession with intent to sell."

"I agree," Jeremy said. "It's better to be safe than sorry."

"This is our chance to make the big time," Bryan added, "so let's make it work. As soon as your drivers get up there, turn them around for another trip while you get some cash gathered up. You should be back down here in 2 days. Call me every day so I know that everything is going okay."

CHAPTER 6

The Pot Heads North

BOBBY GOT INTO THE KEYS THAT evening and drove directly to Bryan's house. He had brought $10,000 with him. Bryan offered Bobby the same deal he had given Jeremy. Bobby agreed and gave the money to Bryan. Bryan hid the money in the closet in his bedroom. Then Bryan took Bobby's car keys and told him to walk to the Pirate's Bar up by the road. He could wait in the bar while Bryan took his car to get it loaded.

Bobby had driven a Toyota and Bryan could only fit 3 bales in its trunk. Three bales; 180 pounds; $250 a pound; $45,000 worth of pot; $10,000 down; the balance of $35,000 due within a week.

Bobby had been nursing his draft beer for 30 minutes. He didn't want to get a buzz. He had a long way to drive. Bryan parked the Toyota in front of the bar and walked inside. He sat on a stool two stools down from Bobby and set the car keys on the bar. They never acknowledged each other.

Bryan ordered a draft, and got up and walked to the rest room. Bobby nonchalantly reached over and picked up the keys when no one was looking. When Bryan returned from the rest room, Bobby was already halfway across the Seven Mile Bridge heading north.

Jeremy's drivers got in early the next morning. Bryan told Jeremy to have them drive their car to a restaurant on Summerland Key and go in and have breakfast. Bryan would be waiting in the parking lot to get their keys before they went in. While they ate breakfast, Bryan took the Ford Galaxy they had brought to Daryl's shop and loaded 4 bales into the huge trunk. Then he returned to the restaurant parking lot and sat in his own car while he waited for the drivers to leave the restaurant. When Bryan saw them come outside, he walked by the Ford Galaxy and dropped the keys by the driver's door. He didn't acknowledge the drivers at all. If anyone had been looking, all they would have seen was some strangers walking past each other.

He continued to walk inside the restaurant where he would enjoy his own breakfast. The man who would take the first shift driving the Ford bent down and retrieved the keys by the driver-side door. Then he unlocked the doors and the two men got in. By the time Bryan was finishing his last cup of coffee, the Ford was already 20 miles north of the Seven Mile Bridge.

CHAPTER 7

The First Payment

JEREMY CAUGHT A LATE AFTERNOON FLIGHT to Key West two days later. He checked into the Sunset motel and called Bryan. Then he sat in his motel room and drank a cold Saint Pauli Girl while he waited for Bryan to arrive. Jeremy's customers had been pleased with the pot and he had cut them a deal so they would front him some of the money for the next delivery. Jeremy had promised them that the next load would be there in a couple of days. Jeremy had brought $60,000 with him to the Keys. It was hidden under a change of clothes in the small carry-on bag that he had brought. It was the only piece of luggage he had brought on this trip.

* * *

Jeremy's drivers had made it back to Chicago in 21 hours after leaving the Keys. They had been given 4 hours to rest before they were in the Ford Galaxy and on the way back to the Keys for their next load.

Daryl's other customer, Randy, had brought $15,000 with him to the Keys. He went to a pay phone in front of a bar in Marathon and called Daryl. Daryl drove his car to Marathon to meet Randy where they sat at a table in the back corner of the bar and ordered a pitcher of beer.

"I now have the connection we need to expand our enterprise," Daryl said, "so, get your customers ready. I have 240 pounds for you today. Its top quality Colombian and your price is $200 a pound. This is all I have for you right now, but I'll know if there is any more available in a day or two. How much do you think you can move on a regular basis?"

* * *

Like Bryan, Randy had never been able to get more than about 50 pounds at a time in the past. The price had always been about $250 a pound and it had to be paid for when he picked up the pot.

* * *

Randy paused for a moment and took a sip of his cold beer as he did some calculations in his head. At $200 a pound, he would be able to sell it for what he used to have to pay for it. This would allow him to supply the dealers that used to be his competitors.

"I can move a lot," Randy replied. "I'll be able to get rid of this within a couple of days and get the rest of your money back down here in 3 or 4 days."

"Make some calls to your customers from the pay phone outside while I go load your car," Daryl instructed. "Get things set up so you can move this load as soon as you get home. I need you back down here with the rest of the money in 2 days, 3 at the most. I need to impress my supplier with our ability to move large quantities and pay him quickly if we want to get access to more in the future."

Randy went through 2 rolls of quarters on the pay phone in front of the bar while Daryl was gone to load the car. It took him about 30 minutes to return with 4 bales of Colombian Marijuana in the trunk of Randy's car. Randy was back on the road within an hour of arriving in Marathon . . . and the supply of quality pot in Tallahassee was about to become more readily available.

* * *

When Jeremy's drivers got back to the Keys, Bryan again took their Ford Galaxy to get it loaded. He and Daryl weighed the remaining 4 bales and put them into the trunk. Bryan returned the car to the drivers and they were on the road heading back to Chicago less than an hour after they had arrived.

With the $75,000 that Jeremy had paid so far, the $10,000 from Bobby, and the $15,000 that Randy had brought, Daryl now had $100,000 to give Marcos tomorrow.

* * *

"Good job, Daryl," Marcos said when Daryl gave him the $100,000 in a brown paper grocery bag the next day. "This is more than I required of you in one week's time. You will have the balance next week?" he asked, as he looked into the blue eyes of the American.

"No," Daryl started. He paused, as he looked for a reaction in the dark brown eyes of the Cuban. Marcos didn't display any reaction. He just waited for Daryl to continue. "I don't need that long. You'll have the balance in 2 days."

"In that case, I think maybe we can do more business. I'm going to let you move some more of my merchandise," Marcos said. "Get a stash house set up somewhere between Key West and Marathon. Then let Miguel check it out. If he thinks it is OK, then I'll have him move some bales there. How long will it take you to move 5,000 pounds?"

"Until my customers get their dealers geared up," Daryl answered, "it may take a few weeks to move that amount."

"Ok," Marcos said. "Get them geared up. It looks like you have just graduated to the big time. But, until I see what you can really do, I am going to have one of my men stay with you. He will be protection for you and for my money. He will not leave your side until I have been paid in full for the 5,000 pounds. So the quicker you get me paid, the quicker you can get rid of your houseguest. Daryl, I expect you to protect my interests. If I am pleased with how you do, you can expect more responsibility in the future."

CHAPTER 8

The Cop Guards The Pot

DARYL DROVE DIRECTLY TO THE HOUSE of his long-time friend, Manny. He was a retired cop from Michigan who had bought a small house on Big Pine Key to live out his retirement years. There were not many houses on the northern part of the island where Manny lived, and none could be seen from Manny's house. Manny liked this place because it had a dock in the canal behind the house. The water in the canal was deep enough to accommodate a much larger boat, but Manny's boat was a used 15-foot runabout that he kept tied to his dock. This was all he could afford after paying for his house. His only income was his Social Security check and a small pension from his years on the police force.

The 40 horsepower motor on his boat was old but it was still reliable. Those Mercury outboards lasted forever. He used his boat to fish in the grass flats and around the mangrove islands that surrounded Big Pine Key. He dreamed of owning a larger boat someday. He wanted one that could travel the 100 miles one way from his dock to the Dry Tortugas where the dolphin and grouper were so abundant.

Manny quickly agreed when Daryl offered him $10,000 cash if he could use his house as a marijuana stash house for a week or so. Manny smiled when Daryl offered him an extra $5,000 if he would stay there and guard the pot. Manny could already envision that boat he wanted tied to his dock in the canal behind his house.

Miguel was impressed that Daryl had not only secured a perfect stash house, but that a retired cop would be there to guard the pot. It took Miguel 4 trips to deliver the 80 bales of pot in the panel work van that Daryl had given him off his used car lot. The van that Miguel had wrecked and left at Daryl's had now been repaired just enough so it could be driven to Miami. The Miami police finally had it towed away as an abandoned vehicle after it had sat there for a few weeks in front of some run down apartments in Little Havana.

Daryl met with Bryan and called Randy. He told both of them that they were guaranteed 20 bales each. The rest of the bales would be available on a first come, first served basis. Daryl didn't want an officer to have any reason to pull over one of the cars loaded with his pot. So he told Bryan and Randy to give their customers a few instructions.

All drivers were to bring cars with large trunks. Large trunks meant fewer trips. Cars were to have new tires. The rear shocks were to be replaced with air shocks so the cars could be leveled out after the pot was loaded. A car that was sagging in the back was a red flag to a seasoned officer that there was a lot of weight in the trunk. All the lights on the cars were to be checked to ensure they were working. The drivers were to take only a small gym bag with one change of clothes so there would not be a suitcase in the back seat on the way home. A suitcase in the back seat could make an officer wonder why it wasn't in the trunk.

All drivers were to follow all posted speed limits. Every driver had to have a valid license and couldn't drive if he had any outstanding warrants. Current registration and insurance papers were to be readily available inside each vehicle. There was to be no alcohol or empty containers in the car. A new, unopened air freshener had to be inside every car. The air freshener would be opened when the car was loaded to cover the smell of the pot in the trunk. In the event a driver did get pulled over for any reason, he was not to argue with the officer. Just be polite, apologize for any infraction, take any ticket graciously, and wish the officer a good day. This would greatly improve the chances that the officer would just give you a ticket and let you go on your way.

Bryan called Jeremy and Bobby. He also called Byron in Cleveland, Josh in Denver, and Joe in Seattle. Randy called his contacts in Memphis, Fairfax, Atlanta, Ithaca, and Knoxville. All their contacts were informed to get their drivers on the road and then gather as much cash as possible and head to the Keys.

Within hours there were a dozen cars on their way to the Keys from all over the country. In a few days people all around the country would be lighting up joints that would be rolled from pot that was now sitting in a remote house on the north side of Big Pine Key being guarded by a retired cop.

CHAPTER 9
Moving On Up

DARYL DECIDED TO MOVE OUT OF the Keys to Miami where there were a lot of places to spend his money. He had closed his used car lot in Key West months ago because he no longer needed the meager income it provided. Over the past year his income from his marijuana sales had continued to increase. Through Bryan and Randy, he had sold more than 100,000 pounds of Marcos's pot.

He vacated the house he had rented in the Keys and left behind almost everything inside. He wasn't going to need any of those things in his new home. He took only some pictures, a couple changes of clothes, and a few personal items. He paid cash for a 4,000 square foot beachfront home in Miami. His wife picked out all new furniture in the best designer stores in south Florida.

He still bought and sold used cars but they were no longer the old Chevys and Fords that used to fill his lot in Key West. Now he was only interested in collectible cars that were usually sold at auction houses like Mecum's in Kissimmee. He didn't think twice about paying $50,000 or more for a car that was just for show and would never be driven. The cars he bought were changed more often than some people changed their socks.

He rented an opulent office in downtown Miami where he would meet anyone he wanted to impress. He only went there occasionally because no real business was conducted there. With so little to do, his receptionist had the easiest job she had ever had. From the corner glass walls of his office on the 20th floor, Daryl could see the coast for miles in either direction. He enjoyed seeing how small the people looked way down there on the sidewalks…down there where he used to be.

Daryl hired a rather aggressive accountant named John

Taylor who specialized in setting up fake businesses. John was willing to bend the rules of financial accounting since Daryl was willing to pay him more money than he had ever made before. His primary job was to launder the money that Daryl was making.

All of the businesses John set up for Daryl were very profitable. But these businesses existed only on paper. Daryl's only real source of income was from the pot that he got from Marcos and sold to Bryan and Randy

Following John's advice, Daryl no longer went anywhere near the pot or the money before it was laundered. He tried to distance himself from any obvious illegal activities. Marcos's men delivered Daryl's pot to the stash houses that Bryan and Randy secured. Daryl had hired a long-time friend that he trusted to meet with Bryan and Randy to collect their payments.

Daryl's only involvement now was to manage the people that he hired to run his illegal marijuana operation. To the average person, Daryl looked like a very successful businessman. But his bravado was growing and that caused him to be a little too careless. He began to think he would never get caught. Throwing money around the way that Daryl did was sure to draw the attention of some of those 3-letter government agencies sooner or later.

CHAPTER 10

Spring 1977 – Perry

MY NAME IS RYAN O'DAIR. I was born thirty years ago in the hills of West Virginia . . . the son of a poor coal miner and the local high school's homecoming queen. Mom named me after my dad. When Dad held me for the first time, he knew he didn't want me to work in the mines like he had to do. So he moved us north to Akron, the rubber capital of the world, where the economy was booming and there were plenty of jobs.

I married my high school sweetheart, Jessie, the year after I graduated. Our first son, Keith, came along a couple of years later and I joined the Air Force when he was just two.

Join the Air Force and you'll get to see the world, I had been promised. After basic training in Texas and tech school in Mississippi, all I got to see of the world was the red clay of Georgia. Our second son, Billy, was born when I was half way through my 4-year enlistment.

Then trouble found us and we went through a divorce. Jessie got custody of Billy, and I got custody of Keith.

When I was discharged in the spring of 1977, I loaded my old 1962 VW van with all of our worldly possessions, got on I-75, and Keith and I headed south.

My parents had bought an old run down motel on route 27 in Perry, Florida last year. At one time, years ago, it had been profitable. But that was before the I-10 and I-75 interstate highways were opened. Now all the tourists used the interstates and only the Florida natives who wanted to avoid the traffic used route 27 anymore. But my parents didn't think of that when they bought the motel. I was going to help my dad work on his motel for the summer and decide what I was going to do next. I knew I wanted to go back to college. I just didn't know where.

Because I was honorably discharged, I qualified for unemployment benefits and would be getting $90 a week until I found I job. Since I was going to be helping Dad work on the motel, I wouldn't have to pay for rent or food. I figured I'd spend a few dollars a week on some necessities for Keith and me, but I planned on saving up most of that $90 every week.

There was an awful stench in the air that just kept getting worse as we got closer to Perry. I found out later that the smell was from the paper mill in Perry. The process of turning pine trees into paper requires some cooking and chemical processes that expel sulfur compounds into the air. The smell is sickly sweet, but it's hardly noticed by the locals. They get used to it, I guess. Or it smells like jobs to them, since that was the only industry around.

Dad was remodeling all of the motel's rooms and the diner out in front of the motel. The rooms were all getting a fresh coat of paint, new carpet, new air conditioners, new beds, and new televisions. The diner was getting repainted, new carpet, and new tables and chairs. Dad and Mom had sold their house, used all their savings, and went into debt to make this motel work. Dad knew how to do everything. He was a jack-of-all-trades. He was doing all the repairs and remodeling himself.

That summer, he taught me how to run electrical wiring, frame out rooms with 2 by 4's, hang sheetrock, and hook up sewer lines. He was good at plumbing too and taught me how to hook up water heaters, toilets and faucets, and even how to sweat copper water lines.

He said, "Being a plumber is easy. You only have to know 2 things. Sewage runs downhill and payday is on Friday."

I liked being around my dad. He always had a way of making things fun. We worked hard every day, and sometimes in the evenings, Dad and I would take Keith and go fishing for an hour or so.

Occasionally, in the evening, Mom would watch Keith for me and I would go into town to play pool and check out the local female population. I wasn't too impressed with most of the women I met in Perry. They just weren't what I was used to. They all wore jeans and cowboy boots. Most of them were brunettes although there were a few bleached blondes. Some had a missing tooth or two. They say you can tell which girls are new to Perry…they still have all their teeth.

CHAPTER 11

Judy

IN MAY, MY SISTER, SANDI, CAME to Perry to visit us and help out at the motel for a few weeks. When she opened her car door, a little fuzzy black and white puppy with bright blue eyes came scampering out. Keith and the puppy spotted each other at the same time and the puppy ran towards Keith with his tail wagging a hundred miles an hour. In minutes, Keith was lying on his back on the ground and he was giggling while Prince, as we named him later that day, was on top trying his best to lick Keith's face off.

"He's a Siberian Husky," Sandi Said, "and he's a present for you and Keith."

Our family had just been enlarged by one.

Sandi loved working with her hands. Something I guess we both inherited from Dad. So for the next few weeks, she helped paint, nail, dig, carry, and do whatever else Dad needed done. In the evenings, after working at the motel all day, Sandi and I would go into town to play some pool and drink some beer.

One night when we went to play pool at one of the local bars, I spied two girls at one of the pool tables. They both had long dark hair and blue eyes. These weren't your typical redneck Perry girls. These girls were gorgeous…and they had all their teeth. One was a little taller and thinner than the other one, but the shorter one looked more muscular. Naturally, I claimed the pool table next to them while Sandi went to the bar to get us a pitcher of beer.

I went to the cue rack and picked out a cue stick. I laid it on the pool table and then racked the balls. I pocketed the cube of blue cue stick chalk that was on the side of our pool table. Then I turned to the two girls at the next table.

"Excuse me," I said, "do you mind if I use your chalk?

27

There isn't any on our table."

"Sure, go ahead," one of them said. Then she bent over to take her shot. She hit the ball she was aiming at, but it didn't go into the pocket. I picked up the cube of chalk and applied some to the end of my stick.

Sandi returned with a pitcher of beer and two mugs. She poured us each a glass and then picked up a cue stick to break the balls I had racked. I turned back to the girls.

"Thanks," I said, as I replaced the chalk back on their pool table. "By the way, my name is Ryan, and this is my sister, Sandi."

I wanted them to know right away that Sandi wasn't my wife or my girlfriend.

"Hi, I'm Judy Foster," the taller one said, "and this is my sister, Beth."

Judy's hair was longer, darker, and straighter than her sister's. It was almost black with just a hint of auburn, and it came halfway down her back. Her sister's hair was brown and trimmed neatly at shoulder length. Sandi and I played a couple games and then I headed to the bar to get a refill on our pitcher while Sandi racked the balls.

When I returned, I noticed that the girls' pitcher was empty and they were nursing the little beer that was left in their glasses.

"You girls want to share our pitcher of beer?" I asked.

"Sure," Judy answered. "Why not?"

"How about a game of partners?" I asked. "My sister and I will play against your sister and you."

Judy looked at her sister who shrugged like that was okay with her. So I racked our balls and offered to let them break. During the next couple of games of eight ball, and another pitcher of beer, I found out that the shorter one, Beth, was on vacation and had come to Perry to visit Judy for a few days.

Before they left to go home, Judy asked if we knew of a place somewhere near Perry that she could take her sister swimming before she had to leave town. So, I told them about Waldo Springs.

"It's only about five miles out of town," I said, "and the water is crystal clear. We were planning on going there tomorrow," I lied. "Why don't you meet us there around noon? We'll bring food and beer. All you'll need is your swimsuits and some towels."

They agreed, and I told them how to get there.

The next day, Sandi, Keith, and I piled into my orange VW van and we headed to Waldo Springs. When we arrived, Judy and Beth were already there. They had already been in the water and their skin was wet and shiny from the water. They were both wearing bikinis that showed off their sexy bodies. This was turning out to be a nice day.

We swam, ate lunch, and drank some of the cold beer that I had brought in a cooler. Judy really took a liking to Keith. She paid a lot of attention to him and he really liked that. They splashed in the water and chased each other around. I think I was getting a little bit jealous. I wanted Judy to be chasing me around in the water. And, I was also a little jealous because Keith was paying all his attention to her.

I sat on the blanket and wondered how all this was going to turn out. I knew Beth was leaving the next morning, but Judy would still be in town after Beth left. So Judy was the one I wanted to get to know better. After a while, when she finally pried herself away from Keith, she sat down next to me on the blanket. I opened us both a cold beer, and she began to tell me her story.

She was 21. She had grown up in Orlando, but had ended up in Perry to escape from her overbearing father. When she was 16, her father had forced her to give up her own son for adoption the day he was born. That explained why she couldn't take her eyes off Keith. He was 5, the same age as her son.

She had taken a job as a waitress in Perry, but she hated her job. The manager at the restaurant where she was working was hitting on her and giving her a hard time because she didn't want to have anything to do with him. It became so bad that she had finally quit her job just a few days ago. She had been rooming with the head waitress, but since she had quit, she really wanted to find another place to live. She didn't know what she was going to do.

She finished her beer and headed back to the water to play with Keith. This gave me time to think about what was happening.

I think Judy fell in love with Keith that afternoon. Maybe she saw him as a replacement for the son she had been forced to give up for adoption. If she wanted to be around Keith, that was okay with me. That meant I came as part of the package. That sounded like a win-win situation all around. Keith needed a full time mother, Judy wanted a replacement son, and I was on the rebound.

CHAPTER 12

Skinny Dipping

WHEN WE WERE ALL PACKING UP our stuff to go home, I asked Judy if she would like to come and visit me and Keith after her sister left the next day. She said yes. And since she didn't have a car, she told me where I could pick her up the next afternoon.

Keith and I drove into town to pick up Judy the next day. Then we drove back to the motel so she could see where we were living and what we were doing to the motel and diner. I introduced her to Mom and Dad and then gave Judy the grand tour.

Dad almost had the diner ready to open. The black lady that used to be the cook at the diner when it was open several years ago stopped by one day and asked if Dad needed a cook. To prove her qualifications, she made us some collard greens, black-eyed peas, and cornbread. Man, could that lady cook. Her cornbread was even better than Dad's, and that's saying something. Her cornbread cinched it . . . and Dad hired her.

But he still needed a waitress for the diner. I asked him if he would hire Judy. I suggested that since she needed a job and a place to stay that part of her pay could be her room and board…and she already had experience as a waitress. Since most of the rooms were now completed, but sitting empty, this would be a very economical solution to his waitress problem. He talked it over with Mom and she agreed on one condition. Judy was to have her own room and if they ever caught either one of us in each other's room, they would fire Judy, and shoot me.

I told Judy about Dad's offer and she accepted. So now we had to go back into town to get Judy's things. Judy got her things and got settled into her room and went to work helping to get the diner ready for its opening day.

31

Judy and I were both busy working at the motel and diner during the day, and in the evenings, we would go for walks, or head to the springs for a swim, or explore the area in my 1962 orange VW van. I wanted some time with just Judy and me to get to know her better, but she always wanted Keith to join us.

One day, I thought I had Judy all to myself. Mom was going to watch Keith while Judy and I went swimming at the spring. We were halfway there when Keith appeared in the van. She had hidden him in the back under a blanket and told him to be quiet until she told him to come out of hiding. I was a little annoyed at first...but I was overjoyed at the same time. I wanted some time with her alone, but I was elated that she loved Keith so much that she had hidden him to bring him along. We were becoming inseparable . . . like the 3 musketeers.

One afternoon, Judy and I did get away alone. We were going snorkeling for scallops. She wore a bikini and I wore an old tattered pair of cut offs that I used for swimming. We packed a lunch and grabbed two towels and our snorkeling gear. My dad let me borrow his pickup truck to pull his 12 foot aluminum jon boat that had an old 10 horsepower motor on it. We drove to Keaton Beach on the Gulf of Mexico and found the boat ramp.

There were about 20 pickup trucks there with empty boat trailers, and a few people fishing off the beach. The empty boat trailers told me that this was a popular place to go boating. We put our lunch, towels, and gear in the boat and headed out. The water was clear and the sun was shining. It was in the middle of June and it was hot and sunny. It was a typical, beautiful Florida day.

You don't have to go out very far to get scallops because they are in shallow water. We got just out of sight of the boat ramp and headed south parallel to the beach. We found a secluded spot and anchored the boat in about 6 feet of water a couple hundred yards off shore. We started snorkeling around and there were scallops everywhere. In about an hour, we had our mesh bag full of scallops and we swam back to the boat.

We threw our bag of scallops into the boat and decided to go skinny-dipping.

I pulled off my cut-offs and dropped them under the boat. Judy took off her bikini and started to throw it into the boat.

"Don't do that," I said. "Drop it under the boat. That way, if another boat comes around, we won't have to climb back into the boat naked to get our suits. We can just swim down under the boat to retrieve them. Then we can put them on while we are still in the water."

"OK," she replied as she dropped her swimsuit and watched it slowly sink to the bottom.

It was like Christopher Atkins and Brooke Shields swimming in the movie Blue Lagoon...except that movie wouldn't come out until 1980. Judy would swim away from me, her long dark hair flowing behind her. I'd chase her until I caught her and then she'd turn around and wrap her arms around my neck while we treaded water. She'd pull me in close and we would sink into each other's eyes. Then our lips would meet. I could feel her tongue on mine. I felt like I was in heaven.

If you can mark one day as the day when you fell in love with someone, then this was the day we fell in love. But even this day would have to end. Even though we felt like we could stay there forever, we finally decided that it was time to head back to Perry. We swam under the boat to retrieve our swimming clothes. And then we both panicked. Our swimsuits were gone!

If we couldn't find them, all we had in the boat to cover ourselves were the two towels we had brought . . . and they weren't very big ones. It would take both towels just for Judy to cover up and that would leave me naked. Or If took one of the towels, Judy would be topless. This would not be a good way to end this day. We had to find our clothes.

We got our snorkeling gear out of the boat and started franticly searching under and around the boat. We realized the tide had probably drifted our clothes away. We didn't know which way the tide was going, so we had to search in ever widening circles around the boat. After about an hour, we finally found them about a hundred feet away from the boat lying on top of some seaweed in about eight feet of water.

That night, as we were all enjoying our scallops, Judy looked over at me and we started laughing. Everyone looked at us and wondered what we were laughing about. It was funny then, but it wasn't funny earlier when we thought we were going to have to load the boat at the boat ramp and drive home naked.

CHAPTER 13

Watermelons

ON ONE OF OUR AFTERNOON EXCURSIONS, Judy, Keith, and I found a field of watermelons that was being picked. I asked the farmer how much he wanted for a load of melons. He said he'd sell me 200 melons for 25 cents each. That was $50. That was a lot of money to me, but I figured we could put them in front of the motel and sell them for 50 cents and I'd double my money.

We went back to the motel to get dad's truck and a trailer, and returned to the watermelon field. After I paid the farmer, he had his workers load the trailer with the melons. Keith and Judy were helping me unload the melons back at the motel and we stacked them out by the road. Keith was carrying a melon much too big for him and he dropped it. I looked over at him and almost told him he couldn't help anymore.

I looked at the broken melon and then glanced over to Judy but she didn't say anything. She just looked back and waited to see what I was going to do. Keith was still standing there with his arms outstretched and he was looking up at me. He looked like he was about to cry. He knew he was probably in trouble. He was just trying to help. He was one of the 3 musketeers and we were not only the adults in his life, but also his best friends.

I couldn't break his heart. I picked up a smaller melon and handed it to him.

"Why don't you carry the little ones," I said, "and Judy can carry the medium ones, and I'll get the big ones."

Relief swelled over Keith's face and a smile broke out revealing the gap where he had lost one of his baby teeth. The sweat dripping off his blonde hair was running down his little face and his sunglasses were streaked with sweat and dust. He took the melon and carried it over to the ever-growing pile by the road.

We kept dropping the price on the watermelons because they just weren't selling. We couldn't even get cars to stop when we wrote 'FREE' on the sign in front of the melon pile. I figured if I could give them away, at least I wouldn't have to move them again to dispose of them when they started to rot. We finally sold enough melons to get about $25 of my $50 investment back. I think I ate more watermelons that week than I had eaten in my entire life.

CHAPTER 14

Key West

IN THE MIDDLE OF JULY I found a truck that I wanted to buy. I had been saving the $90 a week I was getting for unemployment and had enough money to pay for the truck if I traded in my van. I knew I wanted to leave Perry in time to attend college somewhere that fall, and I wanted a vehicle that would be more reliable. So I got rid of the van and bought a 1972 Dodge Ram pickup truck. It had an extended cab with fold up seats behind the front bench seat.

Then I found a used pressure washer that someone wanted to sell. I thought if I bought that, that I could use it to make a part-time living while going to school. The pressure washer cost me $200 and that about wiped out all the money I had saved, but I thought that was a good investment.

I told Judy that Keith and I were leaving Perry in August. I told her that I still wanted to go to college somewhere in the fall and I wanted her to come with us. She asked where I intended to go and I said I didn't know. I just wanted to go to a college where I could study electronics because that was what I had done in the Air Force and I liked it, and it would provide me with a marketable skill.

I asked her where she would like to go. She thought for a minute and then said she didn't care either as long as it was in Florida and as far away from Orlando and Perry as we could get. So we pulled out a Florida map and looked. The farthest place we could go from both of those places and still stay in Florida was Key West.

It took me a few days to find out that there was a college in the Keys. It's called Key West Jr. College, and they had a Marine Electronics program there. So, in the first week of August 1977, we loaded the Dodge pick-up truck with our clothes, the pressure washer, and a few toys for Keith and said

37

our goodbyes to Mom and Dad. As we were getting ready to pull out of the motel and head south, Judy asked if we could stop to see one of the waitresses she used to work with. She said we needed to get Mr. Pickles.

"Mr. Pickles?" I asked. "Who is that?"

"Mr. Pickles is my dog," she said. "He has been staying at my friend's house since I quit working at the restaurant in town and moved to the motel. I can't abandon him and leave him here. I promised him I'd get him before I left Perry."

So, we made a side trip back into town to get Mr. Pickles. He was a longhaired black and white Irish Setter. When he saw Judy, his tail started going about a hundred miles an hour. After he had time to lick Judy in the face, he and Prince had to do that butt-sniffing thing that dogs do. Everything must have checked out OK, because he then turned his attentions to Keith. In a minute, Keith was on the ground laughing and trying to fend off these 2 dogs that were intent on giving his face a good tongue bath.

We finally got the dogs loaded and headed south. Our entourage had grown and now included Judy, Keith, Prince, Mr. Pickles, and me.

CHAPTER 15

Paradise

WE GOT TO THE KEYS ABOUT 8 hours later in the afternoon. We were crossing the Seven Mile Bridge just south of Marathon and the view was breath taking. I didn't know water that color even existed. It was green and blue and clear as far as we could see. The sun was shining and sparkles of light glistened on top of the water. We could see the Atlantic Ocean on the left, and the Gulf of Mexico on the right. We were starting a new life, and we didn't have a care in the world. Here we were, the 3 musketeers, and 2 dogs, and this was our first day in paradise.

* * *

The Seven Mile Bridge has its own fascinating history. It's a skinny bridge…seven miles long, and just wide enough for 2 cars to barely pass each other. The guardrails on the side to keep you from plummeting over the edge really are rails. They are the rails from the original railroad that connected the Keys to the mainland.

Henry Flagler built the railroad in the early 1900s so his trains could take tourists all the way to Key West. It was called the Overseas Railroad. The bridges didn't have to be very wide. Only one train at a time would ever cross them. The Labor Day hurricane of 1935 destroyed the bridges and the federal government subsequently rebuilt the bridges and converted the railroad into an automobile highway . . . the Overseas Highway.

* * *

As we exited the Seven Mile Bridge on the south side and entered Big Pine Key, we were still in awe. We saw a little deer off the side of the road. It was so small it looked like a fawn. I found out later that it was a Key Deer and that's as big as they get. We saw little crabs scurrying across the road. I'd seen those before in pet shops. They're called hermit crabs…and here they were all over the place. Some were squashed in the road where cars had run over them. There were palm trees with coconuts on them, citrus trees with Key Limes growing on them, and many exotic looking flowers. We wondered what other wonderful things were in store for us in this new world.

After Big Pine Key, we crossed Summerland Key, Big Cudjoe, Sugarloaf, Baypoint, El Chico, Boca Chica, Stock Island, and finally crossed the last bridge as we entered into Key West. It didn't take very long to drive all around Key West. It's only 2 miles wide and 4 miles long. We found this little street called Duval Street in downtown Key West that had tourist shops all along both sides. We stopped at a shop that had a little parking lot out front.

Inside the shop were lots of interesting things I had never seen before. I picked up a swimsuit off the men's rack and stared at it. The label said they were Speedos. They were really tiny and looked like they wouldn't cover all of my man parts. I put them back.

Then I found these funny looking sandals called Kinos. The clerk in the shop said they were made right there in Key West. They cost more than ten times what I had paid for my flip-flops. I put them back too.

And there were tee shirts . . . hundreds of tee shirts. There were tee shirts with pictures of Ernest Hemingway, Sloppy Joes Bar, Jimmy Buffet, sail boats, palm trees, grouper, scuba divers, Mile Marker 0, and Key West printed on them. We looked in amazement but we couldn't afford to buy anything. After all, this was a tourist shop, and we weren't tourists. We were the Keys' newest residents. We just didn't have a house yet.

As we were pulling out of the parking lot, a bicycle coming down the sidewalk crossed the driveway right in front of us. The impact with the bumper sent him sprawling. I didn't see him coming. I couldn't help it. It wasn't my fault. I got distracted. On the other side of the street, I had spotted two guys coming down the sidewalk and they were holding hands! I had never seen that before.

Then I realized, *Oh my God, there are gays in paradise!*

We jumped out of the truck to check the cyclist. He said he wasn't hurt. I helped him up and we looked at his bike. The front rim was bent.

"I'm sorry," I said. "I didn't see you."

"I'm OK," he said, "but my bike needs a little TLC. If you'll pay for a new rim, I'm good."

Our first day in paradise could have been much worse. I pulled a $20 bill out of my wallet and gave it to him.

We watched the bent wheel wobble as he pushed his bike on down Duvall Street.

CHAPTER 16
Big Pine Key

WE ASKED AROUND UNTIL WE FOUND out where Key West Jr. College was located. It was just over that last bridge back onto Stock Island. So we headed back over the bridge and found the college. Now our next priority was to find a place to live. We found places for rent right in Key West but we couldn't afford any of those. So we kept making our way back up the keys searching for rentals on every one. The further we got from Key West, the cheaper the rentals were.

About 25 miles north of Key West we entered Big Pine Key. There wasn't much there. There was a bar right beside the road that had a sign saying they had cold beer and boiled shrimp. Boiled Shrimp? I thought the only way to eat shrimp was breaded and fried. There was some kind of warehouse next door to the bar. Behind the bar and warehouse was a trailer park filled with trailers that obviously had been there a long time. But all the trailers were on a canal . . . and that was definitely a plus.

We drove down through the trailer park and we found a "For Rent" sign on a little 8-foot wide by 24-foot long trailer. It looked really old and you could tell the trailer used to be white. It was kind of dirty white now . . . almost gray. There were palm trees in the yard. There were some coconuts hanging in the palms and a few were scattered around in the small yard. There was an old fence around the back yard. Yes, a place for Prince and Mr. Pickles!

As we were checking out the trailer, an old guy with white hair and a full beard walked over from the trailer next door. He kind of looked a little like Ernest Hemingway. It's funny how many of the old locals in the Keys looked like that. "I own that trailer," he said. "Can I help you?"

"Maybe," I replied. "We're looking for a place to rent. How

much are you asking for this place?"

"It's not quite ready to rent out yet," he said. "There's a hole in the kitchen floor and it doesn't have a refrigerator. By the way, I'm just an old Salty Dog named Darius Lewis."

"My name is Ryan and this is Judy and Keith. And this is Prince and Mr. Pickles," I said as I pointed to the dogs. "Can we see the trailer anyway? I'm kind of handy and I could fix the floor. And I've got a pressure washer and I could pressure wash the exterior and make it look new again."

He looked at the pressure washer and then said, "Sure, I guess so." He fished in his pocket and came out with a set of keys. He found the one he was looking for and led us into the trailer.

The hole in the kitchen floor was about a foot across. It looked like it had gotten wet, probably from a roof leak, and the wood had rotted. Someone probably stepped there and their foot went through the floor making the hole. The rest of the trailer was old and in pretty neglected shape but at least it was livable. The backyard was small. It was only about 10 feet from the trailer to the canal. There was a small dock in the canal. As we stepped on the dock, we could see fish swimming around in the clear water.

"Mangrove snapper," Darius said. "There are some other fish that come up in here, like an occasional barracuda, but mostly it's just mangrove snappers in here. They're small, but they are good to eat."

I told Darius that I recently got discharged from the Air Force and was collecting unemployment. I was planning to attend the junior college on Stock Island, and we needed a place to live. I told Darius that I'd repair the floor if he would provide the wood, and that we'd make do without a refrigerator until he could get us one. And I'd pressure wash this trailer and his for free if he'd rent the trailer to us.

He thought for a minute and then said, "OK . . . if you'll fix the floor, and pressure wash both trailers, I'll rent it to you for $65 a month. But you'll have to give me a month's rent in advance, and a month's rent for the deposit."

"It's a deal," I replied and shook his hand to seal the deal.

This was less than half of the next cheapest place we had found. I figured we could afford $65 a month. Dad had given me $500 when we left Perry for the work I had done over the summer. I gave Darius $130, and we had a place to live. We'd have to spend our remaining money carefully, until I could make some money pressure washing to augment the $90 a week I got from unemployment.

I got the hole in the floor fixed in the next couple of days. But we still didn't have a refrigerator. We didn't have much money so we had brown beans and fried potatoes every night for dinner.

After a couple of days, when we got settled in, we found out where the local elementary school was and got Keith registered for kindergarten. Then I went to the junior college and registered for the fall semester. They offered classes in the evenings, which was perfect. I'd be able to pressure-wash houses during the day and attend classes in the evenings. The counselor at the college said that because of the electronics training I had received in the Air Force and the college classes I had taken while on active duty, I could get my AA degree by next June.

Judy was fitting into her new role as a mom and homemaker and did her best to fix us dinner every day. We were getting a little tired of beans and potatoes, but occasionally I'd manage to catch one of those mangrove snappers off the dock and we'd have fish to go with our beans and potatoes that night.

All in all, this was not a bad first week in the Keys. We now had a home in paradise and Keith and I were both registered to start school. It just couldn't get any better than this I thought, unless my younger son, Billy, was also with us. I missed him so much.

CHAPTER 17

Working Man

I STARTED KNOCKING ON DOORS AT houses, mobile homes, and businesses trying to get some pressure washing work. Most people asked me if I furnished my own water when I pressure washed. "No," I said. "I'll just hook up your garden hose to my pressure washer."

That usually turned them off. As it turned out, the fresh water in the Keys is piped there from the mainland. The water pipes are buried underground until they come to a bridge. Then the pipes are attached to the sides of the bridge where you can see them. Then they disappear underground again on the other side of the bridge. That makes fresh water very expensive in the Keys. It would cost them as much for the water to wash their house as I would charge to wash it. Boy, I wish I had known that before I spent $200 on that pressure washer. So much for that plan. I decided that I'd have to find a regular job.

The next day, I left Keith with Judy and went to Key West to go job hunting. I saw some construction work going on at a 2-story bank building. I parked the truck and found the job supervisor. He said his company had the contract to stucco the side of the bank and he could use one more guy.

There were some guys on the ground mixing up the concrete stucco in a big mixer. When it was ready, it got pumped up through a 4-inch rubber hose. A big heavy construction worker was up on the scaffolding and he was holding the other end of that 4-inch hose. The concrete mixture was coming out of the hose and he was spraying it on the building. He looked to be at least 6 foot tall and about 250 pounds of pure muscle. There were a couple guys following him and they were using trowels to smooth the wet stucco.

The boss said the guy spraying the stucco was named Mark

and he needed a laborer to pull that 4-inch rubber hose around so Mark could concentrate on spraying the stucco. He said the job paid $125 a week but I would have to start tomorrow if I wanted the job. I told him I'd be there in the morning.

To celebrate getting a job, I took Judy shopping for some groceries so we could eat something other than beans and potatoes. I mean, that's my favorite meal, but it gets tiresome if you have to eat them every day. We splurged on some broccoli, a box of pancake mix, a bottle of syrup, and one stick of butter. We couldn't buy a whole carton of butter because we didn't have a refrigerator in which to store it, and it would melt in no time in this heat. Judy was a little apprehensive about us spending some of our limited funds on broccoli. She had never eaten broccoli before, but I was craving some vegetables.

The next day I showed up for work at the construction site in Key West. I climbed up on the scaffolding and Mark put me to work pulling that hose for him. The hose was full of concrete and it weighed hundreds of pounds. I was supposed to drag it around on this scaffolding and keep up with Mark.

I never sweated so much in my life. By lunchtime on the first day, I thought I was going to die. I was sore and exhausted and much too tired to eat. I used my 30-minute lunch break just to lie down and rest. Then it started all over again. Mark was constantly swearing at me to keep up with him. I was trying my best, but the hose kept falling through the gaps in the boards that were on the scaffolding. Then Mark would have to help me hoist it back up onto the boardwalk and he'd start swearing again.

When I got home that evening, Judy had fixed our normal beans and potatoes but this time she had a surprise. She had fixed broccoli too. What a treat. I was looking forward to that. She made me sit at the table while she fixed our plates and brought them over. I looked down at my plate and next to my potatoes and beans was a pile of broccoli stalks.

"Where are the broccoli tops?" I asked.

"What do you mean 'the tops'?" she asked, with a puzzled look on her face. "Are you talking about that fuzzy stuff at the top of the broccoli?"

"Yes," I answered. "That's the best part. Can't I have some of that fuzzy stuff?"

"I didn't know you were supposed to eat that," she said. "I cut the tops off and threw them in the canal."

"What? I can't believe this," I said. "You were a waitress. Didn't you ever notice what broccoli looked like when you served it to your customers?"

That started a flow of tears. She was trying her best to be a mom and a homemaker and I had just shattered her pride over some ruined broccoli.

"It's OK," I said, putting my arms around her. "I'm sorry. I didn't mean to hurt your feelings."

When the sobbing subsided, I sat back down.

"Yum," I said, as I forked a broccoli stalk into my mouth. "These are the best broccoli stalks I ever ate."

At the end of the week, the construction boss paid me in cash. I told him this was really hard work for $125 a week and that I should have just stayed on unemployment. After paying for gas to drive to work, I was making less money than when I was collecting unemployment.

"What do you mean 'when' you were collecting unemployment?" he asked. "This is only a temporary job that'll be over in a couple of weeks. That's why I'm paying you in cash. This is an under-the-table job. You never should have reported this job to unemployment. Now they'll come after me for not paying unemployment taxes."

Great, I thought. *I'm killing myself on this job and I'm not even going to be clearing as much as I was getting in unemployment, and it's only a temporary job . . . so much for trying to be a productive member of society and actually working for a living.*

I had started my classes at the junior college and they were going well. I was tired when I went to class those first couple of weeks after working all day at the construction job. I was glad when the job was over. At least I could start collecting unemployment again.

CHAPTER 18

School Starts

JUDY AND I WALKED KEITH TO his bus stop every day for the first week that he started kindergarten. The first day at the bus stop, there was another boy Keith's age that was also starting kindergarten. He had blonde hair like Keith and freckles showed through his suntanned face. His name was Eric. His parents had walked him to the bus stop as well. Keith and Eric became best friends the first day they met and were inseparable after that.

Every day after school, Keith and Eric went swimming in the canal behind our house. Eric was a good swimmer and it didn't take long before Keith was swimming like a fish as well. Keith and Eric were always together either at our house or at his.

Eric's parents were Bryan Morgan and Renee Thompson. Renee seemed kind of laid back like a lot of people in the Keys are. She was a stay-at-home mom just like Judy, so they hit it off well. But Bryan and I didn't seem to have much in common. He said he was in the construction business, but he looked like a pirate. He had long curly brown hair with just a few stands of grey here and there and he had a full, neatly trimmed beard. Whenever we had to go to Eric's to get Keith to come home, Bryan was either not there or he was in a hurry to go somewhere. I saw him using the pay phone a lot outside the bar in front of the trailer park. I wondered who he had to call all the time.

Renee asked me what I did for a living and I told her that I was going to school in the evenings and collecting unemployment. But I was looking for a job. She suggested that I check the beer and soda distributor that was located in the warehouse in front of the trailer park. I didn't know that was what was in that warehouse. But that got me to thinking. If I could get a job there, I could walk to work in 5 minutes. I decided to check it out first thing Monday morning.

That evening after we got Keith to sleep, Judy and I walked up to the bar by the road. They had a soda machine outside by the pay phone and sodas were 35 cents. We still didn't have a refrigerator, and we had made a habit of walking up there every evening to get a cold soda. It was the only time each day that we had something cold to drink. We could only afford to buy one. So we'd buy just one and we'd split it as we walked back to our trailer. The reason we waited until Keith was asleep was so we didn't have to split it 3 ways. Poor little guy. At least he didn't know what he was missing.

CHAPTER 19

Pancakes

THE NEXT DAY WAS SATURDAY. JUDY was going to make us pancakes for breakfast that morning and then we were going exploring. There were lots of little roads off US 1 that ran back into some of the keys and we were going to see what was down those roads. This was going to be a fun day.

I was drinking some coffee out by the canal while Judy was fixing breakfast. She was taking a long time, and then I heard her crying. I came in to see what was wrong. She was at the stove and tears were running down her face.

"What's wrong?" I asked. "Are you OK? Did you burn yourself?"

"No," she whimpered. "It's just that I am trying hard to make you and Keith a nice breakfast, and the pancake batter won't stay together. When I pour it into the pan, it just all separates into little balls all over the pan."

When I looked into the skillet, it was all I could do to not break out laughing. She had about an inch of oil in the pan and as soon as the batter hit that hot oil, it did just like she said. It just broke up into little balls of batter. It looked like a hundred little fried BBs floating all over that oil, and they were all burned to a crisp.

"Judy, is this the first time you ever made pancakes?" I asked with a smile on my face.

"Yes," she said, "and it's a disaster. Why is this so hard?"

"It's OK," I said, trying to comfort her. "Here, let's pour out this oil and start over. You only need just enough oil to make the bottom of the skillet shiny. Then the pancake batter will stick together and they'll come out just fine."

That didn't help matters. She burst out in tears again. I guess that's just like a guy. Always coming up with a solution when what they really want is some sympathy. After she cried a little more, she wiped away her tears and tried it again . . . my way.

The pancakes were a little burned on the outside and a little doughy on the inside, but we ate them and I told her how good they were. But all the while I was thinking, *Oh my God, we're going to starve. She doesn't know how to cook.*

CHAPTER 20

An Awesome Day

AFTER WE ATE, WE PUT OUR snorkeling gear and my spear gun in the truck. I had used a credit card to buy a spear gun from a local dive shop. I thought that I would be able to get more fish in the canal with it than I could catch off the dock with my fishing rod. That plan didn't work too well because the fish just didn't cooperate. The closer I got to them the farther away they swam. They always seemed to be just out of reach.

We drove down US 1 and explored the little roads that went off into the islands. On one of the side roads we came upon a canal that was very straight and looked deep. It looked like a very likely spot for some fish and I was eager to prove my prowess as a spear fisherman. I put on my snorkeling gear, grabbed my spear gun and jumped in. The water was deep and murky. When I looked down I couldn't see the bottom of the canal. That didn't make me feel very safe. I would have felt a lot better if I could see what was lurking down below me. I wished I had never watched that movie, Jaws. Now, all I could think about was that shark coming up out of that murky water and pulling me down as I thrashed around in a pool of blood.

I quickly got out before Judy and Keith had a chance to get in the water. To preserve my manhood, I said, "The current is really swift in this channel and Keith won't be able to swim here. Let's go find another place."

We found another little road that ended up at a pit that was filled with water. The pit was not connected to any other water source so I knew Jaws couldn't be here.

"This looks great," I declared. "Let's swim here for a while."

We stretched out a blanket and Judy lay down to work on her tan while Keith and I snorkeled in the pit. Amazingly, the water in the pit wasn't salty like the ocean. It had just a slight salty taste to it. It must get filled up from the rain and ocean water must invade it through the soil making it just a little salty. After a while, Keith and I joined Judy on the blanket.

That's when the jeep pulled up.

Four girls jumped out of the jeep. They all looked like they were in their twenties and they were all wearing shorts and tee shirts. As soon as they got out of the jeep, they stripped all their clothes off and jumped into the pit. They were going skinny dipping!

When they climbed out of the water, they were all laughing and sounded like they were having a good time. Then three of them lined up facing the fourth one and they started doing exercises! They did stretches and bends, and then they started doing jumping jacks. The jumping jacks were the real show. Every time they jumped, there were 8 breasts that were bouncing up and down as well. It was hard not to stare. Keith's eyes were as big as saucers.

Judy was trying to ignore the girls, but I think she got annoyed with Keith and me looking like bobble-heads as we followed those 8 breasts up and down.

"Let's see if we can find a little beach," she suggested, "where we can look for some shells."

I was perfectly content to lie on our blanket and let these girls do their thing. They weren't bothering me a bit, and Keith didn't seem to mind either. I really wanted to stay a little longer, but I thought it would be smarter just to agree.

"Ah . . . ah . . . OK," I finally stuttered.

I was trying hard not to show my reluctance to leaving this lovely little swimming hole we had discovered, but I think the whimper in my voice was betraying me.

We loaded our stuff back into the truck and with one last look, just to make sure the girls were okay, I got into the truck and we left. Judy was looking straight ahead. I glanced in the rear view mirror and saw that Keith's face was plastered to the rear window. Then we rounded a curve and the cozy little swimming hole disappeared from our view.

We found a little canal where the water was clear and not very deep. Jaws couldn't possibly be in there. Judy looked for shells while Keith and I snorkeled in the crystal clear water. There were lobsters everywhere and I was able to catch four of them by grabbing their antennas and pulling them out from under the rocks.

We were having an awesome day in paradise. How could life possibly be any better than this?

CHAPTER 21

Lobsters On The Grill

WHEN WE GOT BACK TO THE trailer, Darius was outside tending to some pots of flowers.

"Hey, Darius," I said. "Look what we got." I opened the cooler and proudly showed off the 4 little lobsters I had caught.

"Better be careful," he said, peering into the cooler. "Those are shorts. You don't want to be caught with them."

"What are shorts?" I asked.

"Lobsters have to be a certain size to be legal," he explained. "The ones that are too little to keep are called shorts and you have to throw them back."

"You mean I have to throw these back into the water?"

"Not now," Darius said. "You're home. And I don't think it'd do them any good since they're dead. You're just lucky you didn't get caught. You know how to cook them?"

"Aren't you supposed to boil them?"

"Only if you don't know how to fix them the right way," he said with a twinkle in his eye. "Let me fire up my charcoal grill and I'll show you how."

Darius got his grill going and while the coals were getting ready, he picked up the first lobster. He put one hand around the lobster's head and his other around its tail. With a twist of his wrists, he had the head and tail separated. Then he took a knife and slit the lobster tail open from the top without cutting through the bottom of the shell. He butterflied it open and removed a black vein that ran through the tail.

"That's the gut," he said. "It's full of poop. Just pull it out and throw it away. The heads you can throw in the canal and the fish will take care of them. Now you try one."

I cleaned the other 3 lobsters while Darius went back into his trailer. He wanted to show me something he said. While I

55

was waiting for Darius, I heard a plane coming towards me from the direction of the road and it was getting louder. I looked up to see if I could spot it and all of the sudden, there it was. It was just above the treetops and smoke was pouring out the back of the plane. It was heading straight down the road and it looked like it was going to crash right where I was standing.

"Oh my God!" I screamed. "It's going to crash!"

I took off running across the road so I wouldn't be in its path. As I got across the road, the plane zoomed right past me and the smoke was settling to the ground like a fog. It had a funny smell to it. I ran back into the center of the road so I could keep the plane in sight. I didn't want it to crash, but if it did, I didn't want to miss it. It looked like it was still high enough that it was going to make it as far as the water before it crashed.

Darius came running back outside.

"What's happening?" he asked. "I heard you yelling."

"That plane's on fire," I said, pointing up at the plane. "It's going to crash!"

As we watched, the plane banked right, started climbing, and the smoke quit coming out of its tail.

Darius grabbed his belly and bent over laughing. He was laughing so hard that tears were coming out of his eyes.

"That plane's not crashing," he said. That's the mosquito plane. They fly it all over the Keys. And that wasn't smoke coming out of the plane…it's an insecticide to help control the mosquitos. They fly it that low on purpose so the insecticide will settle to the ground where they want it."

When he finally stopped laughing, he held out his hand to show me a big seashell he was holding. There was something that looked like a big snail hanging out of the shell.

"This is what I wanted to show you. It's a conch," he explained. "If you put them in the freezer for a little while, the conch tries to climb out of his shell. That's what this thing is hanging out. Most people make conch fritters or conch soup out of them, but the best way to eat them is to eat them raw, right out of the shell."

He took the knife we had used to butterfly the lobster tails, and sliced off a piece of the conch and extended his hand for me to take it.

"Try it," he said. "It's good."

"You want me to eat a piece of raw conch?" I asked, as I eyeballed the piece in his hand. I didn't reach out to take it. I just kept my arms pinned to my sides. "I don't think so. It doesn't look very appetizing."

I thought he was playing a trick on me.

"You try it first," I suggested.

Darius popped the piece into his mouth and started chewing. He didn't gag or anything. In fact, he looked like he was enjoying it. He cut off another piece and handed it to me. This time, I took it out of his hand, and stared at it.

"Now you try it," he said.

I slowly took a little bite of the small piece he had given me. To my surprise, it was very sweet and tender.

"Cooking them makes them tough," he explained. "They're good like this. You can eat them just like this or cut them up into bite size pieces and put them in a salad. Since I haven't been able to find you a used refrigerator yet, if you find any when you're snorkeling around, just bring them back and I'll put them in my freezer for you."

The coals were now glowing red on the grill. Darius put the four lobster tails on the grill. He put some butter on them and reached in his pocket and pulled out what looked like a small lemon. It was mostly yellow but had a tint of green to it.

"This is a key lime," he said. "I have a friend with a tree and he keeps me supplied."

He cut open the key lime and squeezed the juice onto the lobster tails.

"You just want to cook them until they turn opaque," he said.

I looked at the lobster tails. The tails looked like raw shrimp when we put them on the grill a few minutes ago. But now, the meat was kind of white.

"If you leave them on too long," he said, "they get tough. They look like they're done. Go enjoy your lobsters."

"Darius," I said, "there's only 3 of us and we have 4 tails. Why don't you take one for your own dinner?"

"Thanks," he said. "I will." He picked out the smallest tail and went back into his trailer.

I put the other 3 on a plate and took them inside. Judy had fried up some potatoes and we sat down to eat our first lobster dinner in the Keys. I had tried a lobster once before in some restaurant up north. It was tough and chewy and I couldn't understand why anyone would pay so much for something that tasted so bad. But these lobsters were different. They were tender and juicy and they just melted in your mouth. Even Judy and Keith liked them. Man, I couldn't wait to catch some more of these.

CHAPTER 22

The Accident

ON MONDAY MORNING AT 7:00 AM sharp, I walked into the warehouse up by the road. Inside there were cases of soda and beer stacked all around the outside walls. There was a delivery truck in the middle of the warehouse and a man was loading cases into the truck.

"Hey," I said. "I'm looking for a job. Are you guys hiring?"

The man loading the truck put down a case of soda and turned towards me. He had long shaggy blonde hair and a scraggly beard. His nose was long and prominent. He looked French to me.

"Maybe," he said. "I'm Jason. What's your name?"

I extended my arm to shake his hand. "Ryan," I answered.

"We need another delivery man. Come on, I'll take you into the office to meet the owner."

He walked towards a small office in the corner and I followed. He opened the door and we walked in.

"Hey, Jack " he said. "This is Ryan and he's looking for a job."

Jack shook my hand and after a quick interview told me I could start to work the next day.

"Jason will train you," he said. "Right now we only have one delivery truck, but we're getting another in a week or so and then you and Jason can split the route. One of you will take Key West north to Marathon, and the other will take Marathon to Key Largo. Be here tomorrow at 6:30 to help load the truck."

The next morning I helped Jason get the truck loaded. He had a sheet that listed what each store was getting so he would know how much of each product to load. In addition to all the soda we loaded, there were about 20 kinds of imported beers.

"After we get all the stuff loaded that we know we need,"

Jason said, "we'll throw on some extra just in case."

Jason got into the driver's seat and I climbed into the passenger seat. He pulled the truck out of the warehouse and turned south on US 1. The first stop was only a couple of miles up the road at a small independent convenience store. Jason got a dolly off the truck and looked at his delivery sheet to see what he needed to load. The inventory was stored in different bays on the truck and each bay had a roll-up door.

We loaded several cases of soda and beer onto the dolly.

"Always close the bay doors before you go inside," he said as he headed for the screen door in the back of the store. "Otherwise people will steal cases off the truck. Bring the dolly and follow me."

He showed the owner what we brought in and then we unloaded the dolly into the walk-in cooler. Then we checked the shelves inside the store. Jason straightened up the soda on the shelves and wiped dust off the inventory with a rag.

"Always straighten up our display and dust it off," he explained. "It makes the owner happy and the stuff sells better if it isn't dusty. Looks like they could use about 6 more cases of cola. Take the dolly and go get them off the truck. Be sure to show the owner what you brought in before you unload the dolly."

I took the dolly and went back out the screen door to the truck. I opened the bay door and peered inside. The cola wasn't in this bay, so I closed the roll-up door and opened another. Here it was. I reached in and grabbed a case of soda and put it on the dolly. As I was bent over reaching into the back of the bay for another case, I thought I heard another bay door opening. I thought Jason had come back outside to get something else on the other side of the truck.

Then the bay door above me hit me across the back and pinned me. The sound I had heard wasn't Jason opening another bay door; it was the door on my bay falling shut. I couldn't get the door off my back and I started yelling for help. Jason heard me from inside the store and came running outside.

"Hold on, I'll help," he said, as he raised it off of me. "I told Jack he needed to get this door fixed before someone got hurt. See those spring mechanisms at the top of the bay on each side of the door?" He asked as he pointed up. "They are supposed to keep the door in any position you leave it so it won't open or close by itself. The springs in this bay are broken so the door won't stay open like it's supposed to. You have to be careful of this door."

Now you tell me, I thought.

My back was killing me. I tried not to let Jason see the tears forming in my eyes.

"I'll take these in," he said. "Wait for me in the truck."

I climbed back into the passenger seat. The pain in my back was excruciating. By the time Jason finished and climbed into the driver's seat, there was a knot the size of a golf ball on the lower part of my back where the door had hit me.

When we finished the route and got back to the warehouse, Jason told Jack what happened to me.

"Are you OK?" Jack asked me.

I'm sure he was thinking about what this could do to his worker's comp insurance premiums.

"I guess so. My back hurts but I should be OK," I replied.

I didn't want to take the chance of losing this job on my first day. We needed the money and I would just have to suck it up and endure the pain. That night, the pain was so bad, I cried myself to sleep.

CHAPTER 23

Stealing Space

THE NEXT MORNING I HELPED LOAD the truck even though my back was killing me. Jason was driving and he turned north on US1. Today, we were going to service the stores as far away as Key Largo. We stopped at the first store and pulled around to the back. There were stacks of wooden crates that were full of empties that we had to take back. The bottles had to be sorted into the crates by type before we loaded them onto the truck.

Jason kicked a pile of crates before he picked up the top one.

"Look at that," he said, pointing at a scorpion scurrying away. "Always kick the cases before you pick them up so you won't get stung by a scorpion. They won't kill you, but if one stings you it really hurts. They like getting in these wooden crates, especially when the crates are outside."

We loaded the empties into the truck and restocked the inventory in the store.

Then we started across the Seven Mile Bridge still heading north towards Marathon. I thought this bridge was skinny when I drove my pickup truck across it, but this delivery truck took up every inch of the lane we were in. Jason was hugging the centerline in the middle of the bridge. I looked out the passenger window to see how close we were to the guardrail. There was only about a foot to spare. Then I saw the Winnebago coming towards us, heading south. Its front wheels were on the centerline.

Jason eased over to the right eating up most of the foot we had to spare. We were only inches from the guardrail and we were doing 50 miles an hour.

"You have to watch out for the tourists in their motor homes," he said. "They use up their entire lane and some of yours. You just get over to the right as far as you can and keep going. Keep your eyes straight ahead. If you watch the motor home, you'll drift. The only thing you can do is to keep your eyes on your own lane and hug the rail as close as you can."

I wasn't driving so I kept my eyes on the motor home. I couldn't help it. It didn't look like there was enough room for the truck and the motor home to pass each other.

CLINK, I heard, as the two vehicles passed. The side mirrors had touched.

"I took a mirror off a motor home one day," Jason said.

"What'd you do?" I wanted to know.

"I just kept going," Jason said. "You can't stop in the middle of the bridge or someone will rear end you. The other guy never slowed down either. But he was going to have to buy a new mirror for his motor home before he headed back up north."

We continued up the Keys stopping at one store after another. We also stopped in on several bars. Some of them were regular customers that bought some of the 20 different kinds of beer we had on the truck. Others were bars that didn't carry any of our products, but Jason said to keep going back to these bars because eventually they would start carrying some of our brands.

The stops that took the longest were in the large chain grocery stores. One was in Marathon and the other was in Key Largo. We would straighten out the existing stock on the shelves, restock with any product they still had in the back of the store, and bring in as much product from the truck as the store would allow us to. Each brand of soft drink was allowed a certain number of feet of shelf space, and Jason was showing me how to get as much of our product on the shelves as possible.

He moved some of the 6-packs of Pepsi and Coke off the shelves that were adjacent to our shelf space and piled them higher. Robbing this space from them gave us enough room to stock another 20 cases of our product.

"They'll steal it back and more when their drivers come in," he said. "It's a never ending battle. They steal space from us, and we steal space from them."

Then he opened up a can of Pepsi, and after making sure no one was watching, he poured it all over the Pepsi and Coke displays on the shelves.

"That'll make their stuff all sticky," he explained, "and no one will want to buy them. So they'll buy ours instead."

By the late afternoon, most of our product was gone and we had a truckload of empty bottles to take back to the warehouse. Jason had me drive the truck on the way back.

CHAPTER 24

The Prognosis

AFTER 2 WEEKS OF HOPING THE pain in my back would ease up, I decided to tell the boss, Jack, that I wasn't getting any better and needed to see a doctor. The lump on my back was getting a little smaller but it was still a rather sickly looking shade of purple, green, and blue. Jack said he'd call and make an appointment for me.

* * *

"The x-rays show a curvature in your Lumbar Spine," the doctor said. "That's called scoliosis and there's a hairline fracture in one of the small bones called the Transverse Process. But there's no evidence that either of these things was caused by your accident. More than likely, you were born like that. If you had really been injured, you would have come to see me the first day. Since you waited 2 weeks, I think you are just trying to get on workman's comp so you don't have to work."

"What?" I exclaimed, not believing my ears.

This guy was supposed to be my doctor and help me get well, I told myself.

"I've never had a problem with my back before," I continued. "The broken door on the delivery truck hit me really hard. What do you think caused this horrible bruise and knot on my back?"

"Oh, I don't doubt that the door hit your back and bruised you. I just don't think it did any more than that. I'm going to give you a back brace to wear and you can go back to work."

"Are you saying it's okay for me to be lifting those cases of soda and climbing in and out of that truck all day while my back is like this?" I asked, questioning his judgment.

"What I'm saying is that you aren't fooling me. I am not restricting your work in any way. Wear the brace and come back to see me in 2 weeks."

And with that, he got up and left the room.

* * *

The brace didn't help at all. It just made me uncomfortable and hot. But I wore it. Before I went back to the doctor, I took a full can of soda and put it in the truck bay with the still broken door and I let the door fall shut on the can…just like it did to my back. It smashed the can flat and the soda exploded everywhere. I took the can with me when I returned for the follow up visit.

* * *

"What's this?" the doctor asked when I handed the can to him.

"I wanted to show you what that door could do to a full can of soda," I explained. "It crushed the can just like it did my back."

He took the can and threw it into the trashcan.

"You'd do anything to get out of work, wouldn't you?" the doctor said without even looking at my back. "I am releasing you from my care. You don't need to wear the brace anymore. You are perfectly okay to work and I don't want to see you back here again."

Then he stood up and walked out of the examining room.

So, I said to myself, *now I know. This is the kind of care you get when the doctor gets paid by workman's comp… Since they're the ones paying him, whose side do you think he's on?*

After 2 more weeks without any improvement, I went to see a chiropractor. When he saw the x-rays he took, he knew how seriously I had been injured.

"You can't work like this," he said, "or you'll never heal. I'm going to realign your spine, and you'll have to come and see me every day for 2 weeks, and then we'll taper off the frequency of the visits. I'm giving you a note for your boss that says you can't work at all for 2 weeks. Then you can only be on light duty for another month after that."

* * *

I never drove the delivery truck again. Jack had me start driving the company car to visit all the stores in the Keys. The car was an old corvette. It was fun to drive, but it wasn't comfortable and it made my back hurt. I would visit our customers the day before they were scheduled for delivery to preorder what needed to be loaded on the truck. I also hit all the bars and stores that weren't already our customers to expand our customer base. I carried a cooler full of ice and beer in the car so the bar owners could try out one of our exotic brands of beer. Of course, I had to join them in the sampling.

Before long, I became a connoisseur of the 20 or so brands we carried. You could put out a dozen glasses and pour a different beer in each one and with one taste I could identify what beer was in each glass. All in all, I guess this wasn't such a bad job…driving around the Keys in a vette, visiting all the local bars, and drinking imported beer with the bar owners. It sure beat trying to keep up with Mark while lugging that big hose full of concrete around on that scaffolding.

CHAPTER 25

The Sand Bar

JASON OWNED AN OLD OUTBOARD MOTORBOAT with a 25 horsepower motor. It looked like crap, but to him it was a magic carpet that allowed him to explore the magical world of the blue-green waters that surrounded the Keys.

"There's no reason to live in the Keys if you don't own a boat," I had heard him say.

He was right. There was not really much to do in the Keys if you couldn't enjoy the fishing and snorkeling. And to do that, you really needed a boat.

Jason had offered to take Judy, Keith, and me out on his boat to fish and snorkel on a Sunday afternoon. The plan was to go out at about noon while it was high tide and come back about 4:00. Then we'd fire up the grill and cook whatever we had caught for dinner that evening.

We brought along a cooler with some beer and soda and a bag of potato chips to snack on. We loaded into the boat and Jason headed west out of a canal that led into the Gulf. This was one of his favorite spots to fish and snorkel so he knew where he was going.

We made our way around lots of mangrove islands. Jason said that when the tide was low and the sun was hot, that the fishing around the mangroves was great. The water around the mangroves was a little deeper and the fish would congregate there. The mangrove roots provided them both shade from the sun and shelter from predators. He said we'd try there later, but first we were going to try and get some lobsters.

The lobsters liked to hide under rocks. And the only rocks in the grass flats were usually in the channels. Jason kept the boat in the channels as we left the mangroves behind us.

"We're going to do some 'sharking' to find the lobsters," Jason said. "You put on some snorkeling gear and jump in behind the boat and hold on to this rope. I'll go slow and pull you through the channels while you look for lobster. Look for their antennas sticking out from the rocks. If you see one, let go of the rope and I'll swing back around to get you."

He handed me a net and a tickle stick. A tickle stick is a wooden dowel rod about 12 inches long and it has a metal rod about 2 feet long stuck into one end.

"Use the tickle stick to get the lobsters out from under the rocks," Jason explained. "Stick it behind a lobster and touch his tail with it. He'll come out into the open. Then put the net behind the lobster and put the tickle stick in front of him. He'll scamper backwards right into your net."

Jason and I took turns 'sharking' behind the boat and soon we had 6 short lobsters in our cooler. We weren't worried about getting caught with them. Jason said the marine patrol never came into this area because it was pretty remote.

Then we found a coral head with hundreds of tropical fish swimming around it. It looked like we were swimming in a tropical fish tank at a pet store. We anchored the boat so we could all snorkel for a while and see all the fish. Before we knew it, it was 5:00.

"Oh my God!" Jason exclaimed, looking at his watch. "It's getting late. We need to go. The tide is going out and we need to get back through the channels while they are still navigable."

We climbed back into the boat and I pulled the anchor up while Jason got the motor started.

"Sit on the bow up front and watch for rocks and sand bars so we don't hit anything," he said.

I climbed up on the bow and took the lookout position while Jason turned the boat around, and then we headed in.

There were sand bars showing that weren't visible on our way out.

"Go right," I shouted as I waved my hand in the direction he should take the boat to miss the sandbar I could see just under the water ahead of the boat. "Now left . . . now right and left again," I directed. We were halfway through the mangrove jungle when I shouted, "Look out! It's shallow up there."

It was too late. The bow of the boat ploughed right into a sand bar.

Jason put the motor into reverse and the prop threw a cascade of water into the boat. But the boat didn't move.

"We'll have to get out and push the boat off the sandbar," Jason said.

Keith stayed in the boat while Jason, Judy, and I jumped out. We pushed, and shoved, and lifted, but it was all to no avail. The tide was really going out fast and soon the boat was sitting on a little island that was just a sandbar a few minutes ago.

There was nothing we could do now but wait for the tide to come back in. We took stock of our food situation. We had a handful of chips left in the bag. There were a few beers and a couple of sodas left in the cooler. And there were the 6 short lobsters.

There was a can of Sterno fuel in my aluminum tackle box that I kept there for emergency purposes. It had been in there for a long time. This was the first time I had ever needed it. I dumped all the tackle out of the box and rinsed it out in the salt water the best I could. Then I scooped up a couple inches of salt water into the tackle box. We searched around the sand bar until we found 4 rocks that we put under the corners of the tackle box. We lit the can of Sterno fuel and put it under our makeshift cooking pot.

Then we twisted off the lobsters' heads just like Darius had taught me. But this time we had to take the lobster tails all the way out of the shells. We put the 6 little tails into the heating water and waited for them to cook. One little can of Sterno fuel was not enough to completely cook the tails. They looked about half done when the fire from the Sterno fuel went out.

Half cooked lobster tails might have been half palatable if there were some key limes to squeeze over them and melted butter to dip them in. Keith had finished off the rest of the potato chips while the lobster tails were taking their sauna bath. So the half cooked tails were the only things on the menu. It's surprising how good they taste when you are hungry. At least we had cold beer to wash them down.

As the sun began to set, the mosquitos found us. There were thousands of them and they swarmed us. They were as hungry as we had been and it seemed like they were the size of robins. I had Keith climb into the storage area under the bow of the boat and covered him the best I could with life preservers and throw cushions. The rest of us became the sacrificial lambs for the mosquitos.

BZZZZ . . . BZZZZ . . . SLAP . . . SLAP.

It didn't matter how many we swatted. For every one we killed, four replacements took their spot.

After the mosquitos were so full of our blood they could hardly fly, most of them went off somewhere to sleep it off and we were able to finally get a little sleep.

I woke up when I felt the boat swaying. I sat up and looked over the side of the boat.

"Wake up!" I yelled. "We're floating!"

We didn't have a flashlight so we were lucky there was a full moon so we could see. It took us a couple of hours to wind our way slowly through the mangroves in the moonlight and find our way back to the dock.

CHAPTER 26

Pina Coladas & Mahi-Mahi

ONE DAY IN THE SPRING OF 1978 Bryan and Renee invited us to their house to eat. Bryan put some charcoal on the grill to get it going. Then he opened a cooler and pulled out a beautiful green and yellow colored fish. He laid it on a table in the yard.

"It's a dolphin fish," he said. "Most restaurants call it Mahi-Mahi on their menus so they can charge more. But a lot of people in the islands call it a Dorado."

He used a thin knife to get two really nice fillets about an inch thick off the Mahi-Mahi. He rinsed them off with the garden hose and laid them on the table to drain.

"I'm going to grill the Mahi-Mahi," he said.

He poured a cup of pineapple juice and a couple ounces of Captain Morgan Rum into a large bowl, cut open 2 Key Limes and squeezed them into the bowl and threw in the rinds, added a couple cloves of crushed garlic, some black pepper, and a couple shakes of Old Bay Seasoning. He stirred this up and slid the filets into the marinade.

"I call this Captain Morgan's Mahi-Mahi," he said. "We'll let those marinate while the grill is getting hot."

He had a blender on the picnic table and it was plugged into an extension cord that ran back onto the porch. He poured 8 ounces of the rum into the blender, added a couple rings of fresh pineapple that he had cut up, half a cup of pineapple juice out of a can, half a can of cream of coconut, and a couple cups of ice. After he blended it, he poured the Pina Coladas into some big plastic cups. He handed one to me. I had never had a Pina Colada before. I could smell the pineapple and the coconut as I brought the cup up to my lips.

It tasted fantastic.

"Renee and I are moving to Fort Lauderdale," Bryan said.

"We're keeping this place for a while so we can come here on the weekends. If we decide we don't like living in the big city, we could just move back here. We'd like you to keep an eye on it for us when we're not here, and we're willing to pay you to do that."

"I don't mind watching it for you," I said, "but you don't have to pay me."

"I'll be making really good money in Fort Lauderdale," Bryan said, "so it's no big deal. I'd have to pay someone to keep an eye on it and I'd rather pay you. I know you could use the extra money."

"OK, thanks," I said. "I appreciate that."

He put the Mahi-Mahi on the grill and refilled my cup. The aroma of the grilled fish was making my mouth water. The only way I had ever eaten fish before was breaded and fried. It seemed that every day in the Keys brought new experiences.

Renee and Judy came outside carrying a salad they had been putting together and joined us at the picnic table. Bryan retrieved the Mahi-Mahi from the grill and we ate. It was the best fish I had ever eaten.

"I'd like you and Judy to go into Key West with us after dinner if you can," Bryan announced. "We've already arranged for a baby sitter to stay with the boys. There's something we'd like your help with."

I looked at Judy and she nodded her OK.

"Sure," I agreed.

The girls took the dirty dishes in and Bryan and I moved to a couple of lawn chairs. He reached into his shirt pocket and pulled out a joint. He lit it, took a couple of hits, and handed it to me.

"Finish it," he said. "I don't want any more."

I took a hit.

"Wow!" I said. "What is this? It doesn't taste like any Mexican pot I've ever smoked before."

"It's not Mexican," Bryan said. "It's from Colombia."

* * *

It was common knowledge that a lot of pot came through the

73

Keys. They even talked about it on the radio.

"The square grouper are biting today in Marathon," the announcer would say.

That meant that someone had found a bale of pot floating in the water on Marathon Key. Jason had told me that the Cubans were the ones bringing in the pot. They bought the pot in Colombia and brought it to the Keys in their boats called Mother Ships.

When a Mother Ship arrived, it stayed well off shore. Local fishermen would be paid to load their fishing boats and bring the pot ashore. They knew the waters well and their boats did not draw any attention. To throw off the DEA and police, the Cubans would load some bales of pot on a speedboat and send it up the Keys 20 or 30 miles. The bales on the speedboat would get thrown overboard near a bridge or a resort where it would quickly be found.

They wanted a tourist to find a bale because they were more likely to call the police. Especially if there were lots of witnesses, like at a resort. Then all the DEA and cops in the Keys would speed to the site where the bale was found and the Marine Patrol would launch their boats so they could search for more bales in that area.

Meanwhile, the Mother Ship could be safely unloaded 30 miles away and the load would make it to a safe house without any interference from the police. This was a cheap decoy for the Cubans. Toss 4 or 5 bales into the water 30 miles away to keep the cops busy so the other 700 bales could make it safely ashore.

The local radio station monitored all the police bands. So when a bale was found and the police were called, the radio station would hear it and tell their listening audience where the square grouper were biting. Then all the locals in that area would get in their boats and head out to scout the surrounding waters in hopes of finding a bale before the cops got it all.

If one of the locals found a bale, he wasn't going to turn it over to the cops. One bale was worth more than a fisherman could make fishing all year. A typical 60-pound bale of marijuana would fetch $15,000 to $20,000 wholesale . . . more if it was sold by the pound, and even more if it was sold by the ounce on the street.

CHAPTER 27

Counting Money

BRYAN ALREADY HAD THE TOP DOWN on his yellow Cadillac convertible. The four of us climbed in and we headed for Key West. The air was blowing through our hair, the sun was shining, and the water was green and blue for as far as you could see. The radio was turned up loud and Jimmy Buffet was singing Margaritaville.

Jimmy wrote this song while he was in Key West and it was released in 1977 along with Changes in Latitudes, Changes in Attitudes. Jimmy's songs epitomized life in the Keys. Every bar in Key West played Jimmy Buffet songs and he quickly became my favorite vocalist. My latitude and attitude had certainly changed since I moved to the Keys.

* * *

We crossed Stock Island on US1 and entered Key West. When you cross the bridge, the road does not go straight ahead. You have to either turn left, or turn right. If you turn left, you are on A1A, and the road is called South Roosevelt Blvd for about 3 miles. If you turn right, you are still on US1 and the road is called North Roosevelt Blvd for about 2 miles before the name changes to Truman Ave for about 1 mile. So Roosevelt got about 5 miles of road named after him and Truman only got 1 mile of road. Wonder which dead president they liked better? Maybe it was because Roosevelt was president for 12 years and Truman was only president for 8 years.

* * *

We drove down North Roosevelt Blvd and turned right on White Street, then onto a smaller street and Bryan parked the caddy on the road in front of a gorgeous Key West style 2-story house.

"This belongs to a friend of mine," he said. "We can use it any time we want when he's not in town, which isn't often."

76

* * *

When we were seated in the living room, Bryan went upstairs and came back down with a briefcase. He put the briefcase on the coffee table, undid the combination lock, opened it up, and spun it around.

My eyes bulged and my mouth fell open, but no words came out. I was staring at the most money I had ever seen in my life. I glanced at Judy, but her eyes were still glued to the cash. The money was in piles with rubber bands around them.

"This is a payment for a business transaction," Bryan explained. "It needs to be counted to ensure it's all there. I would like you two to count it for me while we go run an errand. There are $1,000 bundles. Each $1,000 bundle has 1 rubber band around it. Five of these are stacked together and secured with 2 rubber bands. There are eight 2-band bundles in the case, so there should be $40,000. You'll have to take the rubber bands off to count the money and then band them back together the same way. Take the case upstairs to the bedroom to count it so no one will see it if they walk up to the house. Put the case in the linen closet under the towels when you are done. There is beer and wine in the fridge, and you'll find towels in the linen closet upstairs. When you are done, you can enjoy the Jacuzzi tub out on the deck. We'll be back in about an hour or so."

Judy and I were dumbstruck as we watched Bryan and Renee walk out the front door and drive away in the Cadillac, leaving us alone with all this cash. I carried the briefcase to the upstairs bedroom. We poured the bundles of money out onto the bed and stared at it.

Was there really $40,000 here? I wondered.

I did some quick calculations. If I worked 40 hours a week and earned $8 an hour, I would make $320. Times 52 weeks a year was $16,640. Times 2 years was $33,280. Minus taxes, it would be even less. There was more money in the briefcase than I could earn in 2 years!

I picked up the first stack and pulled off the 2 rubber bands. Then I pulled off the single rubber band holding the first stack that was supposed to contain 50 $20 bills. I held the stack in my left hand and licked my right thumb and finger. Then I pulled one $20 bill off at a time and laid them in a stack on the bed. There were 50 of them, just like there was supposed to be. I put the rubber band back around the stack of twenties and picked up the next stack of twenties. Judy picked up her first $5,000 stack and started the same ritual.

There were 50 of the $20 bills in each $1,000 stack in my first $5,000 bundle. I put both rubber bands around the $5,000 bundle and put it back into the briefcase. There was plenty of room in the briefcase but I made sure I put it in there nice and neat. I put the stack into the bottom left corner of the case. Then I picked up another $5,000 bundle and started again. There were 6 bundles that had all $20 bills and 2 much smaller bundles that had only $100 bills.

All the bundles of twenties were accurate, but one of the bundles of hundreds had 2 extra $100 bills.

"Judy, count this for me. I've counted it twice and it looks like there is $200 too much in this bundle."

She picked up the stack of hundreds.

"1 . . . 2 . . . 3 . . . 4," she counted as she laid them on the bed, "5 . . . 6 . . . 7 . . . 8 . . . 9 . . . 10 . . . 11 . . . 12. You're right, there's $200 too much in this bundle."

We gathered up 10 of the hundred dollar bills and wrapped them with a rubber band. The other 4 bundles had 10 one hundred dollar bills like they were supposed to. We put the 5 one-band bundles together and double banded the $5,000. I placed the money back inside the case with the other 7 bundles, snapped the case closed and put it in the linen closet under the towels. I folded the two extra $100 bills and put them in my pocket.

"What are you doing with those?" Judy asked.

"I'm giving them to Bryan," I said. "Either they are there by accident, or this was a test. In either case, they're not ours. I have never stolen anything before and I'm not starting now. Let's grab some towels and a couple of beers and hit the Jacuzzi."

CHAPTER 28

Honesty Pays

I WAS ON MY SECOND SAINT Pauli Girl, and the cold beer and the warm water in the Jacuzzi had really relaxed me. The pain in my back was a distant memory as the jets of water massaged me. Judy was deep in thought as she sat on the opposite side of the Jacuzzi. She was twirling a strand of her wet long black hair around her finger over and over again.

Then the door to the deck opened and Bryan and Renee walked out of the house. I didn't hear the Cadillac arrive, or hear them enter the house.

"How's the Jacuzzi?" Bryan asked.

He was holding a Saint Pauli Girl in his hand. It was half empty.

"Nice," I replied.

This was the first time I had ever been in a Jacuzzi. Another first!

Bryan sat down on a bench and looked at me.

"Did the money count out correctly?" he asked.

"Yeah...it was right on," I answered, as I looked him right in the eyes. I hesitated for a couple of seconds and then added, "Except there were two extra $100 bills in one of the bundles. They're in the front pocket of my cutoffs . . . on the bench beside you."

Bryan looked at me and didn't say anything for a moment.

"Sometimes that happens," he said. "Sometimes it's over . . . sometimes it's short. It's time to go. You guys can dry off and get dressed while I shut down the Jacuzzi."

He reached into my pocket and pulled out the two $100 bills and stared at them for a moment.

We got out of the water, dried off, and wrapped our towels around us. We picked up our clothes and headed inside to change. We went upstairs to the spare bedroom. I opened the linen closet and lifted the towels. The briefcase was gone!

Oh my God, I thought, *Has someone stolen it?*

We dressed quickly and rushed back downstairs.

Bryan was sitting on the couch and the briefcase was sitting on the coffee table. He obviously had brought the case downstairs when he returned and probably had recounted the money before he ever came outside.

"This is for you," he said as he fanned out five $100 bills in his hand. "I like knowing who I can trust. There is plenty more where this came from if you'll help me again in the future."

I hesitated. Then I reached out and took the $500 and put it into my pocket. We had just been paid $500 for an hour of our time. I didn't know what to say.

"Tha . . . tha . . . thanks," I stammered, "anytime."

CHAPTER 29

The Job Offer

A FEW WEEKS AFTER BRYAN AND Renee moved to Fort Lauderdale, he drove back down to the Keys and stopped by to see me.

"I came down to take care of some business and I wanted to talk with you," he said.

He pulled a wad of $100 bills out of his pocket, counted out five of them, and handed them to me.

"This is for taking care of our trailer, but you don't need to do it anymore. We have decided to stay in Fort Lauderdale and we're giving up the trailer."

I took the $500 and stuffed it into my pocket. I thought that was too much money to pay me, but I needed it and was grateful to get it.

"I need someone to help me in my business," he said. "I trust you and I'd like to offer you the job. And as you can see, I pay very well."

"What kind of job is it?" I wanted to know.

"Nothing hard," he replied. "I have customers that come down to Florida from up north to buy merchandise from me. You'll take their cars to a warehouse where the merchandise will be loaded into the trunks of their cars and return the cars to them."

"What kind of merchandise are we talking about?" I asked.

"Marijuana," he said. "You will only work a few weeks at a time, several times a year, and you'll make 40 or 50 thousand a year doing it. When I don't have you on a job, you're free to do whatever else you want. But you'll have to move to Fort Lauderdale so you are nearby when I need to see you. And you'll have to be available whenever I need you."

"Marijuana?" I repeated.

My suspicions about where the money in the briefcase

came from were now confirmed.

"Bryan, I don't know. I have a family . . . and pot is illegal . . . and what if we get caught . . . and I still have a couple of months before I finish college."

I had so many questions. My mind was racing a hundred miles an hour. I thought about what life could be like if I made that much money a year. I had expected to earn half that much working in electronics after I got my degree. Right now we were eating beans and potatoes every day. We still had no refrigerator in our rented trailer. My back still hurt from the accident and I didn't know if I'd ever be able to do hard physical labor again. I had tried to do the right things, to be a good citizen, to be a productive member of society . . . but it seemed like the system was against me.

What were my other options to provide for my family? If I didn't take this opportunity, was I dooming my family and myself to a life of poverty and welfare?

"Can I finish school first and take that time to think about this?" I asked.

Bryan thought for a moment before he answered.

"You don't need a college degree to do this. If you want to stay in school, I'll understand, but I'll have to get someone else. If you want this job, you'll have to move to Fort Lauderdale now. You can always go back to school sometime in the future and finish your degree, but I need someone now. It's your decision . . . but I have to know before I leave tomorrow."

"I don't have the money to move up there and get a place to live," I said.

"I'll advance you $5,000 so you can move, get set up, and have some money until you go on your first job. Then I'll take that out of what you earn. But you'll need to move there within a week," he said. "We go to work the week after that. If you decide to come to work for me, I'll have Renee start looking for a place for you to rent."

"What are the risks?" I asked. "What if we get caught?"

He laughed.

"It's no big deal. Everyone in the Keys gets involved at one time or another. All the marijuana that came into the states used to come from Mexico. It all came in over the border into Texas. That pot is crap. Everyone wants Colombian pot now. And all that Colombian pot is coming into the states on Cuban ships. They can't bring it up here fast enough. Almost all of it is coming into the states through Florida and most of it comes right here into the Keys. When it gets too dangerous here, it'll come in somewhere else. But right now it is the largest source of income for the Keys. People are making money and they are spending a lot of it right here. It is good for the economy. No one wants that source of income to go away so the local law enforcement doesn't try too hard to catch anyone. And there is a lot of money going to them so they look the other way. Do you think they want to bust their friends and family members and cut their own income? It's only the feds we have to worry about and we'll get plenty of warning from local law enforcement if the feds get wind of a load coming in. So it's pretty safe. But there is always a chance of getting caught. If that happens, we have lawyers on retainer to get us off and you wouldn't have to worry about any legal fees. If you got caught, you'd be out of jail in 24 hours and ready to go back to making money."

"Let me think about it tonight," I said, "and I'll let you know before you leave tomorrow."

CHAPTER 30

We're Moving

"THAT'S CRAZY!" JUDY YELLED. TEARS WERE running down her face as she looked at me. "You only have a couple more months of school before you graduate. Then you'll be able to get a good paying job. That was our plan. That's why we moved here. You wanted to go to school and now you're thinking of throwing that dream away."

Man, I hated it when she threw logic and tears into the mix. It wasn't fair.

"I'll never be able to make this much money with a regular job," I argued. "And I don't know if I'll even be able to get a job when I do get my degree because of my back injury. I can't even buy a refrigerator for us. We eat beans and potatoes every day because that's all we can afford. I want to be able to provide for you and Keith. I feel like a loser because I can't take care of you guys like I want to. This is our opportunity, and I want to take it."

She wrapped her arms around me and buried her face into my neck. She started sobbing. I could feel her tears flowing down my neck and onto my chest. She stayed like that for a long time. She didn't say anything, she just held on.

My arms found their way around her and I pulled her in closer.

The tears I felt running down my face weren't coming from her.

She finally pushed away but her outstretched arms still held onto me.

"I don't want you to do this," she said. "I think we can make it just fine without this. We have everything we need right now and the other stuff can come later. I like our little house. I like knowing that you'll be home every night. I feel safe now. I don't think I'll feel safe and secure any more if you do this. I'll always be worrying about you, about us and about our life. Please don't."

Please Don't. Those words echoed through my head sounding like a crack in her resolve.

* * *

She didn't want me to do this, but she is letting me make my own decision. What she saw as a threat to us, I saw as an opportunity. She was just like a woman. They always want to hug the tree. They don't want to venture out onto the limbs where the fruit is just waiting to be picked by those brave enough to take a risk. A man is willing to do what it takes to provide for his family.

Cavemen were willing to take on behemoths at the risk of their lives to provide food for their families. Astronauts were willing to risk the perils of outer space knowing that just a small hole in their suit would condemn them to death. Policemen were willing to risk their lives to protect someone else's property. Firemen climbed into burning buildings to save someone's life. Surely I was as brave as any of these. I had to provide for my family. And Bryan had assured me that the risk was negligible, and if there was any problem that I would be provided an attorney at no cost.

* * *

"Judy, I have to do this. Just for a little while. Just long enough for us to save up some money so we aren't always struggling. Then I'll go back to school and finish my degree. This isn't an end to that dream; it's just a detour. I'll only do it for a little while, and then when we have some money stashed away, I'll quit."

The next morning I walked out onto the dock behind our trailer. The mug of coffee that I had brought with me was steaming when I first came outside, but I was so deep in thought that I had forgotten to drink it. It was sitting on the railing of the dock and it had gotten cold. The creamer had started to separate and the coffee was turning white on top. I like my coffee hot and couldn't stand the taste of cold coffee. I took a sip without looking and discovered that it was cold. I spit it out. It splashed into the water of the canal, and the mangrove snapper and pinfish swarmed to it.

The fish had heard my footsteps when I walked out onto the dock. I usually threw some bread to them when I came out to the dock. Now every time they heard footsteps on the dock they thought they were going to be fed and they would congregate there. When I tossed bread to them, the water looked like it was boiling as a hundred fish or more splashed the surface, each one trying to get more than his fair share of the bounty. But I hadn't brought any bread for them this morning. My mind was on other things.

I was about to make a life changing decision and there were a million thoughts running through my head; *If I stayed here, I'd finish my degree in a couple more months. Then I'd find a job, probably at some marina where I'd install electronics on boats that I'd never be able to afford. They would pay me $8 to $10 an hour. We'd struggle like everyone else to make ends meet but we'd survive. And I wouldn't have to look over my shoulder all the time wondering if I was about to be arrested. If I went to work for Bryan, we'd have to move to Fort Lauderdale. It would cost more to live there, but I'd make a lot more money. There were lots of stores where Judy could shop which was one of her favorite things to do. But it was crowded, unlike the Keys. Lots of people meant lots of traffic, which I hated. But it also meant lots of houses. And all those houses needed to be pressure washed. I still had the pressure washer I had bought in Perry, so I could start up my pressure cleaning business again. I could do that when I wasn't on a job for Bryan. And there was a flight school at Fort Lauderdale Executive Airport. I could use my VA benefits to work on an advanced pilot's license. I got a private pilot's license while I was in the Air Force. There was an aero club on the base and it was fairly inexpensive to use their planes and instructors. I had discovered that I loved to fly. It was the most exciting thing I had ever done. But I hadn't had the money to do any flying since I got out of the Air Force. If I went to work for Bryan, I would have the money to do that again.*

I picked up my coffee cup and walked back inside. Keith was still asleep and Judy was sitting at the table with a cup of coffee. Her coffee looked cold too. She was twirling her hair around one of her fingers . . . a sign that she was deep in thought. She looked up at me as I walked over and took a chair beside her. Neither of us said anything for a while. Finally, she broke the silence.

"We're moving, aren't we?" she asked. It was more of a statement than a question. A tear was running down her face from the corner of her eye.

"Yes," I replied. "I'm going up to see Bryan and let him know. I'll be back in a little while."

CHAPTER 31

The New House

IT DIDN'T TAKE LONG TO PACK our things. Everything we owned fit into the pickup truck. It took us 4 hours to drive from our trailer in the Keys to whatever awaited us in Fort Lauderdale.

Renee had found three houses for us to look at and said we could stay with them a few days until we chose which house we wanted to rent. One was in Fort Lauderdale and was only a few blocks from the beach. But the rent there was $650 a month. Another was a couple miles from the beach so it was cheaper at only $550 a month. The third house was in the City of Sunrise, just west of Fort Lauderdale. You couldn't tell that you had left Fort Lauderdale and entered the City of Sunrise if you didn't notice the little green city limit sign on the side of the road. It all looked the same.

This house was in a development of nice homes and many of the houses had a canal in their back yard. This one wasn't on a canal but it was nicer and larger than any house either of us had ever lived in. It was a 3-bedroom, 2-bath house and it had a pool with a screen enclosure. The back yard was fenced and the landlord was okay with us having the dogs in the back yard. And the best part was the rent was only $450 a month. Only about 7 times more than we were paying for the trailer in the Keys.

After we got over the sticker shock of the rental prices, we decided on the house in the City of Sunrise. We paid the landlord first and last months' rent and a security deposit on the house. Then we got the utilities turned on . . . including cable TV.

It didn't take long to move all our belongings into the house. Three or four trips from the pickup truck to the house and everything was moved in. Luckily the house came with furniture. But we still needed some other things. So we went shopping to buy some dishes, silverware, towels, and a few other odds and ends. There were so many choices of where to shop, but we settled on the shopping center about 5 minutes from the house. I even bought a charcoal grill to put out by the pool.

Then we went grocery shopping. It had been a long time since I had been able to afford a whole shopping cart full of groceries. Since we needed everything, our cart was heaping. And since we now had a refrigerator we bought some cold cuts, milk, butter, and ice cream. And we even got some vegetables.

Yeah!! I decided I would cook the broccoli this time. It would go great with the potatoes we were going to bake in the oven and the Captain Morgan's Mahi-Mahi that I was going to grill out by the pool.

After dinner, we watched TV for a while and I carried Keith to bed after he fell asleep on the couch. I used the blender we had bought on our shopping trip and whipped up some Pina Coladas using fresh pineapple like I had seen Bryan do at his trailer in the Keys. Judy and I sat out by the pool to enjoy our drinks and talk.

We looked up at the sky to see the stars.

"There were a lot more stars in the sky down in the Keys," she said.

"I think there are just as many in the sky here," I said. "We just can't see them because of all the lights here in the city."

Dumb . . . dumb . . . dumb. Just like a guy, ruin a romantic moment just to get the scientific facts straight.

"Remember all the stars we could see that night we were stranded on the sand bar in Jason's boat?" I asked in an attempt to recover the moment.

"Yeah," she said. Then she pulled her chair over closer to me and sat her drink on the table. She picked up my hands and looked in my eyes. "This isn't so bad. I like our house. I like the pool. I like that we have a refrigerator full of food. And I like all the stores. There's even a card shop in the shopping center we were at today. Renee is picking me up about 10:00 in the morning and after we hit the card shop, she's going to show me where all the great shopping is. We're going to shop til we drop." She laid her head on my shoulder and neither of us said anything for a few minutes.

Then finally she broke the silence.

"I think I'm going to like it here," she said. Then she stood up, reached down, and grabbed my hand.

She led me inside straight to our bedroom.

"Let's break in our new house."

We woke the next morning in each other's arms, young, in love, and happy. As we looked into each other's eyes, I asked Judy if she would marry me. She pulled me tight and kissed me like she was never going to stop.

When we finally came up for air, she said, "Yes!" and a few days later, in front of the clerk of the court, Judy Foster became Judy O'Dair.

CHAPTER 32

The Tallahassee Job

BRYAN CAME TO SEE ME a few days later. He pulled a wad of $100 bills out of his pocket and counted out 40 of them and handed them to me.

"I want you to go buy a used car. Try to find one for around 25 hundred dollars. Make sure it has good tires and runs good. Put the car in your name and add it to your insurance policy. Don't get a sports car or anything fancy. Get one that will blend in with the everyday workingman's car. And the day after tomorrow, I want you to drive it to Tallahassee. It'll take you about 8 hours to get there. I want you there by 4:00 pm, so get on the road early. Get a room at the Holiday Inn on Tennessee Street. You can't miss it. It's the only round hotel in town. Check in as Bob Smith and pay cash for your room. Then wait in your room for my call. Tell Judy that you'll be gone for about 2 weeks and that if she needs anything while you're gone to get in touch with Renee."

* * *

There were a lot of used car lots on A1A in Fort Lauderdale, so that's where I headed. At the third car lot, I found a 1975 white Oldsmobile Cutlass hardtop with good tires. The asking price of $2,800 was written on the windshield in big white numbers. I offered $2,000 for it and of course the salesman said he would have to present the offer to his manager.

After a couple of minutes, the sales manager came out of the office with the salesman following him. After the manager introduced himself and shook my hand, he started telling me why this was such a great car and how it had been owned by some little old lady. He said it only had 15,000 miles on it because she had only driven it to the grocery store and to church once a week. He informed me about the great 30-day warranty that came with every car they sold and the fantastic

91

financing they offered with very little money down and low interest rates. He told me that this was the best deal on the lot and probably in all of Fort Lauderdale. He said I would be smart if I snagged this car before it was gone. Then he said that since he liked me so much, he'd lower the price to $2,600 if I would buy it now.

I suspected that the reason that the mileage was so low was because the slick manager had his mechanic turn back the odometer. That's why the numbers in the odometer didn't line up exactly straight. And I didn't believe for a minute that the previous owner was some little old lady. If it was, she was a smoker because there were a couple of burn holes in the front seat. But the car was in pretty good shape and I didn't see any oil dripping under the engine.

"I don't want to finance the car. I want to pay cash," I told the manager.

I pulled out the wad of $100 bills and counted out 20 of them and laid them on the hood of the car. I laid the keys on top of the stack of hundreds so they wouldn't blow away.

Then I looked the manager in the eyes and said, "You can have the stack of hundreds, or you can have the keys back. It's your choice."

He looked at me for a minute and then at the stack of hundreds on the hood.

A smile broke across his face as he turned to the salesman and said, "Randy, go get the paperwork ready. This guy drives a hard bargain, and he just got himself one heck of a deal."

Where do these used car guys come from? They all sound like they graduated from the same used car salesman school.

After signing the required paperwork, I told them I'd pick up the car later that day. I headed for the tag office to get a regular metal license plate. A temporary tag on the car would have every police officer checking out the tag to make sure it wasn't expired and I didn't want the extra attention.

* * *

I loaded my suitcase in the trunk and was on the road to Tallahassee by 6:00 am the next morning. I wanted plenty of time to get there on time without speeding. I pulled into Tallahassee at 2:00 pm and checked into the Holiday Inn. I could see a lot of Tallahassee from the window in my room, but I wasn't real interested in the scenery. I lay down on the bed and tried to nap while I waited for Bryan's call.

I must have dosed off because the knocking on the door woke me. I opened the door and Bryan walked in.

CHAPTER 33

The Stash House

"LET'S GO," HE SAID. "I'M GOING to take you to the stash house so you know where it is. This evening, you'll start taking cars out to get them loaded and bring them back to the drivers. I want to see the car you bought but we'll take my Caddy out there."

After Bryan checked out the Olds I had bought, we got into his yellow Cadillac. Bryan put the convertible top down, and we headed out of town. I looked over at Bryan as he was driving. His long hair was blowing in the breeze. He was wearing a tropical shirt, shorts, and sandals. His shirt was unbuttoned allowing everyone to see the dozen or so gold chains he wore around his neck.

I looked at the other traffic. There were Hondas, Toyotas, Fords, Chevys, BMWs, and even a few other Cadillacs. But none of them looked like the yellow convertible Cadillac we were in. The drivers in those cars looked like businessmen, students, people on their way to work, or moms driving their kids to school. None of them looked like Jimmy Buffet on his way to a party.

We might as well have a sign on the side of the Caddy that read, *Drug Dealer*.

We drove northeast out of town on a two-lane road for about 15 miles. We came to a section where it was mostly woods on either side of the road and there were very few houses. Then we turned on to a dirt driveway that snaked through the woods for about a quarter of a mile before it ended at a house.

"This house is pretty secluded," Bryan said. "There are no other houses nearby where someone could see you turn into the driveway. The guy that owns the house is staying somewhere else while we are here. We have the house for as long as we need it, but we should be out of here in no more than a couple of weeks."

As we pulled up to the house, there were three guys on the side porch watching us pull up. They were all holding half full Budweiser Long Necks. When we walked onto the porch I could smell steaks cooking on the charcoal grill.

Bryan introduced us.

"Hey, guys, this is Ryan. And this is Stephen, Jimmy, and Striker," he said, as he pointed to each one. "They are here to guard the pot and they will load the cars for you when you bring them out."

Stephen was about 5'6" and weighed about 150 pounds. He had a beard that looked like he hadn't shaved in few days. He wore jeans and a white tee shirt. He was a friend of one of Bryan's customers, Jeremy, from Chicago. Stephen was also a small time pot dealer and had bought pot from Jeremy for years. Jeremy had introduced Stephen to Bryan so Bryan could use him to work at the stash houses. This was the fifth stash house that Stephen had worked at for Bryan.

* * *

What none of us knew at the time was that Stephen was working undercover for the DEA.

Several months prior, Jeremy had let Stephen buy 25 pounds of pot at a wholesale price as a favor. Stephen fronted 10 pounds of that to his cousin, Vinny, who sold one-ounce baggies to his friends and their friends. But, one of Vinny's customers was an undercover narcotics officer with the Chicago police.

When the narc found out that Vinny had several pounds of pot available, he set up a sting operation. Vinny was busted with the 5 pounds he had left. Eager to stay out of jail, he quickly made a deal with the police and told them that he got the pot from his cousin, Stephen. And then the dominoes started to fall.

Stephen was arrested next. He was threatened with a lengthy prison sentence if he didn't turn in his supplier. He quickly told the cops that he got the pot from Jeremy and that

Jeremy got the pot from Bryan. He said Bryan sold thousands of pounds of pot. He thought Bryan got the pot from someone named Daryl. He didn't know who Daryl got it from.

The Chicago police realized they were on to something big and called in the DEA. Stephen didn't want to go to prison and was eager to make a deal. They promised him that he would not face any criminal charges if he became a confidential informant for the DEA.

Stephen would continue to work at the stash houses for Bryan as if nothing had happened. But he would have to record license numbers, car makes and models, amounts of pot in the stash houses, how much pot was loaded into every car, who came and went to the stash houses, and everything else he could find out. He would report to DEA Agent Scott Jones.

Jones was in no hurry to make a bust. He wanted to figure out the whole operation. He wasn't interested in the little guys, they were just peons. He wanted to bust the guys at the top . . . the kingpins. That would make a name for him. He was willing to bide his time. Then when he knew who everyone was, and how the organization worked, it would be time to make one grand sweep and arrest everyone involved from the top down.

Since Daryl used to own a used car lot and he was the highest person Jones currently knew about in the organization, he decided to call this sting "Operation Lemon Lot".

* * *

Jimmy wore jeans, combat boots, and a white tee shirt. He had a short, well-trimmed beard, and shoulder length brown hair that he kept tucked under a baseball cap. Jimmy was a long-time friend of Bryan's. He was a Vietnam vet who had learned the value of loyalty when he was in the service.

His unit had been ambushed in the jungle and Jimmy had risked his life to provide covering fire for the men in his unit while they fell back. Only when the others were safe from the enemy's gunfire did Jimmy retreat to join them.

But they were outnumbered and the Viet Cong kept advancing. Finally Jimmy's unit had to take cover behind some fallen trees. They were pinned down when their radioman called for an airstrike. By the time the airstrike arrived, half of Jimmy's unit had been killed. Jimmy survived but shrapnel from a grenade had torn into his leg. The wound had left Jimmy with a limp and he kept a cane nearby that he sometimes used.

That wasn't the only wound Jimmy received. He suffered Post-Traumatic Stress Disorder. He relived the battle in frequent nightmares where he helplessly watched as bullets from Viet Cong gunfire tore through his friends. He would wake drenched in sweat, screaming at the enemy, and grabbing under his pillow for the gun he always slept with.

He vowed that he would never let anyone else ever harm him or his friends again. So he was extremely loyal to those he cared about. And one of those he cared about was Bryan. Bryan had offered Jimmy a chance to earn some real money so he could take care of his wife and kids. He certainly couldn't do that on the small disability pension he got from the service.

* * *

Striker was on the heavy side. He was about 5' 8" and weighed about 250. Striker had known Bryan for years and had often helped Bryan sell his pot. He was one of Bryan's most trusted friends. He was wearing cut-offs, sandals, and a tee shirt that had a picture of a bikini clad blonde riding a Budweiser Long Neck. She looked like a cowgirl riding a horse with one hand holding the reins and the other hand in the air holding her cowgirl hat.

Striker had an infectious smile and it was showing through his black bushy beard. He just looked like someone you could trust. He also looked like he liked to party. I liked Striker right away.

* * *

Striker reached into a cooler and grabbed 2 more Budweiser Long Necks and handed them to Bryan and me.

"Ryan will be bringing out the cars to be loaded," Bryan said, handing Striker a spiral notebook. "Weigh each bale before you load it into the trunk and record the weight and date into this notebook under the buyer's name. There are 3 cars in town now waiting to get loaded. Ryan will bring out the first car in a couple of hours and we'll try to get these three on the road tonight. The other cars should arrive in town tonight and we'll start loading them in the morning. It'll be a steady stream of cars until they are all back on the road. Now let's go see the pot."

Inside the house, the furniture had been moved out of the way to make room for the pot. It was stacked about six feet high around the perimeter of the rooms. Some bales were burlap bags that looked like what grain would be stored in except these were square. Some bales were in cardboard cigarette boxes that had Marlboro or Winston printed on the sides.

"There are 330 bales here and Randy has about the same in his stash house on the other side of Tallahassee," Bryan said. "At about 60 pounds per bale, there's about 20,000 pounds here. The bales in the cardboard boxes are supposed to contain better quality pot. There are only a hundred of those, so only put one of those into each car. The Colombians use trash compactors to pack the pot into the bags and boxes. That's why the bags are square...and heavy. You should be able to fit 5 bales into each trunk so it'll take about 65 or 70 carloads to get rid of it all. So, if we load 5 cars a day, we should be out of here in about 14 days."

As Bryan and I were getting back into the Caddy to leave, I asked Striker if they needed anything from the store that I could bring them when I came back out.

Striker shouted out a quick list, "Beer, steaks, burgers, buns, beer, eggs, bacon, potatoes, butter, and beer. And anything else you can think of and don't forget the beer, Budweiser Long Necks."

On the way back to town, I had a talk with Bryan.

"Bryan, you had me buy a car that would be inconspicuous, one that would blend in. But you are driving this yellow Cadillac . . . with the top down . . . and wearing so many gold chains you look like Mr. T. If we don't want to draw attention to ourselves, how about if you take off a few chains, and maybe get your hair cut so you don't look like a dealer. And put the convertible top up on the Caddy so we aren't so visible to everyone on the road. And let me buy another used car that's less conspicuous for you to drive around in."

Bryan looked at me and grinned. He liked to show off his affluence, but he knew I was right. This wasn't the time or place to be flashy.

"Ok," he said. "I'll take off some of the chains and put the top up. We don't have time now, but when we get back to Fort Lauderdale, you can shop for a working car for me. But I'm not cutting my hair. You happy now?"

"Well, there is one more thing," I added. "How about we install a security system at the stash house to warn the guys when someone comes down the driveway?"

"What have you got in mind?" Bryan asked.

I told Bryan what I had in mind and he agreed. We'd try to get some security set up as soon as we had time.

CHAPTER 34
The Entertainment

WHEN WE GOT BACK INTO TOWN, we stopped at a pay phone so Bryan could call Jeremy, his buyer from Chicago. Jeremy was waiting in his hotel room for Bryan's call. Then Bryan dropped me off so I could pick up my car and I followed him to Jeremy's hotel. When we got to Jeremy's room, we saw that he wasn't alone.

There was a tall, good-looking, longhaired brunette lying on the bed. She was propped up on some pillows against the headboard. She had applied a generous amount of makeup and painted her lips candy apple red. Mascara made her long eyelashes appear even longer. She was wearing a see through tank top that was knotted under her breasts, and she wasn't wearing a bra. Her short shorts showed off her long tan legs all the way up to where I expected to see a tan line . . . but there wasn't any tan line. The black spiked high heels she was wearing suggested she knew she would have to take a hike after we arrived.

She held a stemmed wine glass in her hand. The bubbles suggested that the amber liquid inside the glass was champagne. There were red lipstick smudges on the rim of the glass. In the ice bucket sitting on the dresser was a half empty bottle of Krug. A second bottle was on its side, lying empty beside the ice bucket.

When we walked into the room, she didn't say anything and there were no introductions. She simply got off the bed, walked over to Jeremy, stuck her tongue out through her red lips, and licked the side of his face from his chin all the way up to his eyebrow. Then she picked up her purse, opened the door, and with one backward glance, she winked at Jeremy and left.

"Same old Jeremy," Bryan said, "always having a good time

with some good looking lady or another. I hope you didn't spend all your down payment on your entertainment."

Jeremy grinned. "No, I saved some for you. There's a hundred grand in the briefcase."

He grabbed the briefcase, opened it, and poured the contents onto the bed. There were 20 double-banded bundles of bills.

Bryan counted the bundles as he put them into the gym bag he had carried in.

"This is Ryan," he said to Jeremy. "He will take your cars to get them loaded. How do you want to do this?"

Jeremy reached into his pocket, pulled out a set of car keys and handed them to me.

"The first car is that blue Ford Galaxy parked right over there," he said as he pointed out the window. "Just park it there when you get back. I'll be able to see you pull in and I'll call my drivers who are in another room. Just sit in the car for a few minutes and one of my drivers will come out to see you. Exchange keys with him and he'll point out the second car for you to take. Do the same thing for the third car."

CHAPTER 35

Loading Cars

I STOPPED AT THE WINN DIXIE on the way out of town and filled a cart with the supplies Striker wanted . . . including a few cases of Budweiser Long Necks. When I arrived at the stash house, it was after dark. I got out of the car and opened the trunk. Striker saw it was me, and he lifted a tarp off a pile on the porch. Under the tarp were 5 bales ready to go. Each bale was sealed inside a black plastic garbage bag to help hold down the smell. The weight of each bale was written on a piece of tape that was stuck on the outside of the garbage bag. Striker and Jimmy put the bales in the trunk while Stephen helped me carry the groceries and beer into the house.

The rear of the car sagged from the weight in the trunk. Striker used the air compressor by the porch to fill the air shocks until the car was level. I pulled the plastic wrapping off the new air freshener hanging from the mirror and I was ready to go.

"I'll see you in about an hour with the next car," I said. And I headed back to town with 300 pounds of Colombian marijuana in the trunk.

I was nervous on the way back into town. I had a right to be. If I got caught with this much pot, I was going to jail. I kept an eye on the speedometer to make sure I didn't exceed the speed limit. I came to a complete stop at each stop sign. I used the turn signal at every turn. And I looked in the rear view mirror every few seconds to make sure I wasn't being followed.

Nothing happened. I made it back to Jeremy's hotel without any incident. What a relief. Now I only had to do this about 65 more times before the stash house was empty. I sat there for about 5 minutes when a man I had never met walked towards the car. We made eye contact. I wondered if he was as nervous as I was. I rolled down the window and waited.

He walked up and held out a set of keys.

"The next car is the white Oldsmobile over there by the black pickup truck," he said, as I got out of the car.

"Ok," I said as we exchanged keys. "Have a safe trip."

"Thanks," he replied. "I should be back in about 3 days. I'll see you then."

* * *

I repeated the trip with the Oldsmobile.

When I got back to the hotel, a different driver met me and we exchanged keys. He pointed out another Ford for the third trip. This one was a green Crown Victoria. After making the trip to the stash house and back with loaded cars 3 times without incident, I felt much better. This was a piece of cake. I got into my car and headed back to the round Holiday Inn where I was staying. I was ready for a steak, a couple of cold beers, and a bed.

CHAPTER 36

The Pickup

THE NEXT MORNING BRYAN CALLED MY room early and told me to meet him at the IHOP down the street. When I got there he was already inside having breakfast with another man. He introduced me to Bobby.

Bobby was from Miami and had a pickup truck to be loaded. He handed me the keys, told me to return it here when it was loaded, put the keys under the floor mat, and lock the doors. A driver would be having breakfast inside IHOP while watching for the truck to return. The driver had an extra set of keys, and after I left, he would get in the pickup truck and get on the road.

After I ate some breakfast, I got into the pickup truck and headed out to the stash house. The pickup truck had a camper top on the bed. The windows on each side of the camper had dark window tint on them so no one could see inside. There were some fishing poles, sleeping bags, a tent, and other camping gear inside the camper.

When I got to the stash house, the guys helped me unload the camping gear from the back of the truck. We put 12 bales inside the camper and covered them with a tarp. Then we put the camping gear back in. If anyone opened the camper top's lift-up door, all they would see was a bunch of camping gear.

Striker used the air compressor to level out the truck by filling the rear air shocks. I opened the plastic on the air freshener and headed back to the IHOP.

I put the keys under the mat and locked the doors.

As I was pulling out of the parking lot, I looked in my rear view mirror. There were 2 guys I had never met getting into the pickup truck.

CHAPTER 37

Security

THE NEXT CARS TO LOAD WOULDN'T be here until that evening, so I had a few hours to shop for the items I needed to install a security system at the stash house. I headed to Lowes where I bought a security light that had a motion sensor built in, two 30-foot pieces of chain, a heavy duty combination lock, a small tool set, five 100-foot extension cords, a no-trespassing sign, and some nails, screws, and bolts that I thought I would need.

Then I headed for Radio Shack where I found a closed circuit television system. It came with a camera, a monitor, and a 20-foot video cable. I had stepped off the distance from the stash house to the halfway point of the driveway on my trip there earlier that morning. So I knew I had to buy 400 extra feet of video cable to cover that distance.

I returned to the stash house and got Striker and Jimmy to help me while Stephen stayed at the house so the pot would not be left unguarded. We put the monitor on the porch and hooked the video cable to it. Jimmy unwound the video cable as he walked through the woods up to the point on the driveway where we were going to mount the system. Striker followed him with the extension cords so we would have power to the camera and security light. I had found a ladder behind the house and I carried it up the drive to meet them.

I chose a point where there was a substantial size tree on either side of the driveway. We bolted a chain around each of the trees. We pulled the ends of the chains across the drive and attached them together with the combination lock. We used some wire to hang the no-trespassing sign on the chain, mainly to make the chain easier to see. We didn't want anyone running into the chain . . . we wanted them to stop there.

Using the ladder, we mounted the video camera in a tree

about 20 feet off the driveway. I wanted the camera mounted where it would be out of sight but still have a good view of the driveway in front of the chain.

We mounted the security light in one of the trees that had a chain around it. We plugged a power cord and video cable into the camera and a power cord into the security light. Then we were ready to test the system. It worked so well, we all had to take turns watching the monitor on the porch while someone else drove my car down the driveway to the chain.

The idea was when a car came down the driveway the driver would see the chain and no-trespassing sign blocking his way and he would stop. If it was dark, then the motion detector would turn the security light on so the driver could see the chain. The light also provided light so the camera could see clearly as well. Human nature would compel the driver to get out of the car and look at his predicament as he figured out what to do next. This provided the guys down at the stash house a great view on the monitor of who was coming and gave them time to react if it was someone they didn't recognize or time to run if it was the cops.

CHAPTER 38

The Receipt

BRYAN'S BUYERS FROM CLEVELAND, DENVER, AND Seattle had also arrived in Tallahassee. I took the cars their drivers had brought and got them all loaded. As soon as the drivers got home, they turned around for another trip. It was a steady flow of pot to all around the country.

Bryan's buyers made flights every couple of days so they could collect money from their buyers up north and bring the cash back to Tallahassee. When Bryan picked up money from a buyer, he only counted the number of double-banded $5,000 bundles. But he wanted every bill counted later. When I wasn't taking cars out to be loaded, Bryan would have me come to his room and count the money. I was no longer a slow counter like the first time in Key West. I had gotten plenty of practice. I could count a hundred grand, in twenties, in about 30 minutes.

Daryl Kirby had his money collector, Danny, staying in town to collect the payments from Bryan and Randy. So every day or so Bryan would have me deliver the money he had collected to Danny. Danny would count the number of double-banded $5,000 bundles to see how much I brought. I'm sure he did a more thorough count after I left . . . just like we did with Bryan's customers.

Danny didn't want a written record of any transaction but I always insisted that he give me a receipt. If I gave him $100 grand, I didn't want him saying later that I only gave him $50k.

He'd reluctantly find a scrap piece of paper and scribble me a receipt. The receipt would only have a number for the month and day, a number representing how many thousands of dollars, and his initial "D." Sometimes he'd tear off a piece of newspaper and write the receipt on it like this one, showing that on March 12th, I gave Danny $95,000.

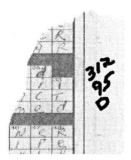

Danny was also a pilot and every couple of days he'd make a flight in his private plane back down to Fort Lauderdale to take the money he had collected to Daryl Kirby.

CHAPTER 39

The Heist

IT HAD BEEN A WEEK SINCE we had installed the security system at the stash house and there was still several thousand pounds of pot inside. It was about 2:00 in the morning and Striker was awake to keep watch. He was sitting on the porch in the dark drinking a beer and listening to the crickets and a hoot owl off in the distance.

Stephen and Jimmy were inside asleep.

With no light outside, the closed circuit monitor's screen was dark and lifeless. But Striker jumped when the black and white monitor screen suddenly came to life.

The motion detector security light had turned on and the camera could now see.

The monitor showed a car stopped in front of the chain. Its headlights were off. And there was a pickup truck stopped behind the car and its lights were also off.

Striker got up from his chair and walked over to the 12-inch monitor for a closer look. He watched as the front doors on the car opened and two men got out. The passenger was carrying a shotgun. Then the driver's door on the pickup opened and another man got out. He was also carrying a shotgun. The three of them were standing in front of the car and were staring at the chain and security light . . . but they had no idea that there was a camera watching them.

Striker couldn't tell what they were saying but it was obvious they were discussing what to do. He could see they were talking and one of the men was gesturing with his hands. He said something and pointed through the woods and the other two nodded in agreement. The two men with the shotguns stepped off the driveway into the woods and headed towards the house. Then they disappeared off the monitor screen.

The third man walked back to the car and reached inside. He retrieved a pistol and stuck it into the waistband on the back of his pants. He stepped over the chain and started walking down the driveway towards the house. Then he too disappeared off the monitor.

Striker turned the monitor off so it wouldn't emit any light. He quickly went inside and shook Stephen to wake him up. He knew better than to touch Jimmy while he was asleep, or he'd wake up fighting. So he whispered Jimmy's name and Jimmy was instantly awake.

"We've got company," Striker said. "A car and a pickup truck just stopped at the chain a minute ago. There's one man walking down the driveway and two others coming through the woods. The one in the driveway has a pistol and the other two have shotguns. Jimmy, go around behind the house. Get on the far side where you can watch for the two guys coming through the woods, but stay out of sight. Don't show yourself unless I call for you to come out. Stephen, grab the shotgun and get out on the porch with me. Stay near the back of the porch so you are also out of sight."

Striker and Stephen went out onto the porch. Standing in the shadows with no lights on, they were not visible to the man on the driveway as he walked up to the house. But there was enough moonlight for Striker and Stephen to see him. He stopped about 20 feet from the porch and looked around, scouting out the situation. Striker flipped a switch that turned on a floodlight and the man was bathed in light. With the light in his eyes, the man couldn't see Striker on the porch.

"That's close enough," Striker said. "Who are you and what are you doing here?" he asked.

Striker stepped out of the shadows so the man on the driveway could see him. Striker was holding a .38 and it was pointed at the man.

"Ah…ah…take it easy," the man said.

* * *

The man's name was Zeke, but he didn't want anyone to know his real name so he lied.

* * *

"I'm David," Zeke said. "I work for Randy. He sent me over here to get one of his customer's cars loaded."

"Why aren't you loading his customer's car at Randy's stash house?" Striker asked.

"This one is closer to town and it's late and we wanted to get the car loaded and on the road," Zeke answered. "So, Randy said it would be okay to load it here."

"Well, Randy is wrong," Striker said. "No one comes here without Bryan telling me personally that they can. How many people do you have with you?"

"I'm alone," Zeke lied again.

"Liar," Striker said. "You have 2 men with shotguns sneaking down through the woods. Holler at them and tell them to stop right where they are."

"Stephen, step out here where our friend can see you," Striker said without taking his eyes off of Zeke.

Stephen stepped out of the shadows on the porch. He was pointing his shotgun right at Zeke.

"Jimmy," Striker shouted, "do you see the two guys in the woods?"

"I see them . . . and I got a bead on them," Jimmy replied from the other side of the house. "Do you want me to shoot them?"

"Not yet . . . but if they come any closer, then you can shoot them," Striker said, loud enough for the men in the woods to hear.

Zeke hesitated for a moment as he took in the situation. Then he yelled to his friends to stop and stay where they were.

"We didn't mean any harm," Zeke said, "we were just trying to get a customer loaded and on the road."

"So that's why you were sneaking up here in the middle of the night?" Striker asked. "I want all of you to turn around, go back to your vehicles and get out of here! And, if you ever come back here again, we're not going to be so hospitable. Do you understand?"

"Yeah, sure," Zeke replied as he turned and headed back up

the driveway.

As Zeke turned the corner in the drive, Striker flipped the monitor back on. He watched as Zeke stepped over the chain and the two men stepped out of the woods. The three men chatted for a minute, and then they got into their vehicles and started backing up. When they were out of sight of the camera, Striker and Stephen walked up the drive to make sure they had left. They couldn't see the car and pickup truck, but they heard them pull away after they got onto the road.

Striker and Stephen went back down to the house and sat on the porch with Jimmy. They all popped open a Budweiser Long Neck. It would be hours before any of them would calm down enough to sleep, so they talked about what happened. Jimmy asked Striker why he let the guys leave with their guns.

Striker explained that he just wanted those guys gone.

"Taking their guns would not have prevented them from coming back again . . . and they could get more guns. And in case the stash house gets busted, I don't want to be in possession of their guns that may have been used in other heists where someone may have been killed. It would be easy for ballistic tests to tie a gun to a previous crime. So letting them leave without disarming them was the easiest and safest way to defuse the situation without anyone getting shot."

* * *

Zeke was pissed. He wanted that pot. At least they didn't know his real name. They'd be looking for someone named David. Zeke had planned on driving the car a little closer to the house while the pickup truck stayed further up the driveway. While he walked to the house, his two accomplices would go through the woods and join him at the house. If everyone at the stash house was asleep, then the three of them would enter the house and surprise the house guards. Then they would tie up the guards and load Zeke's car and the pickup truck with as much pot as they could hold.

If someone at the house was awake, then Zeke would tell them that Randy sent him here to get a customer's car loaded. If he was believed, then his accomplices would ambush the house guards while they were distracted loading Zeke's car. Then they would tie the guards up and load the pickup truck as well.

He wasn't planning on shooting anyone . . . he just wanted the pot. If no one was shot, then no one was going to report the heist to the police. What could they say, *Hey someone just stole my bales of pot?* But you never know what could go wrong in a heist. So he and his men wouldn't hesitate to shoot the guards if they had to.

It seemed like just plain dumb luck that all the house guards were awake. It looked like they were ready and waiting for Zeke and his men but he couldn't figure out how the guards knew his accomplices were sneaking up through the woods. He decided he wouldn't attempt another heist at this stash house. He'd bide his time. There'd be other stash houses and other opportunities. His partner would make sure of that.

When Bryan confronted Randy about David, Randy denied knowing anyone by that name.

CHAPTER 40

Seeds & Shake

WHEN ABOUT THREE QUARTERS OF THE pot had been distributed from the stash house, Jeremy and a couple other customers started complaining that the pot was really dry and that there was too much shake and loose seeds in the pot.

* * *

Pot is more valuable when it is fresh because it is sticky with resin, aromatic, and mellow when smoked. It deteriorates as it ages and eventually becomes so dry that the buds turn into powder and release the seeds. The powder is called shake and is harsh when smoked. And the seeds can't be smoked and are considered worthless.

* * *

So Bryan had me go to the hardware store and pick up some two by fours, a box of nails, 20 feet of chain, a roll of plastic, and some chicken wire mesh.

Using the two by fours, Striker, Stephan and Jimmy helped me make a frame that was 4 feet wide by 10 feet long. We nailed the wire mesh to the frame and, using the chain, suspended it from the ceiling about 3 feet off the floor. We unrolled the plastic sheeting and placed it on the floor under the wire mesh frame. Then we placed a bale on the chicken wire, cut it open, and spread the pot out. This allowed the shake and seeds to fall through the chicken wire onto the plastic sheeting on the floor.

Using big, heavy-duty garbage bags, we repackaged the pot that stayed on top of the wire mesh. We ended up with about 80 garbage bags full of pot that could still be sold. When we finished screening the pot, there was a pile of shake and seeds on the floor that was 3 feet wide, 8 feet long, and 3 feet high. We bagged up the shake and seeds and set those bags in one of the back rooms to keep them separated from the saleable pot.

There were 10 bags of shake and seeds and they weighed about 40 pounds each. Bryan was going to leave these bags in the house as a bonus to Nick, the guy who owned the house. He could sell it at a discounted price.

* * *

I heard later that Nick buried the bags of shake and seeds in the woods. He wanted to wait for things to calm down before he sold it. It rained several times before he dug it up a month later. It had gotten wet and was moldy and worthless.

* * *

In another week, all the pot had been sold. Bryan paid me $10,000 and then it was time to go home. On the drive back to Fort Lauderdale, I felt a lot of different emotions. I missed my family and was glad to be going home. I felt relief that all had gone well and we had not been caught. I felt guilt that I had risked my freedom to do this job because what would my family do without me. But I also felt like a provider for my family because I was going home with a pocketful of cash.

CHAPTER 41
Temptation

I ENJOYED BEING BACK HOME AND spending the next few weeks with Judy and Keith. We'd go to the beach, hang out around our pool, and grill burgers and hotdogs almost every day. Judy liked to go shopping with Renee, so when they went shopping, Keith and I would go fishing in the canals around our neighborhood. There wasn't much to catch except lots of little bluegills but it was fun spending time with Keith.

Then Bryan called and told me to come see him. We had a small job in the Keys. There was a couple thousand pounds in Key West for us. Bryan already had Jeremy and Bobby on the way down. He told me to leave in the morning and get a couple of motel rooms in Key West and he'd meet me there in the late afternoon.

The pot was in a house in downtown Key West just a block off of Duval Street. I would meet Bobby's and Jeremy's drivers in a bar, take their cars, and park them in front of the house. An old Cuban guy would stand out on the sidewalk to watch for cars or people and when it was clear, he would signal to the 2 Cuban guys in the house. Then, one of them would carry out a bale and throw it into the trunk of the car. Then we'd have to wait for a car going down the street until it was clear again.

I couldn't believe we were doing this right on a residential street and asked the old Cuban guy if he was worried about being seen.

"No," he said. "We don't want someone we don't know seeing what we are doing, but we're friends with everyone who lives on the street and they wouldn't say anything. They'd be glad we're helping the economy here."

It only took a couple of days to load all the pot into the trunks of about 8 cars. Bryan had collected down payments from Jeremy and Bobby of $225,000. The money fit into one suitcase. He told me to take the money and drive to Fort Lauderdale, get a motel room, and call Danny. He told me to keep $5,000 as my pay and give the rest to Danny. Then I could go home. Bryan was going to stay in the Keys for a few more days to set up the next job.

* * *

The next job was much larger. There were 12,000 pounds of pot in a house on Summerland Key for Bryan to sell to his customers. And they were eager to get their hands on it. Their customers loved getting this Colombian pot. It sold faster and for more money than the Mexican pot they used to get in the past. As their cash reserves built, they had more money to put down up front to ensure they got a good share of the load.

The buyers brought so much money as down payments that Bryan pulled Striker out of the stash house and put him in a hotel room to guard the money. After the second wave of transport cars had been loaded and were on their way back up north, Bryan told me that he wanted me to deliver the money that Striker was guarding to Danny up in Fort Lauderdale. When we counted out the money in the hotel room, there was $1,130,000. There were some bundles of $100 bills, but most of it was in twenties.

It took one large suitcase, a carry-on bag, a green army duffel bag, a briefcase, and a cardboard box to pack all the stacks of cash. It barely fit into the trunk of the car I was to drive. As I pulled out onto US1 and headed north out of the Keys, crazy thoughts started going through my head.

I had delivered a lot of payments to Danny that he then delivered to Daryl, but this was the first time I had ever considered not completing the delivery. This was the most money that I had ever seen or delivered at one time. I had made lots of deliveries of $50,000 to $250,000, but never a million dollars!

* * *

One million one hundred thirty thousand dollars to be exact, that's 113 followed by a lot of zeroes. I was tempted to keep it.

Hey, don't judge me. What would you have been thinking?

My mind was gong a hundred miles an hour. *Is it worth the risk? Could I get away with it? How long before they started looking for me when I didn't show up in Fort Lauderdale? How long would they look for me before they gave up? Where would I go? How long would this money last on the run? What could I do with a million dollars? What about my wife and kids?*

Then logic started getting in the way. Of course I couldn't get away with it. They would never stop looking for me until they found me. The money would go fast on the run. It wasn't like I could just go home and put it in the bank and live on the interest. And I couldn't leave my wife and sons. And I couldn't stop and get them. If I didn't show up in Fort Lauderdale in the amount of time it should take to drive there, there would be someone at my home before I could even get there. It was foolish to think I could steal a million dollars from the organization and get away with it. But . . . it sure was tempting.

* * *

I stopped at a motel in Fort Lauderdale and got a room. Unfortunately, the only room they had left was on the second floor, and there was no elevator. You had to go up the outside stairs from the parking lot. I had to make several trips to carry the box, the carry-on bag, the suitcase and the briefcase up the stairs and into the room.

Then I had to tackle the duffel bag. It was so heavy that it was difficult just getting it out of the trunk. It hit the ground with a soft *THUD*. I tried to pick it up but it was too heavy. So I dragged it across the parking lot, up the stairs, and into the room.

Then I sat down on the edge of the bed and once more considered what I was going to do. This was more money than I would probably make during my lifetime. Then I thought of Keith . . . and Billy . . . and Judy. They were worth much more.

I picked up the phone and called Danny.

CHAPTER 42
The Barn

IT WAS SEVERAL WEEKS LATER WHEN Bryan called again. There was 10,000 pounds of pot that was waiting for us in a barn up in southern Alabama. Bryan's customers and their drivers were on the way to the nearest town, which was 20 miles from the farm.

Striker, Stephen, and Jimmy were guarding the pot when Bryan took me to the farm. The barn was a quarter mile off the road in the middle of a field. The field was fenced and you had to stop and open a gate by the road to get into the field. Since this was farming community, everyone knew everyone else and they all watched out for each other. A steady stream of cars going across the field to the barn would surely be noticed by the local farmers, so we wanted to keep the daytime traffic limited. We decided we would only load cars after dark.

That evening, I put snapshots of my sons, Keith and Billy, in my shirt pocket for good luck. Then I took the first car out to the farm to be loaded. It was dark and I made sure there were no headlights coming from either direction before I stopped at the gate. I turned off the headlights and the overhead light switch so it wouldn't come on when I opened the door. I jumped out of the car, opened the gate, drove into the field, and shut the gate. I quickly put some duct tape over the taillights so they couldn't be seen when I applied the brakes, and then I drove to the barn.

Striker, Stephen, and Jimmy heard the car coming across the field and were ready to load the car when I got there. I noticed that I could see some of the bales of pot from the open door of the barn. I suggested we move some bales of hay in front of the bales of pot so they couldn't be seen from the door. So after the trunk was loaded, I pulled off my shirt so it wouldn't get sweaty and dirty and helped them move some bales of hay in front of the bales of pot.

Then we heard an engine. We turned off the light in the barn and stepped outside. The engine noise was coming from above the barn. It sounded like a small plane. It was a clear night but we couldn't see the plane. We thought it was odd that the plane didn't have any lights on. We listened as it circled in the air over the barn for about 15 minutes before it left. We listened as the engine noise faded away in the direction of town.

Striker said they needed some food and asked if I'd bring back some supplies on my next trip. I told him the grocery stores were closed but I'd bring them some beer on my next trip and deliver some groceries the next day. I put on my shirt, got into the car and headed back across the field. After I got through the gate, I took the duct tape off the taillights, turned on the headlights, and headed back to town. I still had 2 more cars to bring out here and get loaded up tonight.

The next 2 trips that night were uneventful and I got back to my motel room about 4:00 in the morning. As I undressed to shower I reached for the pictures of my sons in my shirt pocket. They were gone!

CHAPTER 43

The Tail

I MET BRYAN AT NOON FOR breakfast and told him about hearing the plane over the barn. He said it was probably just some pilot out for a joy ride and not to worry about it. He said we had 3 more cars to load tonight and then gave me some money to buy some food and supplies for the guys at the barn.

When I delivered the supplies to the barn, I told the guys I had lost the pictures of my sons and asked them to help me look for them. We searched inside the barn, and where I had parked the cars outside, but we couldn't find the pictures.

* * *

I wouldn't know until much later that they were now in Stephen's pocket; soon to be turned over to DEA Agent Scott Jones as proof that I had been there.

* * *

When I left the barn and headed back towards town, I had a funny feeling that something wasn't right. I kept my speed up until I made the first turn onto a small two-lane road. I knew this road was about 4 miles long and had no turn offs. It started where I turned off the road I was on, and ended at a stop sign where you had to turn either left or right onto another road.

Just as I turned onto the road, there was a long hill in front of me. It was about a quarter mile from the turn to the top of the hill. I slowed down as I approached the hill and watched in my rear view mirror. Just as I reached the top of the hill, three light blue cars made the turn onto the road I was on. They were all bunched up together like they were tailgating each other and they were going pretty fast. Then I was over the crest of the hill and couldn't see them anymore.

I picked up my speed a little, and continued to watch my

121

rearview mirror. I had a long straight stretch of road in front of me, so they had plenty of time to get over that hill. But, I never saw them come over that hill. I stayed under the speed limit all the way to the stop sign at the end of the road so I could continue to watch for the three cars. There was a small country store at the corner, so I pulled in and waited. The blue cars never showed.

When I met Bryan back in town, I told him about the cars. I said that I thought I was being tailed, and when they realized I might have spotted them, they backed off. He said I had an over active imagination and not to worry about it. He said everything was going smoothly and if anything were amiss, we would have been busted.

It took another week to get rid of the rest of the pot in the barn and I didn't notice anything else happen that was out of the ordinary. Maybe Bryan was right.

CHAPTER 44

The DEA Agent

DEA AGENT SCOTT JONES WAS FURIOUS! He had a right to be. He had invested a lot of time learning about Daryl's operation and these agents had screwed up. They were supposed to remain incognito and they had been spotted.

He didn't want anyone in Daryl's organization knowing they were being surveilled, otherwise it would make his job much more difficult. He wanted to gather enough evidence to ensure that when it was time, everyone involved in the organization would face lengthy prison sentences . . . including the Cuban that was bringing the pot up from Colombia and selling it to Daryl.

"How could you be so careless?" he yelled. "All you had to do was tail him. You are supposed to be professionals and you let this country bumpkin see you tailing him? I ought to have every one of you transferred to an office job. Maybe you could handle answering the phones without screwing up."

CHAPTER 45

Heist II

A FEW WEEKS LATER WE WERE on our way back to Tallahassee again. Marcos had provided Daryl with 40,000 pounds of Colombian pot. Daryl gave Randy and Bryan each 20,000 pounds to sell.

Randy's share was in a separate stash house from Bryan's.

The stash house Bryan got was a little one-room house on a two-lane country road about 15 miles out of Tallahassee. The 325 bales of pot were stacked along the walls from floor to ceiling all around the house. There wasn't much room left in the small house, just an aisle from the 2 outside doors to the kitchen and bathroom. The house had a long dirt driveway and you couldn't see any neighboring houses from the driveway. That was good. If we couldn't see them, they couldn't see us.

Jimmy had a family emergency come up so only Striker and Stephen were guarding the house this time. I brought 3 or 4 cars to the stash house every day to be loaded. At this rate it would take us about 3 weeks to get rid of the pot. About 10 days into the job, half the pot had left the stash house and was scattered all around the country.

All the drivers had made several nonstop trips and Bryan wanted everyone to take a couple days break to give the drivers time to rest up. He didn't want some overly tired driver to fall asleep at the wheel and wreck with a trunk full of pot. He told me to drive my car out to the stash house and relieve Striker and Stephen for a couple of days. I would let them take my car and I would stay there until they returned. I wouldn't need the car anyway because I couldn't go anywhere.

On my way to the stash house, I picked up some steaks, beer, and a couple of paperbacks to read because there was no television at the stash house. Striker and Stephen left and I settled in for my two-day stay. I fired up the charcoal grill

124

outside and popped the top off a Budweiser Long Neck as I waited for the coals to be ready. I wrapped a potato in foil and stuck it into the coals. I would give the potato time to cook before I threw a T-bone on the grill. I pulled up a lawn chair under a shade tree and started reading The Stand, one of Stephen King's latest books, while I downed a couple more long necks.

The sun was setting as I finished my steak. I wanted to be inside the house when it got dark and I didn't want the lights on. It's easy to see in through the windows when there are lights on in a house, but hard to see out. I was there alone so there would be no look out when I was asleep so I felt a little uneasy. There were no beds in the house but there were two sleeping bags and a couple of pillows.

Since I was there alone I decided to block the doors and windows with bales of pot so no one could bust in and surprise me when I was asleep. After I blocked the doors and windows, I put some beer bottles on top of the bales in front of the doors so if anyone tried to bust through the doors, the beer bottles would fall and wake me up when they hit the floor.

Then I stacked up some bales to make a fort in the middle of the room and put my sleeping bag inside the fort. That way if someone started shooting into the house, the bales surrounding me would give me protection. My fort looked like the image below:

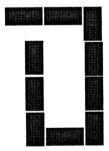

Now, since it was dark, there was nothing else to do but go to sleep. I went inside my fort and lay down on top of my sleeping bag. Striker had left a .38 revolver for me and I laid it on the floor by my pillow. As I lay there, I wondered what Judy and Keith were doing. I missed them and couldn't wait to get back home. Only another week or so and I could be with them again. With them on my mind, I fell asleep.

A few hours later, the sound of a beer bottle hitting the floor startled me awake. My first thought was I had placed a bottle too close to the edge on one of the stacks of bales in front of the doors and it had just fallen over. Then I heard the door rattle. Someone was trying to get in!

I grabbed the .38 and went to one of the windows to peek outside. I could see a car in the driveway with no lights on and a shadowy figure running from the car towards the back of the house.

"Who's there?" I shouted!

* * *

The man's name was Zeke, but he didn't want anyone to know his real name so, again he lied.

* * *

"It's James," Zeke said from right outside the door. So I knew there were at least 2 people outside. "Randy sent me over to get some trash bags. We are loading some customers tonight and we ran out of bags. There aren't any stores open so he told me to come and get some from you."

"You came here in the middle of the night and tried to bust through the door because you needed trash bags?" I replied incredulously. "So why didn't you just knock on the door and why is your buddy sneaking around to the back of the house?" I didn't wait for a reply, "I'm pointing a .38 through the window and it's aimed right at you. You have 5 seconds to turn around and head back to your car before I start shooting. And call out to your buddy behind the house and tell him to get into the car too. Now!" I started counting. "Five, four, three."

"OK . . . OK. Calm down," he said. "We're leaving. Let's go," he shouted out to his buddy behind the house.

I watched in the dim light as the two of them got into the car. His buddy got into the back seat as James climbed into the

126

front passenger seat. That meant there was someone else driving so there were three of them.

I couldn't sleep the rest of the night. My mind was full of unanswered questions. *What would have happened if I hadn't stacked those bales of pot in front of the doors? What if I hadn't put beer bottles on top of the stacks? What if James had called my bluff? Since only Bryan, Striker, Stephen, and I had been to the stash house, how did James know where it was located? Who had masterminded this intended heist? What if they had shot through the window while I was peeking out? How did they pick a night when I was here alone to stage the heist? And who the heck is James? Was Randy involved?*

I still had another day and night to stay here by myself and I had no way to contact anyone. It was going to be a long 36 hours or so before Striker and Stephen returned and I could tell Bryan what had happened.

* * *

Bryan was furious! He trusted Striker and Stephen and he knew I wasn't involved since I had prevented the heist from happening.

"It can't be Randy," Bryan said. "He doesn't know where my stash house is and I don't know where his is located either. I am going to have to have a talk with Daryl and he needs to talk with Marcos. The only other people who knew where the stash house was located are Marcos's men who delivered the pot to the warehouse before we even got here. If one of Marcos's men is involved with James, I don't want to be responsible for the pot if it gets ripped off. And I pity whoever the leak is if Marcos finds him."

* * *

Zeke was disappointed. He thought this heist was going to be a piece of cake. He had been told that there was only going to be one guard at the house that night. Since the guard would have to sleep at some point, the middle of the night seemed like the best time.

There were supposed to be 150 bales still in the house. At an average of 60 pounds per bale, that was 9,000 pounds of pot. Zeke would have sold the pot cheap to get rid of it quickly. But even at $100 a pound, that was $900,000! After paying his men and all his other expenses, he still would have netted half a million dollars. Of course, he had to split that with his partner . . . but still . . . $250,000 was nothing to sneeze at.

* * *

When Bryan confronted Randy . . . Randy again denied any involvement and said he didn't have anyone named James working for him.

It took another 10 days to get the rest of the pot from the stash house sold to Bryan's customers. There were no further incidents. Then, I got to go home once again.

CHAPTER 46
Night Vision

BRYAN DECIDED HE WANTED TO BEEF up security and asked if I could find any night vision equipment. Sure enough, I found a store on Brickell Avenue in Miami that carried night vision goggles. I went to check it out. It was awesome. It was like a toy store for private investigators, spies, and third world dictators. Not only did they have night vision goggles, they had tracking devices you could put on cars, receivers so you could track those cars, small bugs that you could plant in telephones or hide in a lamp or under a table, Taser guns that shot out darts attached with wires so you could immobilize someone with 50,000 volts, wide frequency receivers to detect bugs or tracking devices, voice stress analyzers to tell if someone was lying, phone tap detectors to see if a phone had been tapped, and so much more.

A salesman who was very well dressed asked if he could assist me.

"How well do the night vision goggles work and how much are they?" I asked.

"Let's go in the back where you can test one out," he said. "Then if you like what you see, we'll talk about price. We don't power them up out here because normal light could damage the sensitive receptors."

When we got into a room in the back, he turned out the light and I couldn't see anything. The only light entering the room was from a small crack under the door. Then he turned on the night vision goggles, handed them to me, and walked to the other side of the room. I couldn't see him at all.

"Now look through the goggles," he said.

When I brought the goggles up to my eyes, I could see him very clearly. It was kind of like a black and white image except everything was green and black. I watched him as he moved around the room.

"The goggles magnify existing light," he explained. "They won't work in zero light, but moonlight or starlight is enough for you to be able to see clearly."

"Why does everything look green?" I asked.

"Light that is around 550 nanometers is the easiest for the eyes to distinguish things in the dark," he explained. "Light at that frequency is green. And since the eyes are more sensitive to light at that frequency the goggles don't have to amplify the light as much so the batteries can last longer. As for the price, they are $5,000. Are you interested?"

* * *

After I told Bryan how much they were, he gave me $10,000 and told me to pick up 2 pairs. One pair was for us to take to our next stash house and the other was for Daryl to give to Marcos. Marcos gave his pair to the captain of one of his mother ships. The first time the captain tried out his night vision goggles, he saw a boat that looked like a Coast Guard vessel, jumped, and accidentally dropped the goggles overboard.

CHAPTER 47
Heist III

AFTER BRYAN HAD HIS TALK WITH Daryl about the attempted heist, Daryl wondered if one of Bryan or Randy's stash house guards was involved. He had met another car collector named George who had some big time connections up in Detroit. George had been trying to get Daryl to let him get involved for a couple of years, but Daryl had put him off because Marcos only wanted Daryl to deal with a couple of buyers. But now Daryl thought it was time to give George a chance. He decided he would continue to do business with Bryan and Randy, but he would also sell pot to George and let him run the next stash house.

George set up a stash house in Marathon Key for the 20,000 pounds of pot that Marcos was going to let Daryl sell. George had three of his men from Detroit stationed as guards at the stash house. It took a week for half of the pot to be sold to George, Bryan, and Randy's customers.

* * *

Since Stephen wasn't a guard at this stash house, he was driving a car for Jeremy . . . delivering pot to Chicago. But, he still kept in contact with DEA agent Scott Jones. Stephen couldn't tell Jones about all the drivers and cars that came to this stash house, but he did tell him the location of the stash house and how much pot Jeremy was getting

Jones had two of his agents stake out the stash house, and when George came to check on the stash house, those agents followed George back to his apartment in Miami.

* * *

Everything was running smoothly at the stash house but the men stationed there were letting their guard down. It was a Thursday evening and the guards weren't expecting to see any more vehicles that needed to be loaded until the next day. They grilled some steaks and were eating their dinners and drinking beer while they watched television in the living room. It was hot and humid and there was no air conditioning in the house. So they had opened the front and back doors but had kept the screen doors latched to allow the ever-present breeze in the Keys to flow through the house. Their steaks were about half eaten when both screen doors were kicked open simultaneously. Three armed men rushed into the house. They were all wearing masks so they couldn't be identified.

The stash house guards didn't have time to respond. Their hands were duct taped behind them and pillowcases were put over their heads. Then they lay quietly on the floor as instructed. One of the armed men made a call on a portable CB radio and a few minutes later a U-Haul truck pulled into the driveway and backed up to the house. While one of the armed intruders stood guard over the three tied up men, the other two intruders and the U-Haul driver loaded the 10,000 pounds of pot that was still in the house into the rental truck.

* * *

Zeke smiled as he and his men drove away with their booty. Finally, he had made a successful heist. His partner had been right; there was a lot of pot in this stash house and the guards were inexperienced.

As he followed the U-Haul truck, he was calculating his profit. 10,000 pounds at $100 a pound was a million dollars. He'd pay his men a hundred grand each and still net $700,000. He couldn't wait to tell his partner the good news.

* * *

When Daryl found out that the pot in the stash house had been stolen, he tried to call George, but George wasn't answering his phone. Daryl went to the apartment George had rented in Miami. He knocked on the door but no one answered. He tried the door handle and found the door unlocked, so he walked in.

George was sitting on a chair with his head leaning on the kitchen table in a pool of blood. There was a bullet hole in the middle of his forehead. Daryl was quite shaken up but he made sure he wiped his fingerprints off the door handle as he left. He had no idea who had shot George.

* * *

"You want some more coffee, honey?" the waitress asked, as she started to refill the cup. "Looks like yours is getting cold."

"No, no more," Agent Scott Jones said as he put his hand over the cup. He pulled a five-dollar bill out of his pocket and handed it to her. "Keep the change," he said as he headed for the door.

He had seen the two men pull up outside and now they were waiting for him in the shiny black Chevrolet Suburban parked outside. He walked across the parking lot and climbed into the back seat of the SUV.

"Is it done?" Agent Scott Jones asked.

"George is no longer a problem," the agent in the front passenger seat said. "Do you want us to call in the cleanup crew to sanitize the scene?"

"No," Jones answered. "The neighbors will call the police in a few days to report an awful smell coming from his apartment. So let the police clean up the mess. We've got more important things to do. Zeke called and told me his operation was successful and the U-Haul is on its way to the warehouse in Jacksonville. Stay on him to ensure we get our half of the money, and find out who his customers are. We'll deal with them later."

* * *

Daryl called Bryan with news of the heist and then Bryan called me.

"Remember the store where you bought the night vision goggles?" Bryan asked. "Go back there and get some more equipment. Pick up a voice stress analyzer, a bug detector, and a phone tap detector. And while you're there, pick up another pair of night vision goggles. Then, I need you to go down to the Keys and question everyone down there that was involved in this operation. I'll send Striker and Badge with you for muscle."

"Who's Badge?" I asked.

"He's someone Daryl introduced to me," Bryan said. "He's crazy, but he's loyal, and he'll do anything you ask him to do. A few years ago, he stood up to a mugger that was trying to rob an old lady. The mugger slashed Badge's face before running away. He calls the knife scar he got his Badge of Courage. So now everyone calls him 'Badge'."

CHAPTER 48

The Lie Detector

BRYAN GAVE ME $20,000 AND I went back to the toy store for spies on Brickell Avenue. I bought a voice stress analyzer, a wide frequency receiver to check for bugs and tracking devices, a phone tap analyzer, and another set of night vision goggles to replace the ones Marcos's boat captain had dropped overboard.

"You'll need to take a class on how to use the voice stress analyzer," the salesman said. "The class takes one day and costs $500. The next class is tomorrow from 9:00 until about 2:00 pm."

I paid him the extra $500 for the class. He wrote the address where the class would be held on the back of his business card, and handed it to me.

* * *

When I got to the class, there were about 30 other people in attendance. Some were dressed business casual and some wore suits, neckties, and shiny shoes. The business casual guys were probably private eyes but the shiny shoes guys looked like they were from some official government agency. I knew the CIA, DEA, and FBI all had equipment that made the Brickell Avenue store's merchandise look like toys. So, they were probably there just to see who was buying this kind of merchandise. I really felt out of place in my jeans, t-shirt, and flip-flops.

"The voice stress analyzer detects small changes in a person's voice," the instructor said. "When someone is lying, the muscles in his neck involuntarily tense up and that makes his voice change frequency. Not so much that you could detect it with your ears, but the machine can detect those small changes. Start off by asking the person you are interviewing simple questions that you know to be true. As you do this, use the knobs on the face of the detector to adjust the position of the needle so it points to the middle of the dial. When the dial stays midrange on the known truthful questions, then you can start asking what you really want to know. If the person lies, the needle on the dial will swing to the right. The farther the needle swings to the right, the more stressed the person is about the question you asked."

He then asked for a volunteer and someone actually raised his hand. The volunteer may have been a plant that worked for the company. But as the instructor asked some questions, it appeared that that the volunteer may have cheated on his wife, and on his taxes, sometime in the past.

"Remember," the instructor said, "using the voice stress analyzer is part technology and part technique. You will improve your skill with practice."

* * *

That evening, I tested it out on Judy, and on Keith. The only time the analyzer indicated that either of them was being anything other than truthful was when I asked Keith if he was the one responsible for my new toy remote control car ending up at the bottom of our pool.

"The machine says you're lying, Keith," I said. "Are you telling me the truth?"

Tears welled up in his eyes and he looked guilty as he fidgeted around and started crying.

"I'm sorry, Daddy," he said. "I didn't mean to drive it into the pool. It just happened."

OK . . . this thing works . . . at least on a seven year old.

* * *

Bryan wanted to see the voice stress analyzer demonstrated before I headed to the Keys. Jeremy was in town to make a payment to Bryan, so Bryan told me to bring it over to Jeremy's motel room and he would meet me there.

I explained to Bryan and Jeremy how the sensitive equipment could detect frequency changes caused by minor muscle stresses around the voice box when someone lied. Bryan asked Jeremy if he would volunteer to be the test subject. Jeremy was nervous about being given a lie detector test, but he couldn't very well say "no" to Bryan.

"Ok...but before we get started," Jeremy said, "let me tell you about the weights on the last load. When we got the pot to Chicago and weighed the last driver's load, we had 40 more pounds than what you said we had. Instead of 240 pounds, we actually had 280 pounds. So I owe you an extra $10,000 you didn't know about."

"Is there anything else you want to tell me before we get started?" Bryan asked.

"No . . . no, that's it," Jeremy said.

I closed the lid on the analyzer's case and fastened the latches.

"What are you doing?" Jeremy asked. "Aren't you going to test me?"

"I just did," I replied. "I didn't even have to turn it on to get you to confess to owing Bryan an extra 10 grand. That confession alone paid for the voice stress analyzer twice over."

Jeremy didn't think that was funny, but Bryan was howling in laughter.

I pulled out the new night vision goggles and gave them to Bryan. He turned off the lights and he and Jeremy were playing with them in the darkened room when I left.

CHAPTER 49

Truth Or Lies

THE NEXT MORNING, I HEADED FOR the Keys where I would meet up with Striker and Badge. Bryan had arranged for us to stay at Manny's house, just in case we needed a nice, quiet, isolated place to interview someone. Bryan had given Manny some money to disappear for a few days, and Manny had left us a key hidden under a rock by the front door.

Daryl had provided us with the names of six people that he thought might know something about the heist. I parked my car in Manny's garage and we took the car that Striker had rented in Fort Lauderdale. I didn't want my car and license plate seen by anyone we were going to talk with about the heist.

Our first stop was to see Craig, who lived on Summerland Key. Craig had brought some cars out to the stash house to be loaded, so he knew where the stash house was located. That made him a suspect. He was home when we got there, and he opened the door when I knocked.

"Can I help you?" he asked.

"Are you Craig?" I asked.

"Yes," he replied as he sized us up. "Who are you?"

"You loaded some cars at Daryl's stash house a few days ago. You probably already know that there was a heist at the stash house. Daryl sent us here to ask you some questions. He said you would cooperate."

"Hey, I didn't have anything to do with that," Craig protested.

"Then you won't mind talking to me for a few minutes," I said.

Craig looked behind me at Striker and Badge. "Who are they?" he asked.

"They are just here to make sure you do cooperate. Just

138

answer some questions for me and you won't even know they're here. They'll just sit quietly in a corner until we finish talking. Now, can we come in?"

Craig stood there for a moment sizing up the situation and weighing out his options. He really didn't have any options, but I gave him time to realize this on his own. He opened the door a little wider.

"Sure . . . I guess so," he said, and we all went inside.

"Craig, this is a voice stress analyzer," I said as I opened the case I had set on his kitchen table. "It will tell me if you are answering my questions truthfully. If you tell me the truth, we'll leave in a little bit and you can get back to whatever you were doing. But if it tells me you are lying, you are not going to enjoy the rest of your day. Do you understand?"

"I'm telling you the truth, man. I don't know anything about the heist," he said.

"We'll find out for sure in a few minutes," I said.

"Is your name Craig?" I asked, as I adjusted the dial to record a truthful answer.

"Do you live on Summerland Key? Is this your house? Is today Tuesday? Is it hot today?" The needle stayed in the middle of the dial as he answered all these questions.

"Did you take cars to the stash house to get them loaded with pot?" I asked.

The needle edged to the right as he answered. That question stressed him, but he was telling the truth. He had taken cars to be loaded.

"Were you involved in the heist?" I asked. "Do you know anyone who was involved in the heist? Did you tell anyone where the stash house was located? Would you tell me if you knew who made the heist?"

"No . . . No . . . No . . . Yes," he answered. The needle on the dial stayed in the truthful range.

"Have you ever stolen anything?" I asked.

"No," he said, as a droplet of sweat trickled down his forehead and his eyes averted mine.

The needle on the dial swung all the way to the right.

"The machine says you're lying, Craig! You better tell me the truth."

More sweat beaded up on his forehead. I wouldn't even need the machine to tell me he was nervous now.

"OK . . . OK," he started. "I've stolen a few things in my life. I took an outboard motor off a dingy last year when the owner was out of town. And I pocketed some cigarettes at the store without paying for them. And I took some money out of my girlfriend's purse. But I never stole anything from Daryl. And I didn't steal the pot from the stash house. I swear."

The needle on the dial swung from center to slightly right as he confessed his sins. But he was telling the truth. He wasn't involved in the heist.

"Craig, I believe you," I said. "If you hear anything about the heist, I want you to contact Daryl. Will you do that?"

"Yes, of course," he said. The needle went halfway to the right. Maybe he would . . . and maybe he wouldn't.

"OK, Craig, I think you are in the clear," I said. "Don't tell anyone that we were here. I don't want anyone to be tipped off before I get a chance to talk with them."

"Yeah, sure," he said. "I mean no…I won't say anything to anybody."

"And Craig," I said as we were leaving, "you ought to pay the dingy owner for the motor you stole."

That evening and the next day, we were able to talk with the other five suspects. The results were similar. None of them had been involved in the heist. But, we found out that one had robbed a convenience store, two had stolen from their employers, and one was currently cheating on his wife.

Boy, the things these guys would confess just to prove they were telling us the truth. Everyone that we interviewed was home alone, and very cooperative, so we didn't need to take any of them back to Manny's house for a more private chat.

CHAPTER 50
Badge & The Pool

I WAS READY TO HEAD HOME but Striker and Badge talked me into going into Key West to stay overnight before we headed back to Fort Lauderdale. We got 2 rooms at a hotel right on the beach; one for me, and one for Striker and Badge. While I sipped on Pina Coladas at the cabana bar behind the hotel, Striker and Badge downed rum and cokes at the hotel pool. When I found them there later, it was obvious that they had been drinking a lot. Striker was hitting on some bikini-clad girls and I could see the girls were getting annoyed.

So I talked Striker and Badge into going up to their room to change so we could go out for some dinner. They only agreed after I promised to hit some bars with them after dinner.

We ate at Sloppy Joe's bar. Burgers and beer were the staples for dinner. And then Striker and Badge started hitting the rum and cokes again. After Striker tried to drag an uncooperative girl to the dance floor, one of the bouncers came over and suggested I take my friends elsewhere.

I tried to talk them into going back to the hotel and calling it a night, but they insisted that the night was still young and they wanted to party. So as I headed back towards the hotel, they stumbled down the sidewalk in the other direction.

* * *

The next morning after I showered and changed, I went to Striker's room. Striker finally answered the door after I knocked on it for 10 minutes. His eyes were bloodshot and he reeked of alcohol. Badge was on his bed and I could smell puke. The rest of the room was also a disaster. Clothes were spread everywhere, towels were on the floor, beer bottles littered the floor and there was an empty bottle of Captain Morgan lying on its side. There was also a night table with a broken leg in the corner.

"What happened to the night table?" I asked.

"Badge bit the leg off after I bet him he couldn't do it," Striker said. "Why are you here so early?"

"It's not early," I replied. "It's almost time to check out. You guys need to pack up."

"I think we're going to stay another day," Striker said. "Why don't you stay and party with us tonight?"

"I think I'll just meet you back in Fort Lauderdale," I said. "I'll meet you guys at your place tomorrow evening after I meet with Bryan to get your pay."

* * *

When I got to Striker's the next evening, he had a girl in his apartment.

"Some entertainment," he explained by way of an introduction. "She's from an escort service."

"Where's Badge?" I asked.

"He's in the hospital," Striker said. "He decided to go swimming last night and thought he could dive into the pool from our second story hotel room balcony. He almost made it too. He hit the concrete deck a couple of feet short of the pool and broke his collarbone, two ribs, his nose, and his left arm. It would've been even worse if he had made it to the pool. The pool didn't have any water in it! Maintenance had drained the pool so they could work on it. Someone saw him jump and called the front desk. They called an ambulance and it took him to the hospital. I stopped by to see him this morning before I left the Keys. He said they are going to run some tests to check for internal injuries. I expect he'll be there for a few days. By the way," he continued, "would you mind taking the rental car and turning it in for me since I have company?"

"Is that your rental car parked out front," I asked, "with a busted out window and a huge dent all the way down the passenger side?"

"Yeah," he said. "I had a little mishap on the way back. I was drinking a beer and it spilled in my lap. It was the last one I had so I took my eyes off the road while I tried to keep it from all spilling out. That's when I sideswiped the guardrail. It pissed me off so bad that I kicked the window with my foot."

"Striker, if I was you, I'd park that car in a shopping center somewhere and call the car rental place and tell them it was stolen. I'm sorry, buddy, but I'm not going anywhere near that car. You're on your own with this one."

CHAPTER 51

Phone Tap

BRYAN SAID HE WANTED ME TO take the bug detector and phone tap equipment to Daryl's house and check his house and phones to see if he was being bugged or tapped. So I headed there next.

Daryl had a security gate at the end of his driveway. I pushed the button on the intercom and Daryl buzzed me in. There were two collectible cars parked in his driveway. Each of them was worth more money than I had ever made. My car looked like a servant's car parked next to them. Daryl was waiting for me at the front door and invited me in.

He offered me a drink, which I declined.

"Thanks for doing that little job for me in the Keys," he said. "I didn't think any of them was involved in the heist, but I had to prove that to Marcos. Bryan told me you could check my house for bugs and tell if my phones have been tapped. Is that so?"

"I brought a wide frequency receiver to check for bugs," I explained. "And a phone tap detection device. If someone has placed a bug in your house, or tapped your phone, I should be able to find it."

"OK," he said. "I'll be in my study. Do whatever you need to do and let me know what you find."

I put on the headphones that came with the wide frequency receiver and picked up the handheld antennae. I started sweeping the antennae around tables, lamps, phones, curtains, flower vases and anywhere else I thought someone could plant a bug. It took me an hour to go through the entire house and I didn't get any signals. As far as I could tell, there were no bugs planted in the house.

I unscrewed the mouth and earpieces off the phone and peered inside. There was nothing in the phone that looked like it didn't belong there. I unplugged the telephone cord from the wall and plugged it into the phone tap detector. Using another phone cord, I attached the detector to the telephone outlet in the wall.

When the phone is not being used, the detector should read about 48 volts. That's the voltage supplied by the phone company on their lines to power your phone. That's why a landline phone will still work even when you lose electrical power to your house. When you use your phone, that voltage will drop to about 9 volts. If someone has placed a simple wiretap on your phone, the voltage will be even less.

I looked at the meter. It read 48 volts. I picked up the phone and got a dial tone. The voltage dropped to 5 volts. This line was powering more than just this phone. Daryl's phone was tapped.

You would think that if someone knew their phone was tapped, they would use that information to their advantage . . . like telling someone on the phone that the next shipment was coming in on Friday in Marathon, when it was really coming in on Thursday in Perry.

But noooo . . . not Daryl.

When I informed him that his phone was tapped, he grabbed up the receiver and started swearing into it.

"You lousy SOBs," he yelled into the mouthpiece. "Who do you think you are listening in on my private conversations? I'm going to sue you and see to it that you lose your jobs. Now get off my phone and leave me alone!" he screamed as he slammed the receiver back into the phone cradle.

Then, for good measure, he yanked the phone out of the wall and threw it across the room.

"There . . . that ought to fix things," he said.

CHAPTER 52

The Connie Bust

DARYL NEVER FOUND OUT WHO STOLE the pot from the stash house in Marathon. Marcos informed Daryl that he still had to pay the entire amount he owed. He insisted that the debt be paid in full before he would front Daryl any more pot. But Daryl didn't have $2 million just lying around to cover his debt to Marcos. He was going to have to look for some other way to get the pot he so desperately needed to sell.

In his dealings with antique collectible cars, Daryl had met Ray Foley, another collector. Ray liked cars but he bought and sold airplanes for a living. Daryl called Ray and set up a meeting.

Ray had a Lockheed Constellation Model L049 that he had just finished refurbishing. The 'Connie', Ray explained, was powered by four 18-cylinder radial Wright R-3350 engines. It had a top speed of 330 mph and cruised at 304 mph. It had a range of 5,105 miles with an 18,000 pound payload.

Daryl and Ray struck a deal and Ray became Daryl's partner. Ray would furnish the airplane and Daryl would arrange to import and sell the pot.

The 'Connie' was going to pick up the pot in Colombia and land in the panhandle near Pensacola. The pot would then be trucked to Tallahassee and stashed at Nick's house.

Bryan and I flew to Tallahassee the day before the 'Connie' was to land.

"Go rent us a car," Bryan told me when we landed at the airport in Tallahassee.

I had to use my credit card and driver's license at the Hertz rental counter to get us a car. It was a 4-door, burgundy Chevy Impala. We got in the rental and checked into the round Holiday Inn.

"Now find out where we can rent a big U-Haul truck,"

Bryan said. "We're going to take the truck closer to where the 'Connie' is landing tomorrow. I'll follow you in the Chevy and we'll get a motel room near Pensacola. Tomorrow, we'll be taken to the airstrip where the 'Connie' is landing so we know where to take the U-Haul. Tomorrow night, you'll drive the U-Haul to the strip just before the plane lands. There will be a ground crew there to load the truck and then you'll drive it back to Nick's house. Striker, Stephen, and Jimmy will be there waiting."

I used the phone in the hotel room to call the U-Haul places until I found one with a big truck available. Bryan drove me there and waited until I rented the truck. Then we got on I-10 and headed west. After about an hour on the road, Bryan pulled in front of me and signaled that he was getting off at the next exit.

We went into a restaurant and ordered something to eat.

"I'm going to make some calls on the pay phone outside," Bryan said.

When he came back in, our food had just arrived. I could tell by the look on Bryan's face that something was wrong, but he couldn't talk until the waitress left.

"There's been a delay," Bryan said. "The 'Connie' has some mechanical problems and it's not coming in tomorrow. Daryl expects them to get it fixed in a few days, so he has rescheduled the delivery for next week. So, after we eat, we'll head back to Tallahassee and you can turn the truck in on the way."

When I walked into the U-Haul rental office, everyone in there stopped talking and stared at me. When the manager talked with me, he seemed really nervous. I told him there was a problem with the house my friend was going to rent and I couldn't help him move until he got it sorted out. So I needed to turn the truck back in.

When we got back to the hotel, Bryan said he was going to make some phone calls to let his customers know there had been a delay. He told me to call Nick from a pay phone and meet with him to let him know what was happening. Nick agreed to meet me at the Waffle House.

When I got there, Nick had a table by the window and was watching for me.

As I approached Nick's table, I noticed he had a weird look on his face.

"Were you wearing those clothes earlier today?" he asked. "And driving a U-Haul truck?"

"Yeah . . . why?" I asked.

"And was someone following the U-Haul truck in that car?" he asked.

"Yeah," I replied. "How did you know that?"

"I don't like listening to the radio or watching television," he explained. "I like to listen to my police scanner instead. All day I have been listening as the police and some DEA agents followed a maroon Chevy and a U-Haul truck. The driver of the truck was wearing a shirt that looks like yours. The other guy had a long, wavy hair, and had on a tropical shirt with palm trees and parrots. The car and U-Haul traveled west on I-10 for about 50 miles and then after a stop at a restaurant, they got back on I-10 and came back to Tallahassee."

"Oh my God!" I exclaimed. "Bryan had on a tropical shirt, and we did make that trip today in that car and a U-Haul truck."

"Well, then you guys were being followed," Nick said. "You need to get out of here before they see you with me."

When I left the Waffle House, I decided to stop back by the U-Haul rental office to see if I could find out anything else.

* * *

"I think I left a pair of gloves in the truck I returned earlier. I was wondering if I could check to see if I can find them," I told the manager.

The manager was reluctant, and obviously nervous, but finally told one of his guys to escort me out to the truck so I could look for my gloves.

"I don't know what you guys are up to, or what you are doing," the guy escorting me said, as I opened the truck door and pretended to look for my gloves. "But, as soon as you pulled out of the lot with the truck this morning, four cop cars and two unmarked cars pulled into the lot. The guys in the unmarked cars told the manager that they were with the DEA, and one of them pulled out a badge and identified himself as Agent Scott Jones. He said he wanted copies of the rental paperwork you had filled out. The manager was reluctant, but when Jones threatened to arrest him as an accomplice, he cooperated, and gave them copies of everything."

I looked at the guy and asked, "Why are you telling me this?"

"I don't like cops," he replied. "They gave me a hassle one time when I didn't do anything. And, if I were you, I'd want to know."

"Thanks, man. I appreciate you telling me," I said.

I reached into my jeans pocket and pulled out a $100 bill and handed it to him.

"You don't need to do that," he said. But he took it and put it into his pocket anyway.

When Bryan called Daryl and told him what Nick and the worker at the U-Haul store had told me, Daryl believed the cops were following Bryan, not him. He decided to continue with his plan to have the 'Connie' fly in the following week.

"You stay home next week," Daryl told Bryan. "I don't want you bringing any more heat up here. I'll let Randy get this pot and we'll see where we go from there."

* * *

DEA Agent Scott Jones was under pressure from his superiors to take Operation Lemon Lot to the next level. They wanted a bust. So when the 'Connie' landed the following weekend, 20 cars full of cops and DEA agents swooped in just as the first bales came off the plane. The pilot, co-pilot, and 6 ground crewmen were arrested. The 'Connie' and the 18,000 pounds of pot aboard it were confiscated.

* * *

Daryl was now even further in debt. His empire was starting to fall apart.

CHAPTER 53

The Partnership

JOHN HAD GOTTEN USED TO THE large amounts of money that Daryl had been paying him to set up fake businesses and launder his money. And his wife had gotten used to spending it as fast as John brought it home. Now that the flow of cash from Daryl had dried up, John was getting worried about how he was going to continue living his lavish, new life style.

Bryan was also running low on cash. He liked making money, too, but it looked like the supply of pot that he had been getting from Daryl was about to disappear. He called John and set up a meeting.

"If we want to continue making money, we better go into business for ourselves," Bryan told John. "It doesn't look like Daryl is going to be getting any more pot anytime soon."

"What do you have in mind?" John asked.

"Why don't we start flying pot in?" Bryan suggested. "I met a dealer from Jamaica who says he can get all we want at $100 a pound if we pick it up down there. He'll front half the pot if we pay for half in advance. I've already talked with my customers and they will take all the Jamaican pot we can get at $300 a pound. So we've got a supplier, the distribution network, and the ground crew, but we'll still need to get the pot up here. Do you think you could find us a pilot and a plane?"

"Let me give Danny a call," John said. "I know he wants to work and he has a lot of connections for planes."

"We're also going to need a place to bring in the plane," Bryan added.

"I think I know the perfect place," John said. "An attorney I know told me about a housing development just north of Lake Okeechobee that was started but never finished. It has roads but no houses. The developers ran into some problems and everything came to a standstill. It's all tied up in court and everyone involved is suing each other so the place is deserted. The roads are paved and a small plane would have no problem landing there. How much money do you think we'd need to get started?"

"At $100 a pound, we'd need $100,000 as a down payment on 2000 pounds of pot and about another $50,000 for expenses," Bryan answered, "plus whatever we have to come up with for Danny and the plane."

John grabbed a napkin and then a pen from his pocket. He started doing the math:

2000 pounds X $300/lb = $600,000 wholesale price
2000 pounds X $100/lb = $200,000 cost
Minus $50,000 ground crew expenses
And $50,000 for pilot and plane
= $300,000 profit
Split 2 ways = $150,000 each for a couple of weeks work.

"I can come up with $75,000 if you can," John said. "That'll give us the $150,000 we need to get the pot up here and get it sold. We can pay Danny after we sell the pot."

"Then let's do it," Bryan said. "Call Danny and see if he is interested."

John pulled a small mirror, a single edged razor blade, and a plastic baggie half filled with white powder out of his pocket. He poured a little white powder on the mirror and used the razor blade to chop up the powder real fine. Then he scraped the cocaine into 4 lines. He pulled out his wallet, extracted a $100 bill, and rolled it up like a straw.

"Let's celebrate our new partnership," John said, as he handed the rolled up bill to Bryan.

CHAPTER 54

The Pilot's Plan

JOHN CALLED DANNY AND SET UP a meeting with him and Bryan. They would meet at John's house in Fort Lauderdale. When they met, John and Bryan explained to Danny what they wanted to do.

"Of course I'm interested," Danny said. "I have a friend who has a Beechcraft King Air A100 with a range of 1300 miles loaded. It can carry 2000 pounds. I've rented it from him before so I'm sure I can get the plane."

He asked for a piece of paper and drew a rough map of the Caribbean on it. Then he drew a flight path on the map from Jamaica to Tampa.

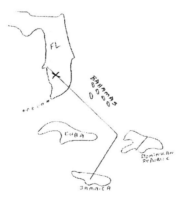

"It looks like this is just a little over 1000 miles, so I won't need to refuel. I'll have to fly from Jamaica northeast through the Windward Passage between Cuba and Haiti. You want to stay on the east side of the Windward Passage so you don't get too close to Cuba. Otherwise they'll send out jets to intercept you. Then I'll fly northwest across the Bahamas. As I cross the Bahamas, I'll call the FAA at Miami Radio and file an en-route flight plan direct from the Bahamas to Tampa. That will take me directly across the road you want me to land on. Once I cross the Florida border, I'll descend to 1500 feet. At that altitude, I'll drop off the radar as I approach Lake Okeechobee. Then I'll increase my speed to bank up a few minutes. That'll give me the few extra minutes I'll need to land and let your men unload the plane. When I take off again and get closer to Tampa, I'll pop back up on their radar just where, and when, they expect to see me so I won't look suspicious."

"Why would you file a flight plan and tell them where you are?" John wanted to know. "Why not just come in low and stay off the radar all the way?"

"That's what an inexperienced pilot would do," Danny explained. "If the Coast Guard sees a plane coming in low as it approaches the coast, then they'll suspect that it's a smuggler. And even if the plane is at an appropriate altitude, but hasn't filed a flight plan, then it is considered an unidentified aircraft and could be a threat. In either case, the Coast Guard would scramble jets to intercept the plane, and force it to land so they could inspect it."

"But I will file a flight plan, and maintain the correct altitude, so there is no reason for anyone to suspect me," Danny continued. "When I land in Tampa, and check in with customs, I'll just be another pilot following all the rules."

CHAPTER 55

The Souvenir

STRIKER, STEPHEN, AND I WERE THE ground crew. I had driven a car and Striker and Stephen had each driven a panel van to transport the pot from the plane to the stash house. It was better to separate the load into two vans. That way, just in case one van got busted, the pot in the second van would still cover all the expenses.

We had brought a portable Navigation and Communications radio, called a NAV/COM for short, so we could talk to Danny on the plane when he got within about 25 miles from us. We also had two scythes that we had picked up at a garden store. When the plane got close, Striker and Stephen would use the scythes to cut down any tall weeds on either side of the road that the plane's wings might hit when it landed.

I had picked up 50 glow sticks that I had already duct taped to 3-foot long 1x2 wooden stakes that would be used as runway lights since it would be getting close to dark when Danny arrived. This way he could see where to land the plane without running off the road. The plan was for Striker and Stephen to cut down the weeds with the scythes, and I would follow them and use a hammer to pound the runway lights into the ground on both sides of the road.

There was nothing to do now but wait.

About 30 minutes later, the NAV/COM came to life as we heard Danny say, "Momma, this is Papa, I'm getting close. Are you home?"

"I'm home, Papa, and anxious to see you. I'll leave the lights on for you," I answered.

It was time to cut the weeds and put up the lights.

We could hear the plane approaching just as I put up the last stake.

"I see the lights," Danny said over the radio. "I'm going to make my approach from the south. See you in a couple of minutes."

We watched as the plane appeared over the tree line. It looked like it was very low. I began to wonder if the road was wide enough for the plane's tires to stay on the pavement. But a minute later, Danny landed the plane right in the middle of the road. He taxied the plane to the next intersection so he could turn it around without going off the pavement. The plane stopped, but the engines kept running.

The door opened from inside the plane. I jumped into the plane and started throwing bales out the door as fast as I could. I had to time throwing them out so I wouldn't hit Striker or Stephen with one. They were loading the bales into the two vans as quickly as I could throw them out.

Danny had put a sheet of plastic on the floor of the plane before it was loaded in Jamaica so any loose pot or seeds would not get down into the carpet of the plane. When all the bales were out of the plane, I rolled up the plastic sheeting and threw that out as well. Striker threw the rolled up plastic into his van. Then he and Stephen threw blankets over the bales in the vans to keep them out of sight.

I jumped out of the plane; the door closed; and the plane took off. It had taken less than five minutes to unload the plane. Striker and Stephen each got into one of the vans and they took off as well. As they exited the subdivision and hit the main road, Striker turned left and Stephen turned right. They would each take different routes to the stash house Bryan had rented. I pulled up all the glow sticks and threw them into the trunk of my car. We didn't want to leave any evidence that a plane had landed there.

Just as I was getting into my car to leave, I noticed a street sign lying on the ground at the intersection where Danny had turned the plane around. The name of the street was on the sign. I knew it was foolish of me, but I wanted the street sign as a souvenir. I picked it up and threw it into the trunk. It hit the NAV/COM radio and broke off one of the dials.

"Dang it," I said to myself. "I knew I shouldn't have picked up that sign." I slammed the trunk lid shut, jumped into the car, and peeled rubber as I left.

We met up at the stash house, unloaded the vans, and weighed the pot. The 34 bales weighed a little bit over 2000 pounds.

Bryan's customers already had their drivers checked into nearby motels. They were resting while they waited for the pot. I picked up the drivers' cars one at a time and took them to the stash house to get each one loaded. It only took two days to get all the pot out of the stash house and on its way up north.

CHAPTER 56

The Everglades Plan

IT WAS ABOUT TWO WEEKS LATER when Bryan called me again and told me to come meet him. He said that Danny had heard of other smugglers who had thrown their pot off their planes instead of landing to unload. They considered this safer because the plane wasn't on the ground where they could get busted if the cops did come. Bryan wanted to try this for the next load. He asked me to scout around for a good spot somewhere west of Homestead where Danny could dump his load without landing.

It took me a week of scouting around until I found a dead-end dirt road that went five miles out into the everglades and then turned left for another half mile. There were a few empty beer cans and some other litter lying around at the end of the road, so it was obvious that people did go down there.

I spent several hours at the end of the road every day for a few days to see if anyone showed up but I never saw anyone. It looked like the road was rarely used. That made sense since it just dead-ended in the everglades.

Bryan and Danny wanted to see the place I had found, so we went out there together in Bryan's car.

"This looks like a good spot to throw the pot out of the plane," Danny said. "This half mile section runs south to north so I can line up the plane as I approach this spot. I'll file a direct flight plan in-flight as I pass the Bahamas, just like I did before. But this time I'll come in over the Keys and then turn northwest to head towards Tampa. That'll put my fight path right over this road. I'll slow down as I approach the south end of the road and the guy in the back of the plane can start throwing the bales out. I'll keep flying north so I won't look suspicious and the bales should all end up on the ground in a straight line on the ground, making them easy to find."

"Sounds good," Bryan said. "A friend of mine, Marc, will join Ryan, Striker, and Stephen on the ground so they can pick up the bales and get out of here quickly. I talked to my Jamaican connection yesterday and he can be ready for us next week. Danny, See if you can get the King Air for next Wednesday and Thursday."

CHAPTER 57
Sky High

DANNY HIRED ONE OF HIS FRIENDS to go with him and throw the bales out while Danny flew the plane. Danny filed a flight plan from Tampa to the Bahamas and they took off Wednesday afternoon. They headed towards the Bahamas but never landed there. They continued towards Jamaica and planned to land there around two in the morning. The ground crew there would have 55 gallon barrels of fuel, and would refuel the plane as the pot was being loaded. Danny expected to be at the drop site in Florida at 10:00 am Thursday morning.

* * *

Bryan met Striker, Stephen, Marc, and me for breakfast at the Waffle House in Homestead at 8 am Thursday morning.

"Bryan," I said. "I just found out that deer season started a few days ago. I think we should go get hunting licenses before we head out there. That way we have an excuse for being out there just in case we get stopped or questioned."

"Good idea," Bryan said. "There's a Kmart down the road where you can get your hunting licenses. But you don't have much time, so you'll have to hurry. I'm going to start calling my buyers to make sure their drivers are ready. Then I'll wait for you to call me at my house after the drop is made and the van is on its way to the stash house."

Striker, Stephen, and Marc went to Kmart in the van they had brought and I drove my car. I let them get their licenses first.

"You guys go on," I said when they were done. "I'm going to buy a shotgun so I look like a hunter. Then I'll meet up with you."

Buying a shotgun took longer than I thought. It was almost 10:00 when I walked out of the store.

No problem, I thought. *I'll just meet up with them at the drop site.*

But as I drove past the Waffle House, I saw them standing outside by their van. I made a u-turn and pulled in beside them.

"Why are you guys still here?" I asked.

"We thought we should wait on you," Striker explained.

"You guys should have went on out to the drop site. I would have just met you there. It's already 10:00. I hope we're not late. Let's go!" I yelled as I took off.

The van caught up with me as I turned onto the dirt road. We were doing about 60 mph down the dirt road and that was creating a really big dust cloud behind us. As we got about halfway down the dirt road, I could see another dust cloud on the road in front of us. A moment later, I could see a pickup truck heading towards us. Judging from the cloud of dust it was creating, it was traveling pretty fast too. The dirt road was only one lane wide, so we all had to slow down, and pull over a little, so we could pass each other.

As the truck went past us, I could see 2 guys in the front seat. They were probably deer hunters because they were wearing camouflage. The men stared at us just as hard as we stared at them, but nobody stopped. The scared look on their faces made a cold chill run through me. I hoped the plane hadn't arrived when these guys were at the drop site trying to shoot a deer. I prayed the plane was running a few minutes late, as if God would answer a prayer to help me commit a crime!

We got to the end of the road but didn't make the left turn onto the last half-mile section where the pot was to be dropped. We didn't want 60-pound bales of pot falling through the air and landing on our vehicles. We jumped out and looked around. We didn't see any bales of pot lying around so all we could do was to stand there and wait. We couldn't call Danny on the NAV/COM radio because it was still in the shop being repaired. So we listened for the plane and waited . . . and waited . . . and waited.

After waiting for almost two hours, we figured something was wrong.

"I'm going to go back up to the main highway and find a pay phone to call Bryan," I said. "You guys wait here for the plane. I'll be back as soon as possible."

* * *

"Bryan, we are still waiting on the plane. Have you heard anything?" I asked when I got him on the phone.

"I just got off the phone with Danny," Bryan said. "They dropped the pot just like they were supposed to. He said they saw you guys waiting down there with a pickup truck. He thought you were going to be in a van so he made a flyby and waved his wings. When you guys waved back, he circled back and they threw out the pot. I thought you guys only had a van and your car."

"Bryan, we did only have a van and my car," I answered. "As we were heading down the dirt road, a pickup truck with two hunters in it came past us heading in the other direction. That's who Danny must have seen. I hope they just got scared off when bales of pot started falling out the sky. I hope they didn't get any."

"Oh My God!" Bryan exclaimed. "Get out there and start looking. I'll meet you there as soon as I can get there." He slammed down the phone.

* * *

By the time I got back out there, the guys had already started looking around. When they found their first bale, they realized that the plane had made the drop before we got there. They had four bales in the van when I got there. We continued searching up and down in a line from where the other bales had been found. By the time Bryan arrived, we had found three more bales.

"Danny said he made two circles to drop the pot because it took longer than he thought it would to throw them out of the plane," Bryan told us. "He said each drop path is about a mile or so long, and the second path is about a quarter mile east of the first. After the first drop, he saw the two guys dressed as hunters throwing bales into the back of the pickup truck, but he thought they were you guys. He doesn't know how many bales they got, but they probably got the ones that fell closest to the road. They probably took off when they saw the dust cloud you were making on your way out. So let's assume they got 5 bales. Danny said there were 24 bales total. Since you guys found 7, there should be 12 more bales out here somewhere."

Bryan instructed Marc to take the van with the 7 bales we had found and take them to the stash house. The rest of us would continue to look for bales and meet up with him later.

We got in a line abreast of each other with about 50 feet between us. We walked north in a line from where the other bales had been found. The ground was covered in limestone rocks that have been eroded away by water over eons of time. The rocks looked like Swiss cheese and were a couple of feet high making it difficult to walk. It took us more than an hour to hike what we thought was a mile.

Weeds sprouted up everywhere they could find a clump of dirt making it almost impossible to see where you were stepping. The weeds were so thick we could have walked right past a bale of pot and never saw it.

After we hiked north for an hour in one direction, we turned around, moved east about 400 feet, and headed back south searching new territory. We found 2 more bales and we hid them under some weeds near the cars. We didn't want the bales in the car until we were ready to leave just in case some cop or game warden came along and wanted to see in the trunk. We continued searching until it got too dark to see. Then we loaded the 2 bales into my car trunk and quit for the night.

CHAPTER 58

The Search

BRYAN TOLD US TO MEET HIM at John's house at 8:00 am in the morning. When we got there, John had a pad of paper with lots of scribbling on it.

"The 24 bales were about 60 pounds each," he started, "so we have to pay for 1440 pounds. At $100 a pound, we owe $144,000 for the pot. The plane, pilot, and a crewmember cost us another $50,000. So we need $194,000 to break even. Since we sell the pot for $300 a pound, each bale is worth $18,000 to us. That means we have to find 11 bales just to break even."

"We have recovered 9 bales so far," Bryan added. "We need 2 more bales to keep from losing money. Since you guys were late getting to the drop site, you aren't getting paid unless we actually make a profit. But John and I have decided to pay a $1,000 reward for every new bale you find just to keep you motivated. If the hunters in the pickup truck got 5 bales, there should be 19 bales left. So far we have only found 9 of them, so there should still be 10 more bales out there somewhere. You have to keep searching until they are all found, or until we call off the search."

"Bryan, I have a private pilot's license," I said. "How about if I rent a small plane and use it to search from the air? Marc can ride with me and look out the passenger side window while I look out the window on my side. Striker and Stephen can continue searching on the ground. When we spot a bale from the air, we'll throw a roll of toilet paper out the window to mark the spot. The toilet paper will unroll on the way down so Striker and Stephen can see where it is falling. I called the repair shop on my way here and the NAV/COM radio should be ready for us to pick up today. Striker can carry the NAV/COM so we can communicate with him from the plane."

Bryan looked at John who nodded in agreement.

"OK," Bryan said. "Here is some money for the plane rental." He reached in his pocket and pulled out a wad of $100 bills. He counted out ten of them and handed them to me. "Let's try that for a few days and see how it goes."

CHAPTER 59

The 150

AFTER SHOWING MY LICENSE, LOGBOOK AND medical certification, I still had to take a check ride with one of their pilots before they would rent me a plane at the Homestead airport. I chose a Cessna 150. The 150 is a small two-seater commuter and training aircraft. It's light and could fly slower than any of the other planes they had to rent. Flying slower meant we had more time to look. The faster we flew, the harder it would be to spot any bales on the ground.

A plane has to move through the air fast enough for the wings to generate lift. If the plane goes too slow, gravity will overcome the lift generated by the wings and the plane will stall. That means the plane quits flying and starts falling. Stalls generally occur during landing because the plane is approaching the runway at a slow speed. The stall speed on a Cessna 150 varies from 42-48 knots depending on the total weight, flap angle, and atmospheric conditions.

When a plane stalls, the pilot must apply full power and push the nose forward towards the ground. The plane will lose altitude during this maneuver but will quickly pick up speed. As the speed gets above the stall speed, the plane will start flying once again. Pilots practice this maneuver so they can recover from stalls with minimal loss of altitude. But they do this at a safe altitude.

We wouldn't be at a safe altitude. We needed to be close to the ground if we had any hope of spotting any bales. Since we would be flying at an altitude of about 500 feet, I definitely didn't want to go into a stall. With full flaps, I knew the 150 shouldn't stall unless the speed dropped to 42 knots. But no amount of pot is worth crashing and dying for. So even though I decided to use full flaps so I could go as slow as possible, I wanted to keep my airspeed no less than 52 knots.

* * *

I did the preflight checklist and Marc and I climbed into the 150. I taxied the plane onto the runway. I applied forward pressure on the control yoke to keep the plane on the ground and pushed the throttle all the way in. I watched our speed increase while I kept the plane centered on the runway. When our airspeed got to 50 knots, I released some of the forward pressure on the yoke and the plane lifted gently off the ground.

When the plane was airborne, I maintained some forward pressure on the yoke and let the plane gain some speed. When the speed reached 65 knots, I pulled gently on the yoke and the plane started to climb. We were on our way.

I didn't want to make a beeline and fly straight out to the drop site where Striker and Stephen were already staged. So I headed north while I climbed to 1500 feet. Then I leveled off and adjusted my power to cruise at 100 knots. I flew north about 10 miles and then headed west for another 10 miles before turning south. After turning south, I decreased power so I could start a descent. I wanted to be about 500 feet high when we got to the drop site.

CHAPTER 60

Eye In The Sky

"HEY MOMMA, THIS IS PAPA," I said into the microphone. "Do you copy?"

"Hey, Papa," Striker answered, "I copy. Are you on your way?"

"Be there in a few minutes," I replied.

We could see the road as it cut through the swamp. Striker's van was parked at the far end of the road. As we crossed over the van, we spotted Striker and Stephen about half a mile away. We were 500 feet off the ground. I decreased the power until we slowed to 65 knots and applied full flaps. That slowed us down to about 55 knots. I lined the plane up on the east side of the road and we made our first pass.

The ground looked all green and brown from the air. It was going to be hard to spot any bales. We didn't see anything on the first pass. After we went a couple miles, I turned the plane around for another pass; this time heading north. I had to watch my airspeed and my heading while trying to look at the ground for bales. I was glad I had Marc in the plane. He could look without having the distraction of flying a plane.

We continued searching north and south for several passes. Then Marc spoke up.

"I see one. Over there," he said as he pointed. "It's at our 2:00 position; by that big rock."

I looked where he was pointing . . . and there it was.

"Get on the radio and let Striker know," I said. "I've got my hands full flying."

"Momma," Marc said into the microphone, "there's one about a quarter mile west of your position. I'll mark it for you."

As I flew the plane over the bale, Marc grabbed a roll of toilet paper and pitched it out the window. The toilet paper unrolled as it fell. It made a 100 foot long white streamer as it fell. There was no doubt that Striker and Stephen could see the streamer. Anyone could have seen it from miles away.

We continued searching with the plane for a couple more hours and located one more bale. That made 11 bales total that we had recovered so far. The two bales we found today generated a $2,000 reward for the ground crew. Split between the four of us was only $500 each. Bryan and John may not make any money, but at least they wouldn't go into the hole for this operation.

I had only reserved the plane for three hours, so it was time to head back to the airport. I got on the radio and called Striker.

"Hey Momma, Papa has to go home. We'll talk to you later."

I applied power and started climbing to 1500 feet as I headed north. I'd follow the same route back to the airport that I had used when I flew out to the drop site earlier.

The next day Marc and I took the plane out again. We located one more bale. So there were still seven more out there somewhere. The third day out in the plane we didn't find any bales. After three days of repeatedly flying a grid over the search area, it looked like we had found as many bales as we were going to find using an airplane.

Even though we were flying as slow as possible, it is almost impossible to spot something as small as a bale on the ground when you are 500 feet up in the air going over 50 miles per hour. We were lucky to have spotted the three we did find using the plane.

When we landed back at the airport, I saw something I had never seen before.

CHAPTER 61

The Gyrocopter

PARKED BY THE HANGER WAS WHAT looked like a small helicopter . . . but different. We parked the plane and went over to check it out. It had a helicopter blade on top of a mast and an airplane propeller was mounted to an engine on back of the contraption. There was no cockpit like on a regular helicopter so the pilot's seat was out in the open. A man was standing by the machine looking at the engine. We walked over to get a closer look.

"Hi," I said to the stranger. "I'm Ryan and this is Marc. This thing looks really interesting. What in the heck is it?"

"Hi," he replied. "Glad to meet you. I'm David. And this," he said pointing, "is a Benson gyrocopter."

"A gyrocopter?" I repeated. "Does this thing actually fly?"

"Oh yeah. You bet it does," David answered. "I'm just checking everything out before I take it for a spin. Stick around for a few minutes and you can watch."

"Awesome," I said.

"Wow," Marc added.

"How does it work?" I asked.

"The engine is a 90 horsepower McCulloch," David said. "It spins the airplane propeller to give you forward speed. The forward speed causes the helicopter blade on top to spin and that gives you lift. You ever take a toy pinwheel and blow straight into it to make it spin?"

"Of course," I answered.

"Well if you turn that pinwheel on its side and blow on it," David explained. "It'll spin just like it does when you blow straight into it. The same thing happens with the helicopter blade. As your forward speed creates airflow across the helicopter blade, the blade starts spinning. When it spins fast enough, it generates sufficient lift to get the gyrocopter off the

169

ground. Because you have to have forward speed for the blade to spin, you can't take off or land the gyrocopter like a helicopter. It takes off and lands more like an airplane."

"How fast do you have to be going to take off?" I asked.

"It'll take off and fly at about 25 mph," David answered. "It has a top speed of about 75 mph and a cruising speed of 55 mph. But I'm in no hurry when I'm flying it and I like looking at the scenery, so I like to cruise around at a more leisurely 40-45 mph. The tank you see mounted by the seat holds enough fuel for an hour and a half of flight time. So it has a range of about 50 miles with a 30 minute fuel reserve left in the tank."

"I've flown it now for several years but I recently retired. The wife and I are going to move back up to Minnesota to be near the kids and I would only be able to use it for a few months a year up there. So I have decided to sell it. I saw you in the Cessna earlier. Would you be interested in buying it?" David asked. "I'm only asking $3,500 for it."

"Maybe," I replied. "Is it hard to fly?"

"It's different from flying either a helicopter or an airplane," David said. "It's easier to teach someone to fly it if they aren't already a pilot. Pilots tend to try and fly it like what they are already used to flying. But if you do decide to buy it, I'll give you a few lessons. You'll be a pro in a couple of days. It's not really hard . . . it's just different. Well, I'm going out for a spin if you guys want to watch."

David got on the gyrocopter, started it, and taxied to the runway. We heard the engine rev up as he applied full power and he started his take off run. He only used about 250 feet of runway before he eased back on the stick and the gyrocopter rose off the ground. I ran to my car and got my camera so I could take a picture when he landed.

CHAPTER 62

The Deal

WE WATCHED AS DAVID TOOK OFF in the gyrocopter and flew it around the airport a couple of times. Then he made a few touch-and-goes. It looked like it would be a blast to fly.

"Marc," I said, "if we bought the gyrocopter, we could use it to continue searching for the bales. It flies a lot slower than an airplane and with no cockpit in the way there would be great visibility. I think it would be much easier than using a plane to look for those bales. And think of the fun we could have flying this thing around. What do you think?" I asked. "You want to be part owner of a gyrocopter?"

"I think that's a great idea," Marc said. "Let's make him an offer when he comes back. He was asking $3,500, so he'll probably take less."

After 30 minutes of having fun, David landed the gyrocopter, taxied it back over to where we were waiting, and turned off the engine. I took a picture while he was still sitting on the gyrocopter.

"David," I said. We think we may be interested in buying the gyrocopter. Would you take "$2,500 for it?" I asked.

"I don't think I'd let it go that cheap," he said. "How about we meet in the middle at $3,000?"

I looked over at Marc and he nodded.

"You've got a deal," I said, and I reached out to shake his hand.

CHAPTER 63

Airborne

"THE HARDEST PART OF FLYING A gyrocopter is learning how to taxi it on the ground with the nose wheel," David explained, "and then transitioning to the rudder pedals after the nose wheel leaves the ground. When the nose wheel is on the ground, you use the nose wheel pegs to steer the gyrocopter. If you want to go left, you push the right foot peg to turn the nose wheel to the left. If you want to go right, you push the left foot peg to turn the nose wheel to the right. But, as you increase speed during your takeoff run, the nose wheel comes off the ground at about 20 mph. Then you are balancing the gyrocopter on the two main wheels. Since the front wheel is no longer touching the ground, you can't use it to steer anymore. So you have to move your feet to the rudder pedals and use the rudder to steer," he continued. "Then, if you want to turn right, you push the right rudder pedal. And you push the left rudder pedal to turn left. It sounds confusing, but it's not hard once you get used to it. Go ahead and get on and try taxing the gyrocopter around. Just keep your speed below 20 mph and keep the control yoke pushed forward to keep the nose wheel on the ground."

I tried it first and then so did Marc. Steering the gyrocopter with the nose wheel was a piece of cake. David made us practice taxiing around for a couple of hours until we were both very comfortable doing it.

"Now, this time as you taxi down the runway, increase your speed to about 20 mph," David instructed, "and then apply just a little back pressure on the yoke . . . just enough to get the front wheel off the ground. Then you can practice balancing on the main gear and using the rudder to steer."

Again, I went first. I taxied the gyrocopter onto the runway and started applying power. I used the nose wheel to keep the gyrocopter centered as I went down the runway. As I approached 20 mph, I pulled gently back on the yoke and the front wheel lifted off the ground. As I moved my feet to the rudder pedals, the gyrocopter started to drift to the left. My brain was still in the nose-wheel-on-the-ground mode, and I pushed the wrong rudder pedal. The gyrocopter swerved to the left and almost ran off the runway and into the grass.

I taxied back to the center of the runway and tried again. This time when the nose wheel came off the ground and the gyrocopter started to drift left off the centerline, I pushed the right rudder pedal. The gyrocopter turned gently to the right, and I got the gyrocopter back on the centerline. I practiced this for an hour and then let Marc try.

Marc had a hard time transitioning from using the nose wheel to using the rudder to steer the gyrocopter. He got frustrated after an hour of trying and taxied back so I could practice some more.

This time, as I practiced balancing on the main gear, I added a little too much power. It didn't take much. The gyrocopter jumped off the runway, and in seconds I was a hundred feet off the ground! I wasn't ready to actually fly this thing and when it became airborne, all I could think was, *I'm about to die.* I let loose of the control yoke and tried to jump! Luckily, my seat belt kept me in my seat. Otherwise, I would have jumped to my death.

Still safely in my seat, I quickly regained my sanity and grabbed the control yoke again with my right hand. I pulled back on the throttle with my left hand to decrease power, and the gyrocopter started to descend. I made a rather bumpy landing and taxied back over to Marc and David. I was shaking so bad, both of them started laughing at me.

I got off the gyrocopter and sat down in the shade by the hanger.

"Marc, I think I'm done for a while. Why don't you go practice and let me take a break."

I pulled out a pack of cigarettes and smoked almost half a pack to calm my nerves while I watched Marc snake the gyrocopter right and left all over the runway for an hour.

"Marc needs more practice before he's ready to fly," David said. "But you have been airborne, landed, and lived to tell about it. You just need to hop on that thing and fly it next time."

By the time Marc came back, I had quit shaking. What David said made sense. I got back on the gyrocopter and taxied back onto the runway. This time I planned on taking off. I raised the nose wheel at 20 mph like I was supposed to and balanced the gyrocopter on the main gear. Then I increased power and applied a little backpressure on the yoke. When my speed got to 25 mph the gyrocopter gracefully became airborne. I continued climbing to about 1000 feet and headed away from the airport towards the beach.

When I got to the beach, I decreased power and descended to about 500 feet. I stayed about a quarter mile out over the water so I wouldn't endanger all the sun worshippers on the beach. I could see all the people on the beach watching and pointing me out to their friends.

Then I saw a cargo ship a couple of miles offshore in the gulfstream. It was heading north; probably to the port in Miami. I applied power to increase my speed to 60 mph and headed out towards the ship. I made a couple of circles around the ship and a couple of crewmembers on deck waved at me. I waved back and then turned back towards shore. I made one more pass down the beach and then headed for the airport. I was having a blast.

I lined up on the runway and slowly decreased the power. The gyrocopter sank smoothly towards the runway while I kept my speed at 25 mph. When I was cruising down the runway about a foot off the ground, I pulled the throttle back and applied just enough backpressure on the yoke to keep the front wheel off the ground. The gyrocopter landed gracefully on the main gear, and settled down slowly until the front wheel touched the runway.

I was in seventh heaven as I taxied back to the hanger. I had done it! I had flown the gyrocopter! My pride was portrayed by the smile on my face that went from ear to ear. This was easier and a whole lot more fun than flying an airplane. It took work to fly an airplane. This thing practically flew itself.

"OK," David said, as I unbuckled my seat belt and got off the gyrocopter. "You are now a pro. Marc needs some more practice but he'll get the hang of it soon enough. You can coach him now just as well as I can. So you guys don't need me anymore. Enjoy your new toy," he said as he headed for his car. And with one final wave to us, he was gone.

CHAPTER 64

Gyrocopter Success

"MARC," I SAID, "I KNOW YOU want to learn to fly the gyrocopter, but right now, time is of the essence. I think I need to go ahead and start using it to search for the rest of the bales. You can practice some more with it in a few days."

Marc agreed. We decided he'd join Striker and Stephen to help search on the ground while I searched from the air in the gyrocopter. Since I couldn't take the NAV/COM radio with me on the gyrocopter, they would have to watch for me to throw a toilet paper streamer if I found a bale. He watched me take off on the gyrocopter and then headed for his car.

Striker and Stephen knew that Marc and I were learning to fly the gyrocopter, so they weren't surprised when I flew over them. They waved at me and I waved back. I started searching in a grid just like we had done in the airplane. It was much easier to see the details on the ground flying at 25-30 mph, at an altitude of only 200 feet, and with no cockpit blocking my view. After a half hour of searching, I spotted a bale.

I threw a roll of toilet paper and watched it unroll as it fell.

The guys on the ground waved to me as a signal that they saw the toilet paper streamer. I was low on fuel so it was time for me to head back to the airport.

The next day I spotted another bale. That made 14 that we had recovered. If the hunters in the pickup truck got 5, then there should still be 5 more out there somewhere. I continued searching with the gyrocopter for two more days, but I didn't find any more bales. I had thoroughly searched the area from the air and was convinced I wasn't going to find any more bales with the gyrocopter.

I decided to join Striker and Stephen on the ground and let Marc take a few days to continue practicing on the gyrocopter. Then he could take a shot at it. Maybe he'd spot one I missed.

CHAPTER 65

Cops In A Copter

THE NEXT DAY, STRIKER, STEPHEN AND I expanded the ground search farther than they had searched before. If there were any bales left out there, they were either farther out from the drop site than we originally thought, or they had fallen under something and were hidden from view. It took us all day to search the west side of the road, but we didn't find anything.

The following day, we searched the east side of the road. That was fruitless as well. We had searched all day, and it was late in the afternoon when we got back to the car. We put our shotguns in the trunk of the car, and I started plinking at a beer can with a BB pistol I had brought along. Then we saw a cloud of dust up the road . . . a sign that someone was coming . . . and they were coming fast.

I was standing there with the BB pistol in my hand when a police car pulled up and stopped. A cop got out. When he saw my pistol, he drew his weapon and aimed it at me.

"Drop it!" he yelled.

I looked at him dumbfounded.

"It's just a BB gun," I said.

"Drop it now!" he screamed.

I decided it wasn't wise to argue with a cop . . . especially if he is aiming a gun at you. I dropped the BB pistol.

"Now, put your hands up and back away," he instructed.

I put my hands in the air and took a few steps backward. The cop eased forward until he got to my BB pistol lying on the ground. He bent over and picked it up, never taking his eyes off me.

He examined the BB pistol. Then he said, "It's a BB gun."

"I told you that," I said.

"Hey, all I saw was you holding a gun. I couldn't take the

chance," he said, as he handed the BB pistol to me. He holstered his own weapon and told me to put the BB gun in my car.

I did as he instructed.

Then he asked what we were doing out here.

"We were deer hunting," I replied. "We didn't see any and we were just getting ready to leave. Do you want to see our licenses?"

"No," he answered. "I'm not a game warden. I don't care if you have a hunting license or not. I'm here because we got a tip that there was some suspicious activity out here. I'm here to check it out."

I could see another dust cloud down the road. Someone else was coming. It only took a couple of minutes for two more cop cars and an unmarked car to join us. Two men in suits exited the unmarked car.

"We need to take your statements," one of the cops said.

They put me in one cop car, Striker in another one, and Stephen in the third one.

The cop in the car I was in started asking me questions, "What is your name? Where did you live? What are you doing out here?" I was answering his questions when I heard the 'whoop, whoop, whoop', of helicopter blades approaching.

What a great time for Marc to figure out how to fly the gyrocopter, I thought. *Surely he sees all these cops. Why does he keep getting closer? Why doesn't he turn around and get the heck out of here?*

Only it wasn't Marc with the gyrocopter. A real helicopter landed on the road about 100 feet away. I watched as a cop exited the passenger side door. The pilot stayed in the helicopter and kept the engine running. One of the 'suits' got into the helicopter and the helicopter took off. It stayed close to the ground and started flying a search grid over the swampy area near the road.

I wasn't too concerned that they would spot any bales. We had searched pretty thoroughly and if there were any bales to be spotted, we would have already found them. But who knows . . . maybe they'd get lucky and spot one we missed.

They didn't. Their cursory search only lasted about 15 minutes and they landed again. What arrogance. They thought they could find something in 15 minutes that we couldn't find in days? The 'suit' exited the helicopter and the original cop that was in it got back in. The helicopter created a huge cloud of dust as it rose into the air . . . and then it was gone.

The 'suits' never spoke to us . . . only the cops. After the helicopter left, the 'suits' conferred with a couple of the cops and since they didn't find anything illegal, they all got into their cars and left.

* * *

"I told you we should have waited," DEA Agent Jones said to his superior in the car with him. "Now they know that we know about this drop and they'll be more careful in the future."

* * *

"I think we have found all the bales that we are going to find out here," I said to Striker and Stephen. "I think we need to call this search over."

We waited a half hour after the cops left before we got into my car and left as well.

No one said anything. We were all deep in thought.

I was thinking about the close call we had today. I was glad to be going home instead of going to jail.

* * *

Striker was thinking about how happy he was that this search was over. Now he could go back to partying late and sleeping in again.

* * *

Stephen wondered why Jones had tried to make a bust for such a small amount of pot.

* * *

Since Bryan and John made a little money on this operation, they paid us $1,000 each. They also gave us a $5,000 reward to split between us for the 5 new bales we had found as they had promised.

At least Marc and I had enough to pay for our new toy.

CHAPTER 66
The Tennessee Plan

BRYAN CALLED A MEETING WITH JOHN and Danny to plan the next operation.

"I have a friend who is the chief of police in the small town of Zanesville, Tennessee," Danny said, and there is a small airport on the edge of town. The police chief has a wife who likes to spend money, and a house that he can't afford on his salary. So, he collects protection money from some of the moonshiners around there to augment his salary. But, he wants to put something away for his kids' college fund. He is willing to let us land a plane there, and to let your buyers come into his town to pick up the pot. He said he can even provide a small isolated farmhouse we can use as a stash house. He controls his officers with kickbacks as well. So, he guarantees there won't be any problems from the local police."

"How much money will we have to pay him," John asked, "for his police protection and for the stash house?"

"He said we can land the plane there for $10,000 and he wants another $10,000 for the farmhouse," Danny answered.

"Well, that's a no-brainer," Bryan said. "Police protection and a stash house only add about ten dollars to the cost of each pound. But what about fuel? Will you have enough fuel to get to Tennessee from Jamaica?"

"No," Danny replied. "I'd have to refuel somewhere en-route. But, I know a gal named Bridgett Hargrave who lives in Freeport, Bahamas. She owns a small fuel distributorship there called The Bahamas' Fuel Company. She delivers fuel to the marinas and to some farms there that grow sugarcane and citrus. Bridgett said the airport there is closed from dark until dawn, so I can land there in the middle of the night without any problems. She is willing to meet me on the airstrip there when I land, and refuel the plane. Then I'll have the range I need to fly the rest of the way to Tennessee. She said she would charge $10,000 for her time and the fuel."

"The other times you flew in," said Bryan, "you filed a flight plan direct to Tampa and unloaded before you got there. Obviously, you can't do that if you can't unload until you get to Tennessee. So what'll you do?"

"I'll still need to file a flight plan so the Coast Guard won't scramble jets to intercept an unidentified aircraft entering U.S. airspace. But I'll look around before I leave and find another Beechcraft King Air and record its tail number. After I take off from Freeport I'll call Miami Radio and file an en-route flight plan direct from Freeport to Tallahassee. That will put Boca Raton in my flight path as I enter Florida. When I hit the coastline, I'll start an approach to the Boca Raton airport as if I was going to land there. That is an uncontrolled airport so there is no control tower. The closest FAA radar is so far away that it can't see anything at Boca Raton below 1500 feet. I'll fly low right over the airport and then head west. I'll turn off the transponder in the plane and stay under 1,000 feet until I get south of Lake Okeechobee. Then I'll turn right and head north. When I get near Orlando, I'll start increasing my altitude until I reach 3,000 feet. I'll stay at that altitude so I'll be flying under visual flight rules with no requirement to file a flight plan. When I finally do pop back up on radar near Orlando, I'll just be another blip on an FAA controller's screen. Of course the FAA will start looking for the King Air with the tail number that I used when I filed the flight plan. But I will be in the clear and on my way to Zanesville."

"I love it," Bryan said.

"Me too," John added, as he pulled a little baggie out of his pocket and poured some white powder on the table. "How about we do a couple lines to celebrate?"

CHAPTER 67

The Deliverymen

BEFORE STRIKER, STEPHEN AND I LEFT Fort Lauderdale, I had some magnetic signs made at a local sign shop. The signs read: 'Knoxville Delivery Services' on top, and had a bogus phone number on the bottom. The three of us went shopping the day before we left to buy khaki pants, light blue golf shirts, and matching ball caps. Wearing our 'uniforms', we would look like real cargo deliverymen when we met the plane at the airport up in Tennessee.

We stopped by Knoxville on our way up so I could rent a white panel van. We wanted a van with Tennessee plates. A Knoxville Delivery Services van would look suspicious with Florida tags on it and we didn't want to draw any unwanted attention. After we picked up a van, we continued on to Zanesville and checked into a motel. We left the van at the motel and took my car so we could check out the stash house. Using the address and directions we had been given, it was easy to find. Then we had dinner and settled in for the night. Danny was due in the next morning and we wanted to be rested and alert.

Before we headed out to the airport the next morning, we put on our delivery men outfits and put the Knoxville Delivery Services signs on the front doors of the van. We were at the airport by 9:00 am and Danny wasn't expected to land until about 10:00. We had brought along the portable NAV/COM radio so Danny could call us when he got close. The call came just after 10:00. We watched Danny land, and taxi the plane over close to the small terminal. Then he stopped and opened the door to the plane.

There were three old men sitting on some benches in front of the terminal. They were either waiting on a plane to pick them up or they were just there to watch the planes take off and land. They watched as we drove the panel van over to the plane. I parked the van close to the plane and tried to block their view as much as possible. We just took our time unloading the bales off the plane and putting them into the van. We didn't want to seem as if we were in any hurry. We wanted to look like some deliverymen doing our job.

When the plane was unloaded, Danny closed the door and taxied back out to the runway to take off. Striker, Stephen, and I got into the van and drove away. As we passed the terminal, I waved to the men sitting in front of the terminal. They all smiled and waved back.

It only took a couple of days to get rid of the pot . . . and as promised, we never saw any cops.

* * *

Stephen hadn't been able to get away alone so he could use a pay phone to call Jones until the pot was all gone. Then he told Jones who got the pot and where we were staying.

* * *

When we checked out of the motel to leave, I noticed two men sitting in a car across the street. I probably would not have noticed them if they hadn't been in a shiny new car and wearing suits. Most of the locals around here wore jeans or bib overalls and drove old cars or pickup trucks. When they saw me eyeballing them, they started their car and drove away. They would make their report to Jones later that day.

CHAPTER 68
The Captain

DANNY HAD MADE THREE TRIPS AS a pilot for Bryan and John. With the money he had saved, he decided to strike out on his own. He informed Bryan and John that the Tennessee trip would be his last.

John suggested they meet with a pilot he knew named Captain Ron who had flown pot in for Daryl Kirby in the past.

* * *

Captain Ron was in his mid-sixties. He was short, thin, and wiry. He constantly had a cup of black coffee in one hand and a cigarette in the other. In the evenings, the coffee was exchanged for bourbon . . . *neat*. He had been flying almost as long as he had been driving. He owned a one-man air transport company called 30-30 Air Transport, Inc. based out of Fort Lauderdale. He ferried used appliances, cars, food, and other cargo primarily south to islands and countries between the northern and southern 30th latitude lines.

At the time, Daryl had convinced Captain Ron that flying marijuana in the opposite direction, back to the states, could be a lot more lucrative. Daryl paid for an old DC-3 and listed 30-30 Air Transport, Inc. as the owner.

Captain Ron flew the DC-3 to the Guajira Peninsula in Colombia and picked up 4,000 pounds of pot. A ground crew was supposed to be waiting at a small airstrip near Lake Okeechobee where the plane would be unloaded. The ground crew wasn't there so the captain flew the plane back to the Fort Lauderdale airport instead.

Unbeknown to Captain Ron, the DC-3 had been put on a watch list so when Captain Ron radioed for landing instructions, the control tower immediately contacted customs. Customs met the plane as it was parked for an inspection of its cargo. The pot and the plane were confiscated and Captain

Ron was arrested. Lawyers delayed his trial for several years but he was promptly listed in the DEA and Customs computer systems as a suspected smuggler.

When John introduced Bryan to Captain Ron, the captain's case had not yet gone to trial and he was still flying cargo south to the islands.

The captain handed Bryan one of his business cards:

Captain Ron White, ATP

30-30 Air Transport, Inc.
Fort Lauderdale, FL

* * *

The *ATP* after his name meant the captain was licensed as an Air Transport Pilot.

Student Pilots can fly solo only with an endorsement from their Flight Instructor. When they have completed their training, and pass their written and flight tests, they can get their Private Pilot license.

Private Pilots can fly for their own business and personal use, but they cannot be paid for being a pilot. If they continue training, and meet the higher required standards, they can qualify for a Commercial Pilot's license.

Commercial Pilots are professionals and are required to have mutli-engine and instrument ratings to be hired as a charter pilot or to fly cargo.

But to fly passengers on scheduled flights for an air carrier, a pilot must continue training to get an Air Transport Pilot's license. This is the highest level of pilot licenses and is often called an ATP. In addition, an ATP must be type rated in every type of plane he flies that is over 12,500 pounds. As an honorarium, a pilot holding an ATP license is legally allowed to use 'ATP' as a name suffix.

* * *

"What kind of planes can you fly?" John asked.

Captain Ron pulled out his wallet and extracted his ATP pilot's license. Most pilots have a license on one card, like a driver's license, but not his. He held it up and let it unfold . . . and unfold . . . and unfold. There were at least a dozen cards. One for each of the heavy planes for which he was type rated.

He could fly the Douglas DC-3, the Douglas DC-6, the Douglas DC-8, the Lockheed Constellation, the Vickers Viscount 700, the Lockheed L-188 Electra, and many more.

John and Bryan stared at the license.

"Is there anything you can't fly?" Bryan asked, laughing.

"If it's got a prop, I can fly it," Captain Ron said. "And I am willing to fly whatever you want to wherever you want for the right price. But I want a co-pilot."

"Hmmm . . . I have in mind a private pilot with low hours. Would you be willing take him under your wing and train him?" Bryan asked.

"That shouldn't be a problem," Captain Ron agreed.

"Then I think we have a new pilot," Bryan said.

"I think you're right," John added. "Captain Ron, we'll be in touch with you soon."

Bryan called me later that day, "Ryan how would you like to get off the ground crew, start flying as a co-pilot, and make twice as much money?"

I didn't even have to think about this one.

"Bryan," I replied, "That sounds great. I'd fly as a co-pilot for half as much money. But, since you already offered, I'll take the pay increase."

CHAPTER 69

The Rastafarian Strip

BRYAN CONTACTED, JAMIE, HIS SUPPLIER IN Jamaica.

"Danny won't be flying for us anymore," Bryan told Jamie. "We have a new pilot named Captain Ron that will be coming to see you. When can you have 2000 pounds ready for us?"

"I can have the pot ready next Wednesday", Jamie said. "Have Captain Ron get the air strip coordinates and radio frequency we'll use from Danny. Have your pilot plan his flight to arrive here at 2:00 am Thursday morning. Tell him to call me on the radio when he is 15 minutes from the strip and we'll turn on some lights for him. I'll have some men refuel his plane while others are loading the pot."

* * *

Captain Ron knew where he could rent a Cessna 402A for our first trip. It could carry 2,000 pounds of cargo and had a range of 1,100 miles. That was enough to go from Jamaica to south Florida without refueling, but it would be close.

When Captain Ron checked the weather reports on Wednesday, he saw that we would have a 10 mph headwind on the return trip. He did some calculations and called Bryan.

"Due to the headwind on the way back," Captain Ron said, "there won't be enough fuel to bring back 2,000 pounds without stopping to refuel. We'll have to lighten the load a little. We can still make it back non-stop if we only bring back 1,800 pounds."

"I'll call Jaime and let him know," Bryan said. "Striker and Stephen will be waiting for you at the strip tomorrow, and I'll see you tomorrow afternoon."

As soon as he got off the phone with Captain Ron, Bryan got another call. One of his customers just arrived in town with a payment. With that on his mind, the call to Jamie never happened.

Captain Ron filed a flight plan and we took off in the Cessna 402A from Fort Lauderdale and headed for the Bahamas. But we didn't land there. We continued through the Windward Passage and set course for the eastern tip of Jamaica. When we were about 50 miles away from Jamaica, we could see the lights from Port Antonio.

After we passed the eastern tip of Jamaica, Captain Ron kept the plane about 20 miles offshore as we followed the coastline. We could see the lights from Morant Bay, Yallas, Kingston, and Spanish Town as we circumvented the island. When we were due south of the strip, we headed north and called Jamie on the radio so he could get some lights on for us.

The 2,200 foot airstrip wasn't paved; it was hard packed dirt. The north end of the strip abutted a mountain, so you had to land from the south, and take off toward the south. Since we were approaching from the south, we were set up for a straight in approach. The strip was only 5 miles inland from the coast.

We soon spotted the lights on the strip and Captain Ron lowered the landing gear and turned on the landing lights. Just before we landed, we could see a pile of dirt that stretched all the way across the approach end of the runway. That prevented us from landing at the beginning of the runway, and the plane touched down a couple hundred feet past the dirt pile. We were almost at the end of the strip before the plane slowed down enough for us to turn it around. Captain Ron shut down the engines as I opened the door.

There were 2 flatbed trucks off to the side. One was loaded with bales of pot and the other with 55 gallon barrels of fuel. There were 6 black men with the trucks. They looked like Rastafarians with their long dreadlocks.

One of them approached the plane.

"I'm Jamie," he said. "Welcome to Jamaica. My men will get you loaded and refueled and you'll be out of here in 10 minutes. We must be quick because the army patrol will have heard your plane approaching and will be here soon. But you will be gone by then and so will we."

"What is that pile of dirt at the south end of the runway?" Captain Ron asked.

"The local army commander wants us to pay him to use this strip," Jamie explained. "If we pay him his extortion money, he leaves us alone. If we don't, he has his men blow up the strip to make it unusable. We don't want to pay him. So when we have a plane coming in to get loaded, we bulldoze the strip to make it level again. That creates that pile. We bulldozed the strip about an hour ago so it would be ready for you, but the army patrol will blow it up again tomorrow."

"Well, the dirt pile is in our way," Captain Ron said. "You'll have to put a light on the top of the pile so I can see to make sure I clear it when I take off."

"No problem, man," Jamie said. "I will have one of my men climb on top of the pile with a lantern."

Three of the men put down a sheet of plastic on the floor of the plane and loaded the pot into the plane while Jamie supervised. Two of the other men used a pump to transfer the fuel in the 55 gallon barrels into the wing tanks of the plane. In eight minutes, the pot was loaded and the plane was refueled.

"Good luck," Jamie said, as he extended his hand. I shook his hand and shut the door.

Captain Ron was already starting the engines when I buckled myself into my seat. He revved up the engines as he held the brakes on. When the engines were at full power, he released the brakes and the plane started rolling down the runway. Captain Ron was pushing the control yoke forward to hold the nose of the plane on the ground. The pile of dirt at the end of the runway was getting closer and closer.

Just seconds before we hit the dirt pile, Captain Ron pulled back hard on the yoke. The plane lurched off the ground and the landing gear cleared the top of the pile by about a foot. I watched as the man holding the lantern dived off the dirt pile so he wouldn't get hit.

CHAPTER 70
Out Of Fuel

WE RETRACED OUR FLIGHT PATH AROUND Jamaica, through the Windward Passage, and up to the Bahamas. As we crossed the Bahamas, Captain Ron called Miami Radio and filed an en-route flight plan direct from Nassau to Tallahassee. He had written down the tail number of another plane that he had seen at the Fort Lauderdale airport and used that plane's number on the flight plan. When we didn't land in Tallahassee as expected, they would be looking for that plane instead of ours.

We knew we would be cutting it close on fuel and had been monitoring the fuel gauges all the way back. But for the past hour, Captain Ron had been looking at the gauges more and more often. I could tell he was getting concerned.

When we were about 70 miles from Miami, Captain Ron said, "They must have put more than 1,800 pounds of pot on the plane so we used fuel faster than we should have. We're not going to make it to our destination at this rate."

"What are we going to do?" I asked. "We can't just land and refuel with all this pot on board."

"I'm going to shut down one engine to reduce our rate of fuel consumption. We'll have to make it the rest of the way with one engine," he said. "We're at 10,000 feet now but we can't maintain a level altitude with only one engine and this load. So we'll start a slow descent from here all the way to our landing site. That will help conserve fuel and keep our air speed up."

Captain Ron reduced the power on the starboard engine. When the engine was at an idle, he turned off the switch that provided power to that engine. I watched as the propeller on my side slowed and then stopped.

"This plane has variable pitch propellers. So I'm going to

feather the prop to reduce drag," he said as he toggled a switch.

The blades of the propeller turned until the edges were pointed into the airflow.

"How does that help?" I asked.

"Think about putting your hand out the window when your car is speeding down a highway," he explained. "With the palm of your hand facing forward, the wind pushes your arm back. If you turn your hand sideways so your palm is facing down, the wind will hit the edge of your hand and the drag is reduced. The same principle applies to an airplane propeller. Turning the edges of prop into the wind to reduce drag is called 'feathering the prop'. Less drag means less fuel consumption."

We continued our slow descent for the last 200 miles of our flight. When we reached the small airport where we were to land our fuel gauges were on "E". We hoped we had enough fuel to make a controlled landing.

There was a Fixed Base Operator (FBO) at the north end of airport. They sold fuel and rented hanger space and parking spots for planes. Our plan was to land from the north end of the field and stop at the south end where Striker and Stephen would meet us with a cargo van. It would be hard for anyone at the FBO to see what we were doing at the other end of the runway. After we unloaded the pot, we would taxi up to the FBO and refuel the plane. Then we'd take off and fly it back to the Fort Lauderdale airport.

There was no control tower at this airport so pilots announced their intentions on a Unicom frequency before landing or taking off. As we entered the down-wind leg of our approach, we were at an altitude of 1,500 feet. Captain Ron tuned the radio to 122.8 MHZ and announced, "Cessna 402 on down-wind leg, approaching to land."

He slowed our speed and put down the landing gear.

"Cessna 402 on base leg," he said into the radio as he turned left and continued our descent. We were now 1,000 feet off the ground.

"Cessna 402 on final approach," he said into the radio as

we made the final turn towards the runway. We were now about 800 feet off the ground. Then a plane on the ground taxied onto the runway and started his take off roll.

"Oh my God," Captain Ron shouted. "Look at that guy. He must not have his radio on and he obviously didn't see us. We're going to hit him."

"Go around!" I yelled, "Go around!"

"We can't do that on one engine...and we don't have enough fuel," the captain said.

"If we try to go around, maybe we'll make it and maybe we won't," I said. "But if we continue our landing, we're going to crash into him for sure."

"We'll try," Captain Ron said, "but I don't think we can make it." He applied full power to the one engine. "We'll have to turn now," he said as he banked the plane to the left. "Otherwise, we're going to have a mid-air collision when he gets off the ground."

* * *

Planes require more power in a turn to maintain airspeed and altitude. But there was no more power available with only one engine running. If Captain Ron had not been as experienced as he was, we would have never made it around the field for another approach.

* * *

He dipped the nose of the plane down to keep the airspeed up during the turn so the plane wouldn't stall. But the cost of keeping the airspeed above stall speed was a loss in altitude. And we didn't have much altitude to spare, 700 feet . . . 600 feet . . . 500 feet as the captain made the last turn onto a very short final approach.

We made it!

The plane settled down gently onto the airstrip. The captain continued our roll to the south end of the strip, turned the plane around, and shut down the engine.

A white panel van pulled up to the plane as I opened the door. Striker and Stephen jumped out of the van and opened the rear doors so they could load the pot into the van. I started throwing the pot out of the plane and Striker and Stephen threw it into the van.

Off to the side of the runway was a road that circled the airfield. An old red pickup truck was parked on the side of the road. Jerry was in the pickup truck. He was a local real estate agent and a friend of John. Jerry had suggested this airport to John as a place for us to land the plane. Jerry managed several rental homes for absentee owners and had rented one to John, under a false name, for us to use as a stash house.

It only took a few minutes to get the pot out of the plane and into the van. Then Striker and Stephen took off. I closed the plane door and Captain Ron turned the first engine over to get it started. The engine turned over but it wouldn't start. We were out of fuel!

CHAPTER 71

One Seed

I WAVED AT JERRY TO COME over and he drove his truck over to the plane.

"We're out of fuel," I said. "Do you have any extra gas?"

"No," he answered. "But, I do have an empty five gallon can in the back of my truck. Hop in and I'll take you down to the FBO to get it filled."

I hopped into the truck and Jerry pulled back onto the road and we headed to the FBO at the other end of the airport. We paid them for the 5 gallons of fuel and went back to the plane. I climbed onto the wing and poured the 5 gallons of fuel into the wing tank. Then Captain Ron tried to start the engine again.

The engine turned over at first but quickly slowed down. Great . . . now the battery was dead! We had drained the battery trying to start the plane with no fuel.

"Do you have jumper cables?" I asked Jerry.

"Not in my truck," he said. "Let's run back down to the FBO and see if they have any."

They didn't. "I have some at home," Jerry said. "Let's stop back by the plane and let Captain Ron know. Then I'll run home and get them."

As we were telling Captain Ron the plan, two cop cars, with their red and blue lights flashing, pulled up beside the plane. The cops were accompanied by 2 men wearing suits. The 'suits' came in a black sedan.

"What's going on here?" one of the cops asked.

Captain Ron was the first one to answer.

"I was doing a test flight on this plane for a potential buyer," he said. "I had an engine problem so I landed it here. After I landed, the engines quit and here I am . . . stuck at the end of the runway."

"And what about you guys?" the cop asked, looking at Jerry and me.

"Jerry is a real estate agent. He was showing me some property around the airport," I said. "As we were driving by, we saw this plane sitting here and the pilot looked like he was having a problem. We stopped to see if we could offer some help."

"Did you go inside the plane?" one of the suits asked.

I had to think fast. If I said "no", and they dusted for prints, they would know I was lying. "Yeah", I said. "I've never been in a plane like this. So, I asked the captain here if I could come in and look around. He said 'sure', so I did. It's really a nice plane."

The man who asked me looked at the other suit and said, "Pretty good answer. Sounds to me like they've been through this before." Then turning back to Jerry and me, he said, "You guys stand over there by the pickup truck."

The suit walked over to the plane and went inside. He got on his hands and knees and started looking closely at the carpet on the floor of the plane. After a few minutes, he motioned Captain Ron over.

"Well . . . look at what I found," the suit said. "Here is a pot seed."

"Where?" Captain Ron asked.

"Right there," the suit said, pointing down into the seat track on the floor.

Captain Ron adjusted his glasses and peered into the seat track.

"That?" he asked. "Are you sure that is a pot seed?"

"Don't act like you're stupid," the suit said.

"I'm not," Captain Ron replied. "I've never seen one before. Looks like a little rock to me. I always wondered what a pot seed looked like."

"Well," the suit said. "It's a pot seed. It may not be enough for me to hold you on, but it's enough for me to confiscate the plane."

"Then you don't mind if I catch a ride with the two guys in

the pickup truck?" the captain asked. "I'll let the owner of the plane deal with you about the pot seed."

"As soon as you provide the cops over there with identification, you guys are free to go," the suit said. "Here's my card. Give it to the plane's owner and have him contact me."

Jerry, Captain Ron, and I all showed our IDs to the uniformed cops. They wrote down all of our information and let us go. We piled into the front seat of Jerry's truck and left.

"What are we going to do about the plane?" I asked the captain.

"That's a problem for the attorneys . . . let them deal with it." Captain Ron replied.

* * *

Jones was disappointed. When he had received the call from Stephen that morning about the plane coming in, he had contacted the agent in charge of the DEA office in Fort Lauderdale. He wanted some agents stationed at the airport so they could bust us when we landed. The agents just didn't get to the strip in time to catch us with the pot.

When Striker and Stephen got the pot to the stash house, they weighed all the bales. There were 2010 pounds of pot. Within 24 hours, all the pot was on its way to the eager customers up north.

CHAPTER 72

The Call

"I'M NOT FLYING INTO THAT DIRT strip again," Captain Ron said to Bryan. "And we need to have a refueling stop in the Bahamas. We cut it way too close last time."

"I'll have John call Danny. He knows a woman down in Freeport named Bridgett who can refuel you on the way back," Bryan said. "And I'll tell Jamie he has to find us another strip to land on. Anything else?"

"Yeah, the captain answered, "We need another plane."

"I'll have John ask Danny if he can find us another plane," Bryan said.

It took a couple of weeks for all the pieces to come together. Danny located another Cessna 402 for us to use; Bridgett told John that she could refuel us with a 24-hour notice; and Jamie told Bryan that there was another strip that we could use.

"After Michael Manley, the head of the People's National Party, won the election and became the Prime Minister in 1972, he became close friends with Castro," Jamie said to Bryan. "Castro was getting a lot of money and military equipment from the USSR to expand the Communist presence in the Caribbean. Manley allowed Castro to build a military airstrip in Jamaica in exchange for military jets and training for the Jamaican Air Force. But, when Edward Seaga, the head of the Jamaica Labour Party, won the next election, he kicked the Cubans out of Jamaica. This strip is mainly abandoned now, but the army patrols and protects it. It is a paved strip and is only a few miles from the dirt strip you used before. This is the strip the Army wants us to use to load pot planes, but we have to pay them in advance."

"How much does it cost to use this strip?" Bryan asked.

"The Commander charges $20,000 to land and load there,

and an extra $5,000 to refuel the plane. But, it will be completely safe."

"We should have done this the first time," Bryan said.

With everything set, John wanted to celebrate. He picked up a couple grams of cocaine and a bottle of Crown Royal. Then he rented a penthouse suite at a beachside hotel in Fort Lauderdale and called a couple party girls. He forgot to call Bridgett and schedule the refueling.

CHAPTER 73

The New Strip

CAPTAIN RON AND I PICKED UP the Cessna 402 in Tampa. As we were walking out to the plane, Captain Ron wrote down the tail number of another plane sitting on the ramp. Captain Ron filed a flight plan direct to the Bahamas and we took off.

We retraced our steps around Jamaica like we did on the last trip and called Jamie on the radio when we got close to the new airstrip. This airstrip was great! It had 5,000 feet of concrete. Captain Ron set the plane down with lots of room to spare. Then he taxied to the end of the strip where there were some metal hangers. A man with a flashlight guided us to where he wanted us to park.

I opened the door and Captain Ron and I exited the plane. Then we saw the army!

We both froze in fear as we watched a jeep and an army truck loaded with soldiers come out of the hanger. They sped over to the plane and the soldiers jumped out of the truck. They were all armed with M-16s. We knew we were busted!

The soldiers surrounded the plane in a circle with their rifles pointed at us. Then an officer exited the jeep and shouted an order to his men. The soldiers all did an about face and their backs were now towards the plane and their guns pointed away from us.

The message was clear. If you landed here, the army would surround your plane. Which way their guns pointed depended on if you had paid for protection or not.

The soldiers opened their circle to allow a flatbed truck through. There was a tarp covering the bales of pot on back of the truck. Jamie waved at us as he pulled the truck up to the airplane. A refueling truck came next and the soldiers once again closed the gap in the circle.

"How do you like my friends?" Jamie asked as he motioned towards all the soldiers.

"They scared the bejesus out of us!" Captain Ron said. "I thought we were busted for sure."

"They are here to protect you tonight," Jamie said. "How do you like your new landing strip?"

"Jamie, I have to hand it to you. These are first class accommodations," the Captain answered. "But there is one thing . . . you overloaded us last time. You were only supposed to put 1,800 pounds on the plane, and you put over 2,000 pounds on the plane. That caused us to use too much fuel and we almost crashed."

"I was told to provide you with 2,000 pounds last time and that is what I did," Jamie said.

"Bryan said he would call you to change the order to 1,800 pounds," Captain Ron said.

"I never got that call," Jamie said. "But since you have this nice strip to take off from, and you are going to stop to refuel, Bryan said you could take 2,400 pounds this time. Is that a problem?"

"That is really pushing it. But I think we can handle that," the Captain said.

It only took a few minutes to get the plane loaded and refueled. Then the officer in charge barked an order to his men. They all jumped back into the army truck and it pulled out of our way.

Captain Ron started the engines and taxied off the ramp towards the huge runway. We still had half the runway left when we became airborne.

CHAPTER 74
Piles Of Pot

THE HEADWINDS AND THE 2,400 POUNDS of pot on the plane caused the engines to use a lot of fuel. The gauges were on "E" as we set up the approach into Freeport. The airport was closed but it was a clear night and we could see the runway well enough. We could also see construction equipment where they were building a new runway. Captain Ron landed the plane and taxied to the end of the runway. He shut the engines down and I opened the door and stepped outside.

Captain Ron finished securing the plane and joined me outside. It was eerily quiet. Even the crickets and frogs had stopped their chatter when we landed. We expected to hear a refueling truck rushing over to meet us, but we heard nothing. We just stood there waiting. After a few minutes the crickets and frogs started up again, but that was all we heard.

"Where's the truck?" Captain Ron asked. "We've been waiting for over an hour."

"How do I know?" I answered. "It was supposed to be here waiting for us."

"Well, we have to do something. We can't wait much longer. It'll be daylight in a couple of hours and we don't want this plane sitting out here on the runway when everyone shows up for work in the morning," he said. "Get back in the plane. I'm going to start it up and taxi it up there where all the other planes are parked. If we park it amongst all the other planes, maybe no one will even notice it."

Captain Ron started the plane and started taxiing it to the parking area. We almost made it, but then the engines quit. Out of fuel . . . again! We got out and tried to push the plane the last 100 feet to a parking space. Try as we could, we couldn't budge the plane.

"We'll have to get the pot off the plane," Captain Ron said. "Then we can say we ran out of fuel and made an emergency landing. If the pot is still on the plane, then we're going to get busted."

"There are some woods over there," I said, pointing to the woods about a quarter mile away. "We'll have to carry the bales over to the woods."

I grabbed a bale and slung it over my shoulder. The captain did the same. We had to cross some of the new construction area on our way to the woods. We carried the bales a little way into the woods and dropped them. There were 40 bales on the plane, so it was going to take us 20 trips to get it all off the plane.

By the tenth trip, we were both exhausted. We couldn't stop, but we were slowing down. We could tell by the change in the sky that daybreak was coming. We had to keep going. We knew we didn't have much time left.

We had carried 34 bales off the plane and there were only six more to go. We both hoisted a bale onto our shoulders and stepped out of the plane. Then, across the runway, in the new construction area, a pickup truck pulled up and stopped. There were two men in the front and six men in the back of the truck. The construction crew had arrived . . . and they were right between us and the woods.

"Quick," Captain Ron said. "Get back in the plane. I don't know if they saw us or not, but the rest of the pot will have to stay in the plane."

We carried the bales back into the plane and dumped them.

The captain opened his flight case and pulled out a pair of boxer shorts and an extra shirt he carried. He handed me the shirt, thank God, and he used the boxer shorts to start wiping down the controls.

"Help me," he said. "Start wiping down everything we may have touched. We don't want to leave any fingerprints in here."

We wiped the throttles, the control yokes, the seat belt buckles, the door handles, and everything else we thought we might have touched.

"Now grab your flight bag," he instructed. "And that empty soda can. It'll have your finger prints on it too."

Then we walked out of the plane and closed the door. Captain Ron fished a key out of his pocket and locked the plane door.

"That'll slow them down a little, but they'll still get in," he said. "Let's go."

We walked away from the plane in the opposite direction of the construction workers. Then we headed around the perimeter of the airport, keeping off the road. It took us 30 minutes to circle around back to the woods while staying out of sight of the construction crew. We found our pile of 34 bales easy enough. I took 6 of the bales and set them off to the side. Then we started finding branches and palmetto fronds to cover the big pile.

"What's the deal with the six bales?" Captain Ron asked.

"When they find the bales on the plane, they will probably look for the rest," I explained. "If they find the big pile, maybe they'll think that's all of it and they'll quit looking. So, I want to carry the six bales further into the woods and make a second cache. Maybe they won't find those and we can try to recover them later."

It took us 3 trips to carry the 6 bales another quarter mile into the woods. We covered them with branches, sticks, and palm fronds as well. This pile was much smaller and was pretty well hidden. Someone could walk within 50 feet of it and not see it.

We figured if we walked in one direction, we would eventually find a road. When we had walked about half a mile, we found a hollow log where we could stash our flight bags. We didn't want flight bags with us if we got stopped. We took everything thing out of the bags that could identify us, and pushed the bags inside the log. Then we stuffed some moss, sticks, and leaves into the log to conceal the bags. In another quarter mile, we came upon a road.

We started walking down the road towards town. We walked about a mile when a pickup truck heading in the same direction pulled up beside us. "You guys need a ride?" the man in the truck asked.

"Sure," I said, and we got into the truck.

"What are you doing way out here?" he asked.

"We are staying in town and just went for an early morning hike. We just walked farther than we probably should have," I answered. "Sure glad for the ride back. You can just drop us off anywhere in town."

I didn't want to ask the man who picked us up near the airport to take us directly to the Bahamas' Fuel Company.

When we got dropped off in town, we looked around for a cab. There were several sitting in front of a hotel down the street. I asked the cab driver if he could take us to the Bahamas' Fuel Company.

"Sure," he said. "Hop in."

The cab dropped us off in front of a business. The sign said hanging outside read:

Bahamas' Fuel Company, LTD.

There were a couple of refueling trucks sitting in the yard and we could see someone in the office.

We walked into the office and saw a woman doing some paperwork at her desk. "Can I help you?" she asked.

"I hope so," I said. "We're looking for Bridgett."

"I'm Bridgett," she said. "Who are you?"

"John said you were going to meet us this morning," I started. Then I waited to get her reaction. It took a moment.

"Are you the pilots?" she asked.

"We are," I stated. "And we landed at the airport early this morning. Only problem was that you didn't show up to refuel us."

"John had talked to me about refueling you guys," she said. "I told him I could with a 24 hour notice. That was a couple of weeks ago. I haven't heard from him since. Oh my God! If you are here, where is your plane?"

We told her the plane was stranded on the ramp near the parking area. We also told her we had unloaded 28 bales of pot and hid them in the woods before the construction crew showed up, but there were still 6 bales on the plane. We didn't tell her about the second cache of 6 bales.

"Oh, no! You gotta be kidding me," Bridgett said. "I need to get out to the airport as quickly as possible. I know the airport manager and his crew. They'll help me park the plane and keep it from getting busted. But I'll have to get there before Customs shows up and gets involved. Otherwise, it'll be too late. You guys just stay here and wait. I'll come back as soon as I can."

* * *

Before Bridgett drove out to the airport, she made a call to Danny in the states.

"I wasn't notified that they were coming in last night," she explained to Danny. "The pilots told me they ran out of fuel and the plane is stranded on the taxiway. They said they got 28 bales off the plane and hid them in the woods before the construction workers showed up, but there are still 6 more on the plane."

"Something doesn't add up," Danny said. "I was told that they were bringing back 2,400 pounds. Each bale averages 60 pounds, so there should be about 40 bales total. Either they miscounted, or there are some more bales somewhere. Can you get your friends at the airport and customs to work with you? If you can secure the pot, I'll get it back to the states and get it sold. Then we can cut your friends in and split the proceeds. We'll just have to make Bryan and John believe that Customs got all the pot."

"I'll see what I can do," Bridgett answered. "Let me get out there and I'll call you later."

* * *

When Bridgett pulled into the airport parking lot, she could see some activity already around the airplane. She quickly went inside and found Hank, the airport manager. She and Hank had known each other all their lives. Bridgett told Hank that there were 6 bales of pot on the plane, but there were more hidden in the woods. Then, she told Hank about the plan she and Danny had hatched up.

"Do you think Jeffery will go along with us?" she asked Hank.

"Maybe," Hank said. "He and his men are already trying to get into the plane. Wait here while I go out and talk with him."

Hank walked out to the plane to speak with his friend, Jeffery, the Customs Agent in charge. They talked for a moment and then Hank walked back inside the airport.

"Jeffery has agreed," Hank told Bridgett. "He said they have to confiscate the plane and the 6 bales inside because his superiors have already been notified about the plane. But, he won't have his men search the woods. He's even going to loan us the customs' search dog so we can find the bales the pilots hid in the woods later."

CHAPTER 75

Smuggled Home

"IT WAS TOO LATE," BRIDGETT TOLD us when she got back 2 hours later. "Customs had already found the plane before I got there. They took their drug sniffing dog out to the plane and it alerted them that there were drugs on the plane. It didn't take them long to get into the plane and they found the 6 bales inside and immediately confiscated the plane. Then the dog followed your trail into the woods and they found the 28 bales you hid there as well."

"So they must be looking for us," I added.

"True, but they don't know who you are, or where you went. I'm going to take you to an apartment where you can stay until we figure out how to get you back home."

Bridgett dropped us off at an apartment and told us to stay inside. She said she'd pick us up some food and bring it back after she called John to let him know what happened. Captain Ron and I both took showers while we waited for Bridgett to return.

Bridgett came back shortly with two Styrofoam take-out boxes. I didn't realize how hungry I was until I smelled the food. Inside the boxes was rice covered in a medley of seafood including fish, scallops, shrimp, and crab. The seafood had been seasoned with chilies, cilantro, lime, onions, garlic, cinnamon, and coconut. Fresh fruit was on the side and included ripe bananas, orange sections, and papaya. A piece of flattened garlic bread completed the meal.

"You guys eat and rest," Bridgett said. "I'll pick up some clothes for you bring them back later. Do you need anything else?"

"Can you pick us up a couple of tooth brushes and some toothpaste?" I asked.

"No problem," Bridgett said. "Don't go out for any reason.

The police are looking for the pilot of that plane. You'll be safe here as long as you stay inside. I'll be back in a few hours."

Bridgett came back later that evening. As promised, she brought us some clean clothes, some tooth brushes, toothpaste, and some more food. This time, it was flank steak with onions and peppers, a small lobster tail, some rice and peas, more fresh fruit, and some more garlic bread. The smell of the Caribbean spices they had used to season the food made my mouth water. Captain Ron set his food aside, but I dug right in. I always did like to eat when I was nervous.

"I talked with John this afternoon," Bridgett said. "He is going to have Danny fly down tomorrow and pick you guys up. You can't just go to the airport to get on his plane though. The police have heard that there were 2 people on the plane and they are looking for you. Since you didn't check in through customs and get the required paperwork like every other tourist, they would arrest you when you tried to leave."

"So, how is he going to pick us up?" I asked.

"He is going to land at another island about 20 miles from here that has a private airstrip. I will have you there waiting for him when he arrives," Bridgett explained. "I'll be here at daybreak. Be ready to go."

The next morning, we were ready when Bridgett arrived. We all got into her pickup truck and she drove us to a marina.

"We are going fishing," she announced. "Get in the boat."

Bridgett parked her truck and joined us in the boat. Then we took off. It took an hour for us to get to the island where Danny was going to land. Bridgett stopped the boat about a quarter mile away from a dock on the island.

"Hold these poles and act like you're fishing," she said as she handed each of us a fishing pole.

We 'fished' for about 45 minutes before we heard a small plane approaching.

"Get ready," Bridgett said. "That's Danny. As soon as I get you to the dock, hop out and run up that hill as fast as you can. The airstrip is on top the hill. Danny will stop to pick you up and immediately take off. He doesn't have permission to land here, so he will be in a hurry."

As soon as we hopped off the boat, Bridgett took off.

We ran up the hill and reached the airstrip just as Danny landed. He taxied the plane to us and we jumped in.

"Buckle up," he said as he turned the plane around.

He applied power and we took off.

Danny called on the radio and filed an en-route flight plan direct to Tallahassee.

"I'm going to drop you off at the Boca Raton airport on the way," he said. "I can drop in there without being seen on radar. You guys jump out and I'll take off and continue my flight to Tallahassee. Someone will be waiting to pick you up."

Danny set the plane down on the runway at the Boca Raton airport. He kept the engine running as we jumped out. Then he took off again.

Striker was there waiting for us, and drove over to pick us up before Danny was even off the ground. We had just been smuggled back into the country.

Bryan was furious. John was supposed to call Bridgett and let her know that the plane was coming in. Instead, John had focused on his little vacation and forgot to make the call. That little slip-up cost them a ton of money. And they still had to finish paying Jamie for the pot.

CHAPTER 76

Six Bales

EVEN THOUGH IT WASN'T OUR FAULT, Captain Ron and I didn't get paid for that trip. That's what I thought would happen. That's why I made a second stash with those 6 bales. Now, I just needed to figure out a way to go get them.

I couldn't just fly right back into Freeport and check in through customs. What if they had discovered who the pilots were on the plane they had confiscated? As soon as I produced my identification, I'd be arrested.

So, I hatched a crazy plan. I called a friend of mine who was also a pilot and was about my age.

"Richard, I need to talk with you," I said, when he answered his phone. "I need to come over and see you now."

When I got to Richard's house, I explained to him what happened.

"The 6 bales I hid further back in the woods are very well hidden," I said. "There is a good chance they are still there. I want to rent a Cessna and go back and get them. They may be looking for me; so, I can't fly in and use my ID. I'd like to borrow yours. We look similar enough that unless they look really close, I'll pass for you."

"Are you nuts?" he asked. "Why would I take that kind of risk?"

"There's really no risk to you," I explained. "If I get caught, you simply say that someone stole your wallet, or that you lost it. But, if I get those bales, there's $10 grand in it for you. And I'll only need to be you for 2 days."

"I want half," he said.

"If the pot is there, I'm going to need someone on the ground here with a van. I'll land on a back road up near Lake Okeechobee long enough for us to get the 6 bales out of the plane and into the van. If you'll do that, I'll cut you in for

25%," I countered.

He didn't need to think about it very long. He pulled out his wallet and handed me his pilot's license and his driver's license.

I rented a Cessna 182 the next morning and filed a flight plan to Freeport. When I landed, I taxied up to the parking area, parked the plane, and went in to check through customs. I filled out the required paperwork and handed it to the customs agent along with Richard's driver license. I hoped the agent didn't notice how nervous I was.

The agent checked the paperwork I had filed out, glanced at the driver license, and took a cursory look inside my shoulder bag. Then he reached over and grabbed his stamp. I felt relief when he smacked the stamp onto the paperwork. He looked up at me, smiled, and told me to have a good day. They were used to treating tourists well. Tourists meant money and jobs.

I grabbed a cab in front of the airport and asked to be taken into town. The cabbie said he knew of a reasonable motel and took me there. In reality, he probably got a kickback for taking tourists there. Oh, well . . . that was fine. The place was small, but neat and clean. It was on the beach and they had bicycles there for their guests.

After I checked in, I borrowed one of the bikes and went for a ride. It took about an hour and a half to pedal the bike out to the road on the backside of the airport and find the spot where Captain Ron and I had hitched a ride with the man in the pickup truck. About a mile up the road, I spotted where we had exited the woods.

I pushed the bike into the woods and hid it behind some bushes. Then I headed through the woods towards the airport. When I could see the airport construction through the trees, I was able to get my bearings.

The spot where we had left the 28 bales was all trampled down. It looked like someone, or rather a bunch of someones, had used machetes to chop down all the vegetation in the whole area. They obviously didn't want to miss any bales. Well, I knew they had found the big pile. I was interested in finding out if the second cache was still there.

I retraced the steps we had taken through the woods just a few days before. When I got to the second location, I was disappointed. It too had been all chopped down. The pot was gone!

I headed for the log where we had hidden our flight bags. I found the log easily enough since I knew where it was. But when I peered into the hollow log, I couldn't believe it. The bags were gone too! Good thing we had taken everything out of the flight bags that could identify them as ours.

I hiked back to where I had hidden the bike. At least it was still there. As I pedaled back into town, I had to wonder how in the heck they had found our flight bags in the hollow log. Someone must have used dogs to track our path through the woods.

When I got back to the motel, I cleaned up and went out to eat. This may have been a wasted flight, but at least tonight I was going to enjoy some of the fabulous seafood that the Bahamas has to offer. Tomorrow, I'd fly back to the states.

CHAPTER 77

The Big Time Plan

BRYAN AND JOHN MET TO FIGURE out their next move. They had 2 planes that had been confiscated that they still had to get released, and they still owed Jamie $120,000 for the pot they lost in the Bahamas.

* * *

John had hired an attorney he knew to work on getting the two planes released.

"Getting the Cessna 402 that was confiscated in Florida released shouldn't be too hard," the attorney said. "After all, they only found one pot seed on the plane and there was no way to prove how it got there. The plane that was confiscated in Freeport is a different story. Only Bahamians can practice law in the Bahamas," the attorney explained. "So, in addition to me, you are going to have to hire an attorney in the Bahamas to petition the courts to release the plane. And since there were still 6 bales on the plane when it was confiscated, they know it was being used to smuggle pot. The government there could keep the plane and sell it, or, some magistrate may be willing to take a bribe to release the plane on some technicality. Either way, getting that plane back is going to be expensive."

* * *

"We need a big score if we're going to stay in business," John said to Bryan. "Ever hear the saying 'in for a penny, in for a pound'? Well, I think it is time we quit playing around with these little trips and go for the big time."

"What have you got in mind?" Bryan asked.

"Through a friend of mine," John said. "I met an affiliate of one of the cartels in Colombia. He said he can get us enough pot in Colombia to fill a big plane."

"Where are we going to get a big plane?" Bryan asked.

"Let me talk with Ray about getting us a plane," John said. "He's the one who furnished the 'Connie' to Daryl. Are you okay with him partnering with us if he furnishes the plane?"

"We don't have the money to do it ourselves," Bryan said. "Let's talk to him and see what he says."

* * *

John made the call and Ray agreed to meet with him and Bryan in Fort Lauderdale.

"Tell me what you have in mind," Ray said when they got together a few days later.

"We have a contact in Colombia who is willing to front us 20,000 pounds of pot, but we have to pick it up down there," John said. "We have a pilot, and we have the customers. We just need a plane that can get that pot up here. If you'll furnish the plane, and a place to land it, we'll make you an equal partner."

"How much money can we make?" Ray asked.

"The pot is grown by small farmers in the jungles of Colombia," John answered. "They try to grow enough to support their families. On average, each farmer may be able to grow anywhere from one to two hundred pounds of pot in a season. To get 20,000 pounds together, someone has to buy pot from a lot of farmers. It takes several buyers to deal with that many farmers. A buyer in each area may deal with anywhere from 5 to 20 farmers. The buyers pay the farmers anywhere from $5 to $10 a pound for their pot. The buyers then sell the hundreds of pounds of pot they have gathered to another middleman for around $25 a pound. These middlemen sell the thousands of pounds of pot they have gathered to the cartels for about $50 a pound. The cartel we are dealing with will sell the pot to us for $125 a pound. Our customers will pay us $250 a pound. So, after expenses, we make about $100 a pound. We put 20,000 pounds on that plane and we're looking at $2 million in profit."

"Wow! Now I'm interested," Ray said. "I am working on a DC-6. It should be ready to go in a few weeks. It has a range of about 2,500 miles and it can carry 28,000 pounds of cargo.

What are your plans for getting the plane there and back?"

"We'll stage the plane in the Caicos Islands while the pot is being staged for us in Colombia," John said. "When they are ready for us, they will give us 2 days' notice. When we get that call, the pilots will take the plane to Great Inagua. We have a contact in Great Inagua, named Tom, who has the local officials on his payroll so they won't be a problem. Tom will get the plane refueled before it takes off for Colombia. The pilots will fly the loaded plane back to Great Inagua. Tom will have his men unload the plane there, and store the pot in a warehouse for us. From there, we'll get the pot into the states on smaller planes and speedboats."

"I like it. Here's to my new partners," Ray said as he raised his beer bottle.

Bryan and John raised theirs as well, and they CLINKED them together.

"All right," John said, as he reached into his pocket for the little plastic baggie he knew was there. "Let's celebrate."

CHAPTER 78

The DEA Plan

RAY HAD BEEN APPROACHED BY THE DEA after the 'Connie' had been busted in the panhandle. They knew he had supplied the plane for Daryl and had threatened him with prosecution and a lengthy prison sentence if he didn't cooperate. The wire he wore when he met with Bryan and John had performed beautifully. They hadn't suspected a thing, and Agent Scott Jones had recorded the whole conversation. Now he was meeting with his team.

"Operation Lemon Lot is on track and we will eventually bust this smuggling organization," he said. "I know we've had all of them under surveillance for almost 2 years, but be patient, we are getting close. Now that we know how the entire organization works, we can go after the federal indictments we need. But until then, we're going to hurt them every time we get a chance. I want to send 2 of you down to the Caicos Islands and 2 of you to Great Inagua. You're going to need some bribe money to get the local officials there to give you their complete cooperation. That shouldn't be a problem . . . you just have to pay them more than the smugglers are paying them. They'll get to double dip and collect from both them and from us."

"How are we going to come up with the bribe money?" one of the team members asked. "We can't just take it out of our budget. That's illegal."

"Why do you think I kept furnishing that low life, Zeke, with information about the location of the stash houses?" Jones asked. "We let him steal the smugglers' pot, sell it, and split the profits with us. I have a lot of money that I got from Zeke stashed away in a secret account to pay for any covert operations we need to finance. We're basically using the smugglers' own money to finance their demise."

Laughter came from all around the table.

* * *

It was ironic. A DEA Agent tells a drug-dealing thief where some smugglers have a large stash of pot. Then the thief steals the pot and sells it without interference from the DEA. The thief and the DEA Agent split the money. Then the DEA Agent uses his half of the money as he sees fit to help bust the smugglers . . . and maybe keep a little for his troubles.

Of course Zeke would pay for his crimes when his usefulness was over. And he couldn't just be arrested. If he got to court, he'd tell how he knew the location of the stash houses and to whom he had given half the money. No, one day Zeke would just have to disappear where no one would ever find him.

* * *

"They plan to fly a big bird this time; a DC-6," Jones said to his team. "Let's see if we can't take that albatross down and tie it right around their necks. Here's what we're going to do."

They were all ears.

CHAPTER 79

Gainesville

THERE WERE A LOT OF PEOPLE in Fort Lauderdale. The traffic was bad. The businesses were geared towards tourists. Bars and souvenir shops lined the boulevard in front of the beach. Strip bars had neon signs advertising the naked ladies inside. They should have named this place Sin City instead of Fort Lauderdale.

We decided this wasn't the best place to raise a family. So we pulled out a map and once again studied the state of Florida.

"What do you think about moving to Gainesville?" Judy suggested as she pointed at the map. "The University of Florida is there, so the town caters to students, not tourists. I think it'd be nice to live in a college town. And maybe you could finish your degree there."

"Ok. Gainesville it is," I agreed. "Bryan said we won't be going on another job for a few weeks. So we have time to move. Let's pack up and go."

I let our landlord and Bryan know we were moving. We had bought a few things since we moved here, so now we needed to rent a U-Haul trailer to move our stuff. When we got to Gainesville, we bought a newspaper to look for a house to rent. After we checked out several, we decided on one and moved our things in.

It was just outside of town in a country setting. It was right beside a farm. We'd sit outside on the porch and have our coffee while we watched the birds and cows in the pasture behind the house. There was a rope swing that hung from a big oak tree beside the house. A tire was tied to the bottom of the rope and Keith would climb on the tire and beg me to push him until I gave in.

Since there were a lot of students in town, there was always something going on. There were art shows, restaurants that served healthy food, trails and parks to explore, the Hippodrome Theatre, coffee shops where professors hung out with the students, and of course, the Gators. On game day, everyone in town wore blue and orange as they went to Ben Hill Griffin stadium to watch the Gators kick some butt.

As we settled into our new town, we discovered we really liked Gainesville.

Then one day came the call from Bryan.

"Don't go," Judy pleaded. "You said you would only do this for a couple of years and then get out. It's been 2 years. I don't want you to do this anymore. Every time you leave, I don't know if you'll make it back home, end up in jail, or get killed. I can't take it anymore. I don't want you to go."

"Judy," I replied, as I looked into her eyes. "We still don't have any money set aside. If I don't go, what are we going to do? Are we going to go back to living in a run-down trailer without a refrigerator and eating beans and potatoes?"

"If we have to, then, yes," she answered. "You can go back to school and finish your degree. I'll get a job if I have to. We'll make it somehow. Other people do."

"Judy, we've already invested 2 years of our lives trying to get a stake so we can start over. Now you want me to quit when the big payday is only a few weeks away? Bryan said he'll pay me $50,000 to make this trip and another $50,000 bonus when all the pot is sold. That'll be enough for us start over. Let me make this last trip. Then I'll tell Bryan I'm done."

"I have a bad feeling about this trip," Judy said, as a tear rolled down her cheek. "How long will you be gone?"

"Bryan said it should take a week . . . two at the most. So, I figure it'll probably be three weeks. Then we can start our new life."

I didn't know how true that statement was. It just wasn't the new life I had envisioned.

CHAPTER 80

The DC-6

CAPTAIN RON AND I WENT TO the Fort Lauderdale airport to pick up the DC-6. It was an impressive airplane. As we stood there on the ramp looking up at the plane, Captain Ron started telling me about it.

"There were 704 of them built between 1946 and 1958," he said. "Douglas made several variations of this plane. See the cargo door on the left side behind the wing?" he said, pointing up. "That identifies this one as a DC-6A. It was designed to carry cargo instead of passengers."

Then he pointed up at the wing on our side. "Look at those engines," he said.

There were two on each wing. And they were huge.

"Those are Pratt & Whitney R-2800-CB16 'Double Wasp' radial engines," he continued. "Each one has 2,400 horsepower. With all four engines, that's 9,600 horses. And check out those props. They're Hamilton Standard Hydromatics. They're constant-speed props with auto-feather and reverse thrust capabilities. They can make this baby cruise at 315 miles an hour. This plane is big, and it's heavy. It's 105 feet long, 28 feet high, and has a wingspan of 117 feet. Empty, it weighs over 45,000 pounds. But it's a workhorse. It has a maximum takeoff weight of 107,200 pounds. So it can carry 62,000 pounds of fuel and cargo. But all that power makes it suck a lot of fuel. It has a range of 2,500 miles, but that will use all of the 4,700 gallons of fuel it can hold in its wing tanks."

"You sure know a lot about this airplane," I said.

"I ought to," he said, as he pulled a picture out of his pocket and handed it to me. "I've got over a thousand hours in this one."

* * * Photo used by permission: Malcolm Reid * * *

Ray stuck his head out of the cargo door calling to us, "Hey, I'm up here. Come on up."

We climbed up the stairs that folded down out of the cargo door and we entered the plane. The inside of the plane was huge. There were no passenger seats since this plane was for transporting cargo. There was enough room to put a one-lane bowling alley inside.

"I was just taking a last look around," Ray said, as he reached out to shake our hands and welcome us aboard. "Let me give you the grand tour."

He showed us the new gauges and radios he had installed in the cockpit. He told us what he had done to the engines. He explained what he had done to ensure the hydraulics were in good repair.

"Everything is in good working order," he said, "and has been checked out. You shouldn't have any problems with this plane."

"What about fuel?" Captain Ron asked.

"I took care of that for you. It's all fueled up and ready to go. If you guys are ready, I'll pull the wheel chocks for you when I get outside."

"We're ready," Captain Ron said.

Ray went down the stairs and pulled the wheel chocks for us. We retracted the stairs and shut the cargo door.

Captain Ron took the pilot's seat and I strapped myself into the co-pilot's seat. I took one look at the controls and felt overwhelmed.

Good thing Captain Ron knew what he was doing. I didn't have a clue. This plane was a lot more complicated than anything I had ever flown.

Captain Ron handed me the pre-flight checklist and told me to read out the instructions as he performed each step.

"All ignition switches on," I read.

As I read each step, Captain Ron performed the operation and replied, "Check."

"Start engine 3 first . . . followed by 4, 2, and then 1," I read.

"Engine 3 fuel booster pump on HIGH . . . Engine selector switch to NUMBER 3 . . . Safety switch to ON . . . START and BOOST switches to ON simultaneously."

"Engine 3 started," the captain said when it roared to life.

"Move Mixture Control to Auto-Rich . . . Set Fuel booster pump to OFF . . . adjust throttle to 1000 rpm."

We repeated the steps to start the rest of the engines. When all four engines were running, the captain called the tower on the radio to get our takeoff instructions. He had already filed a flight plan direct from Fort Lauderdale to Lima, Peru. We weren't going to Peru, we were going to the Caicos Islands, but we didn't want to tell them that.

The towers gave us instructions to taxi to the staging area for the runway they wanted to use. While we were waiting for clearance to take off, Captain Ron had me read the checklist for the engine run-up.

"All engines 1500 rpm, check fuel and oil pressures, check cylinder and oil temperatures, set engines 1 and 2 to 30 inches manifold pressure, check magnetos 1 and 2, reduce throttles to 1000 rpm."

Then we repeated the steps for engines 3 and 4.

"DC-6 . . . Foxtrot . . . Echo . . . six . . . five . . . nine . . . you are cleared for takeoff runway nine zero," the control tower instructed us over the radio.

"Roger, Tower," the captain repeated over the radio, "DC-6 . . . Foxtrot . . . Echo . . . six . . . five . . . nine . . . cleared for takeoff runway nine zero,"

Captain Ron taxied the plane onto the runway.

"Put the checklist away and put your hands on the controls so you can feel what I am doing," he instructed, "but don't help. I'll maintain all control."

"I am setting the flaps to 20 degrees and applying full power," he said. The plane started rolling down the runway. Slowly at first, but the speed quickly increased. He held forward pressure on the yoke until we reached 125 mph. Then he pulled smoothly back on the yoke and we became airborne.

"Adjusting power to 80%," he said. "We'll use the control yoke to maintain 160 mph. Now, retract the landing gear," he said as he pointed to the gear-up switch.

I did as he instructed. You could hear the gear coming up and the gear doors shutting. Then the gear-up light came on.

"Now we'll raise the flaps," he said. "Up from 20 to 10 degrees first . . . Good . . . Now we'll let the plane settle for a minute . . . OK, that's good . . . Now up to zero degrees, OK, that's good."

I watched as he alternated from scouring the instrument panel to looking outside.

"When we reach an altitude of 9,000 feet, we'll reduce power and cruise at 310 miles an hour," he explained.

I was excited and a little apprehensive about being in the cockpit of a DC-6. I looked over at Captain Ron. One of his hands gently cradled the control yoke while the other made small adjustments to the throttle and other controls. He was completely at ease as the captain of this plane. His confidence was reassuring.

"Welcome to your inaugural flight in a DC-6," he said.

CHAPTER 81

The Caicos Islands

WHEN YOU'RE 9,000 FEET UP IN the air, it doesn't look like you're going 310 miles an hour. The ocean, boats, and islands below just slowly pass beneath the plane.

It only took us a little over 2 hours to get to the Caicos Islands. When they were in sight, Captain Ron got on the radio and called their control tower for clearance to land.

"Caicos Tower," the captain said into the radio. "This is DC-6 Foxtrot . . . Echo . . . six . . . five . . . nine inbound. We need clearance for landing please."

"DC-6 Foxtrot . . . Echo . . . six . . . five . . . nine, you are cleared to land runway one eight zero," the controller responded.

"Roger, Tower. And please cancel our flight plan to Peru."

Captain Ron made small adjustments to keep the DC-6 centered on the runway. He was in complete control of the huge airplane and it responded to the gentle touches of his hands. It was like he and the airplane were one.

The plane settled onto the runway with a little *PFFFT*, *PFFFT* as each main wheel touched the concrete. Captain Ron taxied the plane over to the parking ramp and shut down the engines. When we exited the plane, Captain Ron said we needed to do a walk around and look for any dripping oil or anything loose on the outside of the plane. Sure enough, there was an oil streak on the cowling of engine number 3 and oil was dripping onto the ground.

"I'll call Bryan after we get checked into the motel here," Captain Ron said. "He's going to have to have Ray come down and see what's going on with that engine."

We walked into the customs office and checked in. The customs Agent looked in each of our small carry-on suitcases and stamped our passports.

"Is there a taxi we can get to take us to the motel?" Captain Ron asked.

He didn't have to specify which motel; there was only one on the island.

"Sure," the agent replied. "I'll call him on the CB radio and tell him he has some customers here."

* * *

"Most of the tourists that come here are scuba divers or fishermen," the taxi driver said, "and they usually don't come here this time of year. You guys don't have diving or fishing gear, so what brings you to our beautiful island?"

"We are delivering a DC-6 to Lima, Peru to a small airline there," I answered. "We had a mechanical problem with one of the engines and had to land here. We'll stay here until the plane is repaired and the airline in Peru transfers the final payment for the plane to our company in the states," I continued, inventing our cover story on the spur of the moment.

Captain Ron looked over at me and nodded his approval.

The motel was only a couple of miles from the airport, so the taxi ride didn't take very long.

"Both the airport and the motel have CB radios," the driver said as he dropped us off in front of the motel. "So whenever you need a ride, just ask them to give me a call. That'll be four dollars."

I pulled out a ten and told him to keep the change.

After we checked in and put our bags in our rooms, we returned to the front desk and Captain Ron asked how he could make a call to the states.

"There is a phone in the library," the desk clerk said. "Give me the number you want to call and go wait in the library. When the phone in the states is ringing, I'll transfer the call to the phone in there and it will ring once. Pick up the phone when you hear it ring."

The walls of the library were lined with shelves and they were full of books. One shelf had a few board games and several decks of tattered cards with rubber bands around them. All the books were old and looked like they had been read hundreds of times. On one wall was a small blackboard and some chalk and an eraser were on the front ledge built onto the blackboard. On the blackboard was a message. It read:

```
Welcome to the
the Admiral's Inn

Today's dinner special
will be whatever
the local fishermen catch
```

There were a couple of armchairs against one wall and a telephone sat on top of an end table between the chairs. We both choose a book to look at and sat in the armchairs while we waited for our call to go through.

After about 20 minutes, the phone rang once. Captain Ron picked up the receiver.

"Hello," he said.

"Please hold while I connect the call," an operator said.

A few seconds later, Bryan came on the phone.

"Bryan, we have a problem with the plane," Captain Ron said. "We just landed at the Caicos Islands a little while ago and one of the engines is leaking oil. It will have to be repaired before we can fly it again. You'll need to send Ray down here."

"What else can go wrong?" Bryan asked, exasperated. "OK, I'll call Ray and see when he can get there. I'll also get ahold of our friends in the south and let them know. I'll call you back when I know something."

* * *

When Bryan got off the phone with Captain Ron, he immediately called Ray and told him about the oil leak.

"There are no scheduled commercial flights there in the off season so I'll have to charter a plane," Ray said. "Let me make some calls and I'll get back to you."

Ray called Bryan back an hour later.

"I was able to charter a plane for tomorrow morning," Ray said. "I should be there by noon. Depending on what I find, I

228

may have to get some parts from the states. So it could take several days to get it fixed."

Bryan's next call was to the Colombia contact, Mauricio, to let him know about the delay.

"We have the load sitting up in the Guajira Peninsula on the northern tip of Colombia," Mauricio said. "I think we'll have to let someone else take it while you get your plane repaired. We'll get another shipment ready for you, but it may take a week or so. I will give you a few days' notice before I want the plane to come."

"I understand," Bryan said. "I'll call you when I find out how long it's going to take to repair the oil leak."

CHAPTER 82

The Photographers

RAY ARRIVED THE NEXT DAY AROUND noon on a chartered plane. We took the taxi and met him at the airport. He borrowed some roll-around stairs from the airport so he could get to the engine, unlatched the cowling and peered inside. It didn't take him long to see the problem. An oil line had ruptured and sprung a small leak.

"Good thing the line didn't burst wide open," he said, "otherwise the engine would have lost all the oil and seized up. I'm going to have to go back to the states to get some parts and the tools I'm going to need. I'll check the other engines while I'm here to make sure those are OK."

He checked the other 3 engines and didn't find any problems with them.

"I'll go back on the charter plane, get what I need, and be back down here in a couple of days," he said. "I'll call Bryan and let him know what's going on when I get back to the states tonight."

He got back on the charter plane and they took off.

Captain Ron and I had nothing better to do, so we decided to walk back to the motel rather than take the taxi. There were no paved roads on the island, only dirt roads. The main road went from the airport, on one end of the island, to the other end of the island where the motel was located. A few smaller roads went off the main road here and there, and small houses lined those roads.

Most of the houses were made of what looked like dried mud, and they all had thatch roofs. Many had doors that were painted blue, yellow, green, or orange that added some character to the otherwise drab looking houses. Every yard had a clothesline and many had clothes hanging on them. The clothes were mostly old and tattered, and looked like Goodwill rejects. Bright colors and stripes seemed to be the clothing of choice. Trash littered the road and the yards. It looked like everyone just threw their trash out in their yard.

Before long, we had a dozen kids and a couple of skinny dogs following us. The kids asked us for money and candy, but Captain Ron told me not to give them anything. He said if we did, they would forever pester us. When we got to the motel, the kids stopped just short of the motel property. They must have been warned before to leave the motel guests alone.

As we walked up the path in the motel's yard, I stopped and turned around. The kids were watching us. I couldn't help myself. I reached into my pocket and pulled out a handful of small Tootsie Rolls I had brought.

Tootsie Rolls are great for 2 reasons; they are chocolate and they don't melt.

Captain Ron just looked at me and shook his head. I tossed the candy to the crowd of kids and they went wild. They scrambled around, each one trying to get one or more of the candies that fell on the ground.

When they had all the Tootsie Rolls picked up, they turned and headed back towards their houses. Their laughter and smiles were worth the pestering we were now going to have to endure every time they saw us.

I watched as they shoved the candies into their mouths and dropped the wrappers onto the ground.

We walked out to the motel's patio to order some dinner where we could watch the sun set as we ate. Two men came out a few minutes later and took a table on the other end of the patio. Our waiter told us that during the scuba diving season, the motel would be full. But right now there were only 4 guests staying at the motel. He said the other 2 guests, sitting on the other end of the patio, were photographers from National Geographic.

I glanced at the camera on their table. It looked a lot like the 35mm SLR film camera I had at home.

That's odd, I thought. *I thought that someone taking pictures for National Geographic would be using something more professional. Maybe they had other equipment back in their room.*

The waiter suggested we try the Dorado. He said it had been caught by one of the local fishermen just that morning, so it was really fresh. I've discovered that it's usually a good idea to order what your waiter recommends. He knows what the best food is in the kitchen and he wants you to be happy with your meal. Good service and good food means a good tip. This case was no exception. The Dorado was excellent.

It was grilled and came with rice and beans, and a skewer of green peppers and onions. Sliced papaya and banana was served on a separate plate for us to share.

"All the fresh food was grown right here on the island," our waiter proudly told us. "But, the yellow rice and red beans, like most of the food here, has to be imported from the states."

The Red Stripe beers that we had with our dinner came from Jamaica.

After we watched the sun set and drained the last of our Red Stripes, we headed for our rooms to read for a while. There was really nothing else to do on the island after dark. The motel ran a generator for a couple of hours after sunset, but then it was turned off and the only light came from the moon and the stars.

I read one of the books I had borrowed from the motel's library until the generator quit and the lights went out. Then I did what everyone else on the island did when it got dark; I went to bed.

* * *

A rooster crowing at 5:00 in the morning woke me up. I had 8 hours of sleep so I was ready to get up and have some coffee out on the patio. We'd have breakfast out there while we watched the sun rise.

"Where'd the coffee come from?" I asked the waiter.

"Colombia," he said.

CHAPTER 83

Good News & Bad News

IT WAS SEVERAL DAYS LATER WHEN Ray came back on the charter plane. The charter pilot and Ray came inside to check in with customs. Then Ray came out to talk with us.

"Sorry it took so long for me to get back," he said. "I had a hard time finding the correct oil line and had to have it flown in from Atlanta. It won't take long to replace the oil line, and then we'll take the plane out for a test flight. The charter pilot is going to wait for me."

Ray had the new line installed in less than an hour, and then we climbed aboard to take it for a test ride. Ray sat in the co-pilot's seat beside Captain Ron, and I sat in the navigator's seat behind the pilots' seats.

Captain Ron called the tower for clearance to take off, and then taxied the plane onto the runway.

I noticed the 2 photographers standing by the customs office. One of them was taking pictures of the plane with his 35mm camera.

When we were airborne, Ray said, "Bryan wanted me to tell you that the Colombians couldn't hold the pot any longer and they sold it to another importer. They are gathering up another load, but it could be a week or so before they get it together. He'll call you in a few days when he knows more. Stay here and stay ready."

We flew the DC-6 for about an hour and then returned to the airport. Ray rechecked all of the engines and said everything looked good. Then he got back into the charter plane and they took off.

Captain Ron and I walked back to the motel. By the time we got there, the entourage of kids following us had grown to about 20.

"Can-dee . . . Can-dee," they pleaded, as they held out their hands.

When we got to the motel's front yard, I threw a handful of Tootsie Rolls that I had in my pocket into the air above them. They laughed and scrambled for the candy as it rained down around them.

Captain Ron and I both smiled as we walked inside.

The motel didn't have any televisions, so we went to the library to peruse the books. That's when I first discovered the author, Zane Grey. His westerns are short, easy to read, and entertaining. With nothing much else to do, I read a dozen of his books while we waited for Bryan's next call to come.

The call finally came a week later.

"I have good news and bad news," Bryan said to Captain Ron on the phone. "The good news is the supplier got another load together. The bad news is there is storm heading for Cuba and it is blocking your flight path. Our friends down south have another customer who has a plane staged in Venezuela. They are going to get the load and fly it to Louisiana before the storm gets any farther west. Then they'll work on getting us some more cargo. Mauricio said he is sending up a Boss Lady to the Caicos Islands as soon as the storm passes to ensure everything there runs smoothly. Her name is Angela Blackman and she will have a few of her men with her. She is renting the nicest, largest house on the Island for her and her entourage. You guys will stay there as well. Now you may not like this part, captain, but Angela will be in charge there. However, you will still have the final say about anything to do with the plane's airworthiness. So don't let her intimidate you into flying in inclement weather. That'll still be your call. I'll get back in touch with you in a few days."

CHAPTER 84

Boss Lady

IN A COUPLE OF DAYS THE storm passed over Cuba and made its way toward Mexico. The clouds disappeared over the Caicos Islands and the blue skies returned. Then Angela arrived.

She sent one of her men to the hotel to get us. He didn't speak English, so the hotel desk clerk interpreted for us.

"This is Fredrico. He says you are to get your luggage and go with him. Evidently you are going to the Harrison house on the east side of the island. It is very nice. You will be very comfortable there. You are still welcome to come here and eat at our restaurant and to borrow books from our library."

"Thank you," I said. We paid our bill, tipped the clerk, and started to pick up our bags.

"Let me do that for you," the clerk said as he ran around to our side of the counter.

He picked up our bags and put them into the trunk of the taxi.

Captain Ron pulled out a five and slipped it into the clerk's hand.

"Thank you, senor."

* * *

"This is the only solid concrete house presently on the island," the taxi driver said as he pulled up in front of the bright blue two-story house. The house sat right on the edge of a cliff overlooking the Atlantic. "It was originally built by a wealthy businessman, and is named after him . . . The Harrison House. But after his death, his estate sold it to an investor who rents it out to tourists. It has 3,000 square feet, 5 bedrooms, and 3 baths. It will accommodate a dozen tourists comfortably . . . or 3-dozen natives."

He laughed at his own joke. Then he opened the trunk and

carried our bags to the front door.

"There is a CB radio in the house for the use of the guests," the driver said. "If you need a ride, just call me. I monitor channel 19."

The taxi left and we went inside the house.

Angela was sitting on the couch in the living room and three men sat on chairs around the room. There were 2 more men sitting on the floor.

"Aaah . . . Captain Ron and Ryan, I presume. Come in and sit down," Angela said. "Let me introduce you to my men." She told us the names of each of the men in the room as she pointed at them and they each nodded their heads at us. "The two men sitting on the floor represent the middleman who buys the pot for us. They will be flying back with you. When you get to the area where you are to land, they will point out the air strip to you."

She said something to one of her men in Spanish and he left the room.

The only word I understood was 'cerveza'.

"Unfortunately, only my man Carlos and I can speak both Spanish and English," she said. "The rest of the men with me can only speak Spanish. That can be a bother at times, but it also has its advantages."

Carlos came back a minute later and handed each of us a cold beer.

"We'll be staying here together until you fly the DC-6 out to Colombia," Angela said. "I talked with Mauricio yesterday and he said it would be several weeks before he can get another load up to the Guajira Peninsula. I think it is a bad idea for your plane to be sitting here for so long. So I want to change the pickup location closer to where the pot is grown. That way, you can pick it up in a week."

"Where is this new location?" Captain Ron asked.

"The pot is grown in the Amazon Basin which is about 800 miles south of the Guajira Peninsula," Angela answered. "There is a 3,000 foot dirt strip there by el Rio Apaporis. In English, it is called the Apaporis River. Many planes have landed there. It is there you will pick up your pot."

A look of concern came over the captain's face.

"Let me pull out a map," he said as he dug in his flight bag and found a flight chart and a map of Colombia. He spread the map out on the table in the living room and studied it for a few minutes. "Our plane has a range of about 2,500 miles, but that's over flat terrain. To get to the Apaporis River, we will have to fly more than 2,000 miles and go over the Andes Mountains. That will use all our available fuel with very little reserves. And coming back loaded will be impossible. We won't have enough fuel."

"Then you must install some bladders in the plane," Angela said.

"What are bladders?" I asked.

"They are rubber tanks made to carry fuel. They look like waterbed bags," Captain Ron explained. "Normally, they are installed in a contained space made for them, like under the floor in a boat or in the wings of an airplane. Extra bladders in the DC-6 would have to be strapped down in the cargo area, and that is dangerous."

"Many pilots down here install them in their planes to increase their range," Angela said. "There aren't airports around every corner where you can just stop and refuel like you can in the states. You are going to fly a plane into the middle of a jungle and pick up pot from people you have never met. There are more dangerous things for you to worry about than having bladders on your plane. Anyway, you have big balls...no?"

Captain Ron and I didn't say anything.

"There are 2 bedrooms downstairs for you," Angela said. "I'm taking the master bedroom and my four men can share the other two bedrooms up here. Our jungle friends over there can sleep on the pull out sofa. Get settled into your rooms and come back upstairs. We're going to dinner at the motel. And while we're there, I'm going to use the motel's phone to call Mauricio."

CHAPTER 85

Bladders

ANGELA TOLD ONE OF HER MEN to call for the taxi on the CB radio. When the taxi arrived, she hopped into the front seat and told Captain Ron, Carlos, and me to hop in the back.

"The others can walk up," she said. "It's only a mile or so."

Angela went to the front desk to initiate the call to Mauricio.

"You'll have to wait in the library for the call to go through," the clerk said. "It should take about 20 or 30 minutes."

"I'm not sitting in the library waiting for the phone to ring. I'm going out on the patio and have a drink while I wait on my dinner. You can come and get me when the call goes through," she said, as she turned and took off for the patio.

The clerk just stared.

I looked at the clerk and shrugged my shoulders. We all followed her out to the patio. The waiter showed us to a table and Angela stood there looking around.

"No . . . we'll take that table over there," she said as she pointed. She didn't hesitate. She just walked over to the other table and sat down. We followed her cue and took seats around the table.

"I have five other men coming," she said to the waiter. "When they get here, seat them at a table on the other end of the patio. What have you got that's fresh?"

"We have fresh caught snapper," the waiter said.

"We'll all have that," she said. "I'll have a Crown and Coke while we wait. Bring cold beer for everyone else. Put it all on one bill. And I'm thirsty, so hurry up."

"Yes ma'am," the waiter replied. He glanced at me and raised one eyebrow.

In response, I raised both of mine back at him. Then he

turned and hurried off.

As we finished our second round of drinks, the desk clerk came to tell Angela that her call was waiting. She followed him to the library.

When she returned, she looked at Captain Ron and said, "Mauricio agrees. You will have bladders installed. He will contact Bryan and instruct him to send your mechanic back down here. He will stay here until the bladders are installed on the plane."

Then she turned to me.

"The mechanic will arrive on a charter plane tomorrow. He will stay to figure out everything he needs to get the bladders installed while you fly back on the charter plane to pick up the parts he needs. He will call and order the parts and tell you where to pick them up. Then you will charter a plane and bring everything back here."

Then she noticed the waiter coming.

"Aaahh . . . look. Here comes our dinner," she announced.

CHAPTER 86
Devil's Triangle

RAY ARRIVED ON A CESSNA 206 charter plane the next afternoon. He and the pilot checked in through customs and the pilot ordered some fuel. Then the pilot filed a flight plan back to Fort Lauderdale and we got on the plane.

The pilot gave me a choice. "You can sit in the back, or you can sit in the co-pilot's seat."

"I'd love to sit up front with you. Thanks," I said, as I climbed up front.

"I'm Bill Bell," the pilot said and reached out to shake my hand. I shook his hand and introduced myself.

Bill called the tower for clearance to takeoff and we taxied onto the runway. I watched as he did the preflight run up. I watched when he looked at the compass and dialed the compass heading into the directional gyros. There were 2 directional gyros in the plane; one for the pilot, and one for the co-pilot.

* * *

A compass in a plane can be inaccurate during flight due to the downward curve of the earth's magnetic field. This error is magnified during a turn, when the plane is accelerating, or when the plane is being bounced around by the wind. Directional gyros on the other hand, are stabilized by built in gyroscopes. So they will read accurately all the time. You just have to adjust them to the compass reading when the plane is steady and level, like on the ground.

* * *

When the tower gave us clearance, Bill applied full power and we took off.

"It is about 600 miles to Fort Lauderdale," he said. "We'll be cruising about 200 miles an hour, so it will take us about 3 hours to get there." He looked at his watch. "It's 5:00 now, so we should get there about 8:00."

I told Bill I was a pilot, but I usually flew the smaller, single engine Cessna's. He told me about the planes he had flown and explained all the controls and gauges in this plane to me. As we cruised along, we talked about planes, and life, and the fact that our flight path took us right through the Bermuda Triangle.

* * *

The Bermuda Triangle is also called the Devil's Triangle. It covers the triangular area between Bermuda, Puerto Rico, and Florida. Officially, this area doesn't exist. But there are many stories of planes and boats that have mysteriously disappeared there. We wondered if any of it was true and what really happened to those boats and planes.

* * *

I looked at my watch. It was 7:00.

"Bill," I said, "we've been flying for 2 hours. Shouldn't we be able to see the lights in Nassau by now? All I see in front of us are stars."

Bill looked at his watch, and I saw his brow furrow a little. He looked at the gauges. He looked at his directional gyro.

"We are still on course," he said. "I've held a heading of 305 degrees all the way. We must have a stronger headwind than I expected. It's just probably taking us longer than I anticipated."

I looked at the directional gyro on my side. It said 335 degrees.

I looked at the compass . . . 335 degrees.

Then, I looked at his directional gyro. It said 305 degrees.

"Bill, look at the heading on your directional gyro and compare it to mine. There's a 30-degree difference. Mine agrees with the compass. I think your gyro is 30 degrees off."

He looked at my gyro . . . then at his . . . then at the compass.

"Something's wrong," he said, as he tapped his finger on his gyro to see if the reading changed. It didn't.

I asked him for a chart of the Caribbean and used a pencil to draw two flight paths from the Caicos Islands; one with a heading of 305 degrees, and one with a heading of 335 degrees.

"Take a look at this chart," I said, as I handed it to him. "We've been flying for 2 hours at 200 miles per hour. If our heading was 305 degrees all the way, we should be just about over Nassau, and we'd be able to see the lights there. But if our heading was 335 degrees all the way, then we're somewhere about 100 miles northeast of Nassau with nothing in front of us but open water."

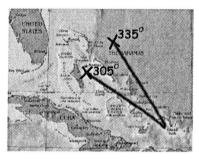

"I know I set my gyro correctly before we took off," he said with an air of confidence. "You watched me do it. Out here, you need to trust your electronics."

"I did watch you set your gyro . . . and you did set it correctly," I assured him. "But, something has happened. If we really are northeast of Nassau, we need to turn left and head west at a heading of 270 degrees."

"I can't believe we're that far off course," Bill said. "I'll reset my gyro, but I think we should still stay on a heading of 305 degrees."

"Can you pick up the VOR in Nassau yet; or the one in Miami?" I asked.

* * *

VOR stands for Very high frequency Omni-directional Radio range. The VOR transmitter on the ground sends out a signal that is picked up by a receiver in the plane to help pilots navigate.

* * *

He dialed in the frequency for the VOR in Nassau. The needle didn't respond. Then he tried Miami.

"I can't get either of them," he said.

"That's because we are too far away," I replied. "At this altitude, a VOR has a range of about 50 miles. Bill, we can't see the lights in Nassau, and we can't receive their VOR. I'm telling you the only thing in front of us is ocean. We need to turn left right now and take up a heading of 270 degrees. If we did that, and I am wrong, what's the worst that could happen?"

He thought about it for a minute.

"We'd come in over the Keys," he said.

"OK. And, if I'm right, and we don't turn, what could happen?" I asked.

He thought for a moment and then banked the plane as he turned left.

"I hope you're right," he said.

"Good," I said as I let out a sigh of relief. Then I looked at the fuel gauge.

"Bill, I saw you get fuel before we took off. Did you fill up?" I asked.

"No," he answered. "The fuel there in the islands is really expensive. I got enough to get us home with an hour of reserve."

"How much do we have left now," I asked.

"About 2 hours," was his reply. "And that's using the reserve," he added.

I looked back at the chart.

"If we really are 100 miles northeast of Nassau, then we're about 450 miles east of Fort Lauderdale. Two hours of fuel will only take us 400 miles. Our flight path should take us right over Freeport. I think we're going to have to make a pit stop. The airport there is only open until 9:00, so we should make it in time."

"You seem to know a lot about Freeport," Bill said.

"Oh, I've stopped there for fuel before," I responded, hoping this time I could actually get some fuel.

Bill set his receiver for the VOR frequency in Freeport. About 8:30, we saw some lights on the horizon in front of us, and the needle on the VOR started to move. Bill adjusted the

VOR receiver until the needle centered. We were about 50 miles east of Freeport.

Bill landed the plane and had the wing tanks filled. Then we took off and headed for Florida.

When we landed in Fort Lauderdale, Bill handed me one of his cards.

"Any time you need a ride, call me," he said, as he shook my hand. "It's been a pleasure flying with you."

CHAPTER 87

Surrounded By Soldiers

I GOT A ROOM AT A hotel and called Bryan the next morning.

"Ray called and ordered everything he needs to install the bladders," Bryan said. "He said they'll have everything ready by noon today. I'll have Striker pick you up at the hotel about 11:00 and you guys can go get the stuff. I've already given cash to Striker to pay for the bladders and for the charter flight back to the Caicos Islands. Call the charter company and schedule a flight back for this afternoon."

I pulled Bill's card out of my wallet and called the charter company.

"I'd like to charter a plane to the Caicos Islands, and I'd like to leave this afternoon," I said. "Bill picked me up there yesterday, and if he is available, I'd like to have him fly me back. I'll pay for Bill to spend the night there. He'll pick up another passenger there and fly back tomorrow."

The agent put me on hold while he checked his docket and called Bill to see if he was available.

"Thanks for holding," the agent said when he came back on the line. "Both the plane and Bill can be available today at 5:00 if that is OK?"

"That's fine," I answered. "I'll see you this afternoon at 5:00."

* * *

Each of the three bladders was packed in its own cardboard box. In another box was the fuel pump, a long rubber fuel line, quick disconnect fittings, tie-down straps, and a roll of wire. Striker paid for the items and they loaded the boxes in Striker's van for us. Since we had a few of hours to kill, Striker asked me if I'd like to go eat somewhere.

"I'd love to have a good steak," I said. "The seafood in the islands is great, but it's impossible to get a good steak there."

Striker laughed. He loved to eat and knew all the best places.

"I know just where to go," he said.

He was right. The steak was excellent and we downed a few Budweiser Long Necks for old time's sake.

When we got to the airport, Bill was there waiting for me.

"I didn't know I'd be seeing you so soon," he said, as he reached out to shake my hand. "The mechanics checked out the directional gyro and couldn't find anything wrong with it. They are going to send it off to be thoroughly inspected and calibrated and they've installed a new one in the plane. So, hopefully, this flight will be a little less exciting."

Striker helped Bill load the cardboard boxes into the plane. Bill had already filed a flight plan so he called the tower for clearance to taxi and takeoff.

The flight back was uneventful and we saw the lights as we approached the island just after dark. Bill called the tower for clearance to land, and got landing instructions.

He taxied the plane up to the customs building and we exited the plane. Three uniformed soldiers came out of the customs building and walked briskly over to the plane. One had a pistol on his belt and the other two were carrying M-16s. The one with the pistol was obviously an officer.

"Who's the pilot?" the officer asked.

"I am," Bill answered. "What's going on?"

"I need to see identification from both of you," the officer said. "Give me your passports."

As we were getting out our passports, I heard a noise across the runway. It sounded like a bunch of people running in cadence. I looked towards the sound. It was too dark to see what was causing the noise, but I could see the runway lights on the other side of the runway blinking on and off.

That's odd, I thought. *Runway lights are solid…they don't blink like that.*

Then the sound across the runway started towards us and the lights stopped blinking. In a minute, we were surrounded by a dozen soldiers who were all armed with rifles. The sound we heard was their boots hitting the concrete as they ran in formation down the edge of the runway. The blinking was caused by them running in front of the lights.

These soldiers had to have been flown here from the main island, I thought.

The officer looked at our passports and handed them back.

"What have you got in the plane?" he asked.

"Just some boxes of cargo that my customer brought," Bill answered. He looked over at me. I could tell he was concerned. He hadn't asked me what was in the boxes. From the look on his face, I could tell he was hoping it was nothing illegal.

"I need to look in those boxes," the officer said.

He pulled out a pocketknife and sliced the tape on top of the boxes and opened them.

"What are these?" he asked, as he peered at the folded up bladders.

"Those are fuel bladders for some fishing boats," I said, "and the wiring, hoses, and pumps that go with them. I have a contract to install some new tanks on some charter boats down here. Is there a problem?"

It was obvious that the soldiers had expected to find some contraband on the plane. The officer just stared at the bladders for a minute while he thought about what to do next.

"I . . . I don't guess so," he stammered. "But you'll have to declare them with customs."

"Of course," I responded, and Bill and I started walking towards the customs building.

After we cleared customs, I asked the agent to call the taxi for us. I told Bill I'd see him tomorrow and we dropped him off at the motel. Then the taxi took me to the rental house.

CHAPTER 88

The Bladder Test

THE NEXT DAY RAY INSTALLED THE bladders in the plane. He put the bladders on the floor of the cargo area and put straps over them to hold them in place. He opened an access panel underneath the belly of the plane and bolted the fuel pump inside. Then, he ran a hose from the input side of the pump up through the floor of the cargo area to the bladders.

Next, he hooked up the output side of the pump up to an existing fuel line that went to the wing tanks. He put quick disconnect fittings on the three bladders and one on the hose that came up through the floor. Then he put a switch in the dashboard in the cockpit and ran wires from it to connect power from the electrical system to the new fuel pump.

When he was satisfied with the installation, he had the fuel truck come out to the plane and fill each of the bladders. He then connected the quick disconnect coupling to the first bladder and flipped the switch he had installed in the cockpit. The pump started and we watched the bladder collapse as the fuel was pumped into the wing tanks. Then he turned off the switch and repeated the test on the other two bladders.

When he was satisfied that everything worked as it was supposed to. He packed up his tools to go while I had the Customs Agent call for the taxi to pick up Bill at the motel.

When Bill got to the airport, he had the fuel truck fill up his plane while Ray loaded his tools on board.

"Oh, so this time you're going to fill up the tanks instead of just getting enough fuel to get back home on?" I jibbed.

"After last time, I think I'd rather be safe than sorry," he said.

Then he reached out to shake my hand.

"By the way," he added, "flying with you is way too

exciting. I think I want my card back."

Ray and Bill got into the plane and I watched as the plane taxied to the runway and took off.

CHAPTER 89
Devilish Entertainment

THE NEXT AFTERNOON I WALKED OUT behind the house and sat on the cliff overlooking the ocean. I was getting really homesick. I wanted this job to be over so I could go home and be with my family. I had already been gone for several weeks and I hadn't been able to call home. Just in case our home phones were bugged, Bryan didn't want us to call and give anyone the ability to trace our calls and discover our location. After I sat there for an hour or so, I walked back into the house.

Angela and her men were sitting around the dining room table and they had been drinking. There were beer bottles and a half empty bottle of whiskey on the table. Angela looked at me as I walked in and said, "Ah, Ryan, grab a cold beer and join us. You are just in time for some entertainment."

I opened a cold beer and sat down at the table.

Angela turned to Carlos and said, "Go get one of our Colombian jungle friends and bring him in here. I'm bored and want to have some fun."

Carlos returned a couple minutes later with Santino, one of the Colombians from the jungle.

"I'm going to talk to him in Spanish," Angela said, looking at me. "But I'm going to repeat everything we say in English so you can understand." Then she turned to Carlos and said, "Bring me the map that is on the dresser in my bedroom."

When Carlos returned with the map, Angela spread it out on the table. It was a map of Colombia.

"Santino," she said, "stand up by the table here so you can see the map. Carlos, you and Santos stand behind him."

"Santino, you know where the landing strip is by the river don't you?" she asked as she looked at him.

Santino nodded affirmatively as he answered her in

250

Spanish.

"Good," she said. "Now I want you to show me where the strip is located on this map."

Santino studied the map but it was obvious he was not familiar with using one.

"Come on Santino," Angela demanded, "we're all waiting for you to show us where the strip is."

When Santino didn't point out the location, Angela asked, "Do you see the Apaporis River on the map, Santino?"

"I'm not very familiar with maps," Santino said. "But I can spot the strip from the airplane when we fly down the river."

"If you can't show me the strip on this map, then how do I know you can show the pilots where the strip is when you get there, Santino?" She jabbed her finger on the Apaporis River on the map. "There's El Rio Apaporis, Santino. Now point out where the strip is," she ordered, raising her voice.

* * *

Santino studied the map as he tried to picture the river as it curved through the jungle. On the map, it just looked like a snake drawn on a piece of paper. He had seen maps before, but he had never used one. His world had consisted of just the area of the jungle where he lived. He knew it like the back of his hand. But . . . on a map . . . it just didn't make sense.

He knew the jungle airstrip was just upstream from the sharp bend in the river near his cousin's village. He had been there many times. He would recognize it if he saw pictures of it, but the map wasn't pictures. It was symbols.

* * *

"Where is it, Santino?" Angela insisted, her voice getting louder.

"Somewhere near here," Santino said, as he pointed a shaking finger towards the line on the map that she said was the Apaporis River.

"Exactly where, Santino?" she screamed, as she bent over the table leaning on the map with her outstretched arms.

Her face was just inches from his. I could see spittle from her lips flying through the air and landing on Santino's face.

Their eyes were locked. Her's looked fierce, like a lioness staring at her prey. And Santino's were filled with fear.

He began to shake.

She reared back and threw her arms up over her head with her palms outstretched.

"What am I going to do with you, Santino?" she said more calmly but still sounding exasperated. "Can't you see I am trying to be reasonable? But, you are not cooperating."

Then she reached over to the far side of the table and picked up a butcher knife that lay there. She twirled it around in her hand as she stared at the blade. Then her eyes went wild. She raised the knife high above her head like she was getting ready to plunge it into Santino's chest. Then with both hands grasping the knife, she plunged it down right through the map and into the wooden table. She released the knife and the handle vibrated back and forth until it finally became still.

Then she sat down and looked into Santino's eyes from across the table.

"I don't want to hurt you, Santino," she said calmly. "But, you have to show me the location of that strip on the map. I want you to drop your pants, Santino."

Santino started shaking his head 'no' and he started sobbing. He was pleading with her to stop as tears started running down his face. He couldn't take his eyes off hers. It was like there was nobody else in the room . . . just them.

"Drop them, Santino," she said again, calmly.

Again Santino started begging for her to stop.

She reached behind her back and pulled out an automatic pistol she had tucked into her waistband. She pulled back the slide on the pistol to load a bullet into the chamber. Then she pushed the barrel of the gun into Santino's crotch.

"If you don't drop those pants, Santino," she screamed, "I'm going to blow your balls off!"

Santino's face had turned ashen like all the blood had drained from his head. His lips were quivering and snot was starting to drip out of his nose. His hands were shaking so bad, he could hardly unbutton his pants and unzip his fly. He released his pants and they fell down around his ankles.

"Good boy, Santino," she said in a calm voice. "I can be nice when you cooperate and do what I say. Don't you like me better this way?"

Santino's head bobbed up and down affirmatively, but his eyes never left hers.

"Now drop your underwear, Santino," she said as she shoved the pistol into his crotch again.

Santino started crying again as he begged her to stop.

"Now, Santino," she said calmly.

Santino hooked his thumbs into the waistband of his underwear and tugged them down until they fell down around his ankles on top of his pants.

"Stand up closer to the table, Santino," she told him.

He shuffled his feet forward until his thighs were touching the table.

"Now put it up on the table, Santino," she said.

Then, in perfect English, Santino pleaded, "Please, Senora, no. I beg you."

It was the only English I had heard Santino speak.

As he tried to back up from the table, Carlos and Santos grabbed him by his shoulders and forced him forward again.

"Santino, if you don't do as I ask, then I will shoot if off," Angela said in a calm voice as she jammed the barrel of the pistol into his crotch.

With loud sobs, and shaking hands, Santino did as she asked.

Angela calmly laid her pistol on her side of the table. Then she reached over the map and grasped the knife handle, and with a jerk, pulled the knife out of the wooden table. She placed the knife across Santino's parts and applied a little downward pressure.

"Now, Santino, you have one last chance to show me the location of the airstrip on the map or I will be forced to chop it off."

Santino was now so overcome with fear that he was having a hard time standing up. Carlos and Santos were holding him up so he wouldn't collapse. Tears and snot were now freely flowing down Santino's face. He was sobbing so much the words coming out of his mouth were incoherent.

Angela yanked the knife up into air and threw her head back as laughter started pouring out of her.

The look on her face was pure evil.

Her eyes almost looked like they were on fire.

She couldn't stop laughing as she plunged the knife down into the table again. The blade sunk an inch into the wood. We all stared at the knife as the handle again vibrated side to side.

Her men stared at her like they had never seen her before. The looks they gave each other showed they were nervous. They were glad her entertainment this evening was Santino and not them.

I sat there dumbfounded as feelings of evil, fear, death, and destruction filled the room. It was as if hundreds of demons were surrounding us in the room, watching the show, and laughing with her.

"Go get the other one," she instructed her men. "Let's do it again."

CHAPTER 90

Seduction

CARLOS AND SANTOS RELEASED SANTINO AND left the room to get the other Colombian.

Santino was still sobbing as he bent over to pull up his pants.

I stood up and walked out.

I didn't want to see any more.

I walked back out to the cliff overlooking the ocean and sat down. A few minutes later, Santino came out and sat down about 50 feet from me. We both stared at the ocean. Neither of us said anything. We both knew what his friend was going through right now inside the house. We also knew we were powerless to stop it.

When the other Colombian came out of the house about 30 minutes later, he joined Santino. He was sobbing and wiping the tears off his face with his sleeve. We could hear Angela laughing inside the house.

I thought the Colombian guys would talk about their ordeal, but they didn't. They just sat there and stared out over the ocean.

When the sun sank below the water on the horizon, I got up and walked to my room.

I tried to read, but I couldn't get my mind off of what had just happened. So, I just sat there on the edge of my bed and thought about how good I had it at home; *there, I was loved, warm, needed, and safe. Nothing like this ever happened at home. Why did I ever leave there and venture into this world?*

I felt tears starting to flow down my cheeks.

Then someone knocked on my door.

I wiped the tears away with the bed sheet and got up to see who was there. When I opened the door, Angela was standing there. She had a drink in one hand and a bottle in the other.

She took a sip of her drink as she leaned up against the doorframe.

"Why did you leave so early?" she asked. "The second show was even better than the first. He was scared so bad, he pissed all over himself."

I didn't answer. I just turned and walked across the room and sat down on the edge of the bed. There was no other place to sit.

Angela followed and sat down beside me.

"Want a drink?" she asked.

"No, I don't want a drink," I replied.

She sat the bottle and her drink on the floor. Then I felt her hand on my leg and she started rubbing my thigh.

"I thought we could have a little fun. Just you, and me," she said as she leaned in for a kiss.

I could smell the alcohol wafting from her. I pulled back and put up a hand to stop her from getting any closer. My mind was going a hundred miles an hour, *Having sex with her would not have a good outcome,* I told myself. *There would be consequences later. What if I didn't please her? Or . . . what if I did? That might be even worse! What if I couldn't perform? What if I was premature? What if she got pregnant? Oh my God . . . I'd have a little demon for a kid! There was just no bright side to this picture. There was no way I could let this happen! How was I going to stop her without insulting her . . . or making her so angry she would want revenge?*

A quote from Daryl Congreve's, The Mourning Bride, raced through my mind . . . *Hell hath no fury like a woman scorned.*

I saw what Angela did when she just wanted a laugh. I couldn't imagine being the object of her fury.

"I'm married," I said, as I lifted my left hand up so she could see the gold on my ring finger.

She brushed my hand out of her face like she was shooing away a fly.

"Your wife is a thousand miles away," Angela countered. "She will never know."

"My religion won't let me have sex outside of marriage," I said and I made the sign of the cross across my chest.

"God will forgive you," she reasoned as she leaned in for another attempt at a kiss.

"OK . . . OK. Look, Angela, I just can't do it. You're good looking and sexy and I know it would probably be the best sex I ever had, and I may regret not doing it later . . . but I just can't. Every time I'd go to bed with my wife, I'd think about this. I just can't carry that kind of burden. Please understand."

She leaned back and looked at me.

I looked right into her eyes. Whatever it was I saw in there was cold and dark. It was nothing that I wanted to be a part of.

She stood up and looked at me without saying anything more. Then she picked up her drink and her bottle and walked out of my room without looking back.

She didn't shut the door behind her.

CHAPTER 91

The Blackboard

THE FOLLOWING DAY, CAPTAIN RON AND I went for a walk. We were going up to the hotel to trade some books we had borrowed from their library. He was in his room napping when all of the prior evening's ordeals took place, so I filled him in on what happened.

"You are lucky to still be alive," he said. "If she didn't need us to go on this flight, she would have had her men hurt you, or worse, for spurning her last night. I wondered why she was in such a bad mood this morning."

As we approached the hotel, we noticed the two National Geographic photographers sitting out on the patio drinking coffee. They sure didn't seem to work very hard. They mostly seemed like they just sat around and showed up where ever we happened to be. They watched us as we stepped off the road and onto the path that lead across the hotel's yard. There were two women on their knees in the sparse grass. They were wearing straw hats to keep the sun off their heads and using scissors to trim the grass around a flowerbed.

We tried to ignore the photographers, but said good morning to the ladies in the yard.

The clerk inside greeted us as we entered the lobby.

"Just trading some books," the Captain said in response.

We walked across the lobby and entered the library.

We walked over to the blackboard to see what was listed for dinner this evening. The menu wasn't on the board today. Instead, someone had drawn a picture on the blackboard. It looked like this:

Two men on top of a plane? That was sinking in the water? And they were yelling for help?

What was this all about? I said to myself.

* * *

If I had had half a brain, I would have caught the next flight home, but nooo . . . not me. Look up 'turning a blind eye' in the dictionary . . . and you'll probably see my picture.

CHAPTER 92

News From The Tower

ANGELA TALKED WITH MAURICIO A COUPLE of days later. He had the load staged for us at the airstrip on the Apaporis River. The plan was for us to fly out of the Caicos Islands that evening. We would land in Great Inagua where Tom would be waiting for us at the airport. Then the next morning we would take off for Colombia.

That afternoon, the Captain had the wing tanks and bladders topped off at the airport. Then he went through a checklist to make sure the plane was ready for our departure.

After dinner, Angela had a meeting with us at the house.

"You are taking Santino with you on the plane," she said to Captain Ron. "But I am keeping the other Colombian here." She looked at Santino as she added, "If you don't spot that airstrip on the Apaporis River for our pilots here, you will never see your friend again. So do not fail me . . . or him."

Captain Ron and I looked at each other. We both knew we couldn't change anything.

Santino grabbed his friend and gave him a hug as he spoke to him in Spanish. I am sure he was assuring his friend that he'd see him soon.

The taxi was waiting outside to take us to the airport, so we grabbed our bags and left. The Captain sat up front with the taxi driver and Santino and I sat in the back.

When we got to the airport, Captain Ron told me to wait with Santino at the plane while he went into the tower to file a flight plan.

* * *

"I want to file a flight plan to Freeport," Captain Ron told the tower operator.

"Leaving kind of late this evening, aren't you?" the tower operator asked.

"Well, you know how the bureaucrats are. When they want something, they want it now," the Captain responded. "By the way, what's your name?"

"Charles," the tower operator said.

"Well, Charles, this is for you," Captain Ron said as he laid a one hundred dollar bill on top of the flight plan.

"What's this for?" the operator asked, looking at the one hundred dollar bill.

"Just for being so patient with us while we've been on your island," the Captain said.

"Look," Charles said. "I don't know what you guys are really doing here and I don't want to know. But the DEA and the FAA from the states got ahold of my superiors the first day you guys got here. They threatened us with all kinds of things if we didn't cooperate. They even sent a couple agents, posing as photographers, down here to watch you guys. And they want to know when you leave and where you are going."

"Thanks, Charles," Captain Ron said. "Just give us a little time after we take off. Then you can let them know we left and headed for the Bahamas." He pulled another hundred out of his pocket and handed it to Charles. "Buy something nice for your wife."

* * *

"Those photographers are agents," Captain Ron told me as he was firing up the plane. "I knew they didn't work for National Geographic with those puny little cameras they had. And all they did was sit around and drink coffee and show up wherever we went. I'd like to kick their butts."

He ranted on for a few minutes about the agents and the FAA and the DEA and the government in general while he maneuvered the DC-6 onto the runway.

As we took off, he said, "I filed a flight plane for Freeport, so we are going to head in that direction for about 50 miles. That will put us out of everyone's radar range. Then we'll turn west for another 50 miles before we turn south and head to Great Inagua."

261

CHAPTER 93
Sabotage

THE FLIGHT TO GREAT INAGUA WAS uneventful and Captain Ron landed the plane like a pro and taxied over to the hanger. Tom was waiting there for us as we exited the plane.

"Welcome to Great Inagua," he said as he shook our hands. "This is my daughter, Mikayla. She is going to take you back to my house where you can rest from your trip. My wife has prepared a dinner for you and you can eat while I get my men to refuel your plane."

"There are three bladder tanks in the cargo hold that need to be filled as well," Captain Ron said. "I want 300 gallons in each of those. Let me show them to you."

A few minutes later, Tom Cleveland and Captain Ron exited the plane.

"Now go and make yourselves at home in my home," Tom said. "We will take care of everything here and I will join you for a drink after dinner."

* * *

Tom's wife had fixed us a really nice meal of fresh fish, rice, and fruits. We were just finishing up when Tom arrived.

"All is ready for your departure in the morning," he said, as he poured all of us a shot of rum. "What time do want to leave in the morning?"

"Get us up at 4:30," the Captain responded. "We need to take off at 6:00."

"Ok," Tom said. "My wife will wake you at 4:30 and have breakfast ready for you at 5:00. Your beds are in the rooms at the end of the hall. Sleep well, and I'll see you in the morning."

* * *

I woke up to the smell of coffee. It was dark in my room. I looked at the luminous dial on my watch. It was 4:30 . . . time to get up.

I followed the sound of dishes clanking in the kitchen and found Captain Ron and Santino already sitting at the table drinking coffee.

"Tom and his daughter have already gone to the airport to make sure everything is ready for us and to pay off the Customs Agent there," Captain Ron said as I sat down. "He said he will be back about 5:30 to take us to the airport."

Tom's wife set breakfast out for us. There were fried eggs, refried beans, fried plantains, white cheese, tortillas, and sliced pineapple. The coffee was strong and black. I added lots of sugar to mine to make it palatable. We finished breakfast and drank more coffee out on the porch while we waited for Tom.

5:30 came and went and we still waited.

6:00 came and went and still there was no sign of Tom. We were starting to get nervous.

Finally, at 6:30, a car pulled up to the house. The headlights went off, the driver's door opened, and we saw someone get out of the car. When she got close to the porch, we could see it was Mikayla, Tom's daughter.

"Why are you so late? Where's Tom? What's going on?" Captain Ron asked as Mikayla walked onto the porch. "We were supposed to take off a half hour ago."

"There was a little problem at the airport," Mikayla said. She seemed nervous as she talked to us. Maybe she thought we were going to be upset and yell at her. "The Custom Agent's superior wants more money than he agreed on. Tom is taking care of it, but it will take a little longer. He sent me here to tell you so you wouldn't worry."

"I'm worried about getting to our destination in the jungle before it gets dark." Captain Ron responded. "That's why we needed to leave at 6:00. If we don't leave soon, it'll be dark when we get there and we won't be able to find the airstrip. Go tell Tom that we need to leave now!"

"I'll tell him what you said," Mikayla replied. "I'll be back as soon as possible."

We watched as Mikayla got back in the car and left. We didn't want any more coffee, but Captain Ron started pacing the porch as he kept eyeing his watch. He smoked non-filters and he kept lighting new ones with the old ones before he put them out. It was the first time I saw him chain smoking.

It was 7:30 when Mikayla returned to pick us up. We jumped in the car and she peeled out, throwing gravel behind the car. It was only ten minutes to the airport and Tom was standing by the plane when we got there.

"You have made us very late," the Captain said to Tom as he was getting out of the car. "If it was any later, we'd have to postpone the flight until tomorrow. It'll almost be dark when we get there." It was obvious that Captain Ron was very upset.

"I am sorry, Captain," Tom said. "There was nothing more I could do. The Custom Agent's superior was being very greedy and was threatening to confiscate the plane. It took a while to get him to be reasonable. I had to double the amount of money he had originally agreed to. But, all is settled now and you can go. Do not wait until tomorrow to leave or we may have more trouble."

Captain Ron just stood there and stared at Tom for a moment. Tom was sweating and acting pretty nervous. He averted eye contact with Captain Ron and he couldn't stand still. He kept shifting his weight from one foot to the other.

Finally Captain Ron turned to Santino and me. "Get in the plane," he said.

"We'll be back in the morning with the load. Is there going to be any problems when we return?" Captain Ron asked Tom.

"No," Tom said. "The Custom Agent's superior is flying out today and the agent on duty here is satisfied with our arrangement. I will be waiting here for you tomorrow and my men will be ready to unload your plane. Good luck, Captain."

Captain Ron sat in the pilot's seat and started flipping switches as I sat in the co-pilot's seat and read off the checklist to him. Santino sat in the navigator's seat, which was in the middle just behind the pilot and co-pilot's seats. We were all buckled in with the 3-point safety belts that were provided for each seat. Santino didn't say anything. He just watched as we readied the plane for takeoff.

* * *

Tom and Mikayla watched as the DC-6 taxied to the runway and took off. Then four men walked out of the hanger and joined them. One of the men was Ray . . . the other three were Agent Jones and the two agents he had sent there two weeks ago.

They all watched as the landing gear was retracting into the belly of the plane.

Jones was the only one in the group with a smile on his face.

"You know you just killed them, don't you?" Ray said to Jones.

"You're the one who reversed the fuel lines on the bladder pump so they won't have any extra fuel," Jones replied. "And, you're the one who installed the timer switch that'll kill the hydraulics when they get about halfway there."

"On your orders," Ray retorted, "and only because you threatened me with a lengthy prison sentence if I didn't do as you instructed."

"Tell that to your conscience, Ray. Whatever you need to do to sleep at night. You are still the one who sabotaged the plane," Jones said. "I did what I needed to do, and I'm going to sleep like a baby tonight."

They watched until they couldn't see the plane any more.

"There they go," Jones said to no one in particular, "on their final flight."

CHAPTER 94

Bad News

WHEN WE GOT TO AN ALTITUDE of 9,000 feet, Captain Ron got on the radio and filed a flight plan to Peru. That flight path would take us right over Colombia. That way, when we entered Colombian airspace, they would see us as a legal aircraft with a flight plan and would not bother us.

We flew the DC-6 south towards the Windward Passage, which lies between Cuba and Haiti. I plotted our course on the chart to make sure we hugged Haiti on the way through the passage. If a plane gets too close to Cuba, they'll scramble jets to intercept it.

As we exited the Windward Passage on the south side, we entered the Caribbean Sea. We changed our course to the southwest towards the Jamaican Channel, which is 120 miles wide and lies between Jamaica and Haiti. We could fly through the center of this passage without any danger from either country.

We were about halfway between Jamaica and Colombia in the middle of the Caribbean Sea when I saw Captain Ron staring at one of the gauges. He reached up and tapped it with his finger but the needle didn't move. The Hydraulic Pressure Indicator was reading *zero*. He checked the second indicator. It too read *zero*.

He turned the control yoke to the left to test the ailerons. The plane banked to the left. Then he turned it to the right. The plane banked to the right. He centered the yoke and the plane straightened out. He pushed the control yoke forward to test the elevators. The nose went down. He pulled back on the yoke and the nose went up. He centered the yoke and the plane leveled out. So the elevators were working. He pushed the rudder pedals one at a time. The plane yawed right and left like it was supposed to. So, all the controls worked.

"Both gauges indicate we've lost all hydraulic pressure," Captain Ron said. "That doesn't make sense. There are redundant hydraulic systems on this plane. If one fails, the other still provides hydraulic pressure to the controls. And even if one indicator failed, the other one would still show hydraulic pressure. And if both indicators are correct and we really don't have any hydraulic pressure, then none of the controls would work."

He scratched his head and I could see he was thinking.

"The hydraulic system powers the rudders, the ailerons, the flaps, the landing gear, and the brakes," he said. "So if you lose hydraulic pressure, all those controls would fail, not just one. The ailerons, elevators, and rudders are still working. I'm going to slow the plane down to landing speed so I can test the flaps and landing gear."

When the plane slowed enough, Captain Ron tried applying 10 degrees of flaps. They didn't move. He tried the landing gear. They didn't deploy. He pushed on the brake pedals. They just went to the floor. He applied power to bring us back up to cruising speed.

"This doesn't make sense," he said. "We can still control the plane, thank God, or else we would be crashing right now. But, we don't have flaps, landing gear, or brakes. That's impossible . . . but that's what we got."

* * *

Thankfully, when Ray was forced to install the timer switch that would close a valve halfway into our flight and shut down the flow of hydraulic fluid, his conscience got the better of him. He had to give us a chance. He installed the shut off valve downstream from the control systems. So even though the brakes, flaps, and landing gear wouldn't work, the pilot could still control the plane.

The lines to the hydraulic pressure indicators are normally upstream from where he installed the shut off valve. So he rerouted them downstream as well so when he operated the shut off valve in front of Jones, the gauges would read zero.

* * *

Captain Ron pointed to a handle between our seats.

"This is the emergency hand pump," he said. "You can pump it up and down to lower the landing gear but it takes a while to get them down. And, we'll have to land at a higher speed than normal since we won't have flaps, but we can still land."

"What about brakes?" I asked the Captain.

"I'll use the reverse thrusters once we're on the ground," he said. "And I'll apply the emergency brake. It isn't made to stop us, but it'll help slow us down."

"What do you think we should do?" I asked.

"Nothing we can do right now," he replied. "Eventually, we'll have to put this baby on the ground somewhere . . . might as well be at our destination as anywhere else. Right now we need to concentrate on staying in the air and getting to where we're supposed to be going. Why don't you flip that auxiliary fuel pump switch on and pump that first bladder of fuel into our wing tanks?"

* * *

There was nothing Ray could do to help us when Jones made him reverse the fuel lines on the auxiliary pump he had installed. Jones watched as he took the lines off the pump and reinstalled them on the opposite ports. Now when the pump was turned on, it would pump fuel out of the wing tanks and into the bladders. The pump was only accessible by removing a panel under the plane, so there was no way to correct this in the air.

* * *

I flipped the switch to the 'on' position and watched the fuel gauge. The gauge wasn't registering any more fuel in the tank.

"Something's wrong, Captain. This gauge isn't going up. If anything, it has gone down," I said, "and that pump has been running about ten minutes."

"Then turn the switch off and go check the connection going to the bladder," he said. "Maybe the quick disconnect isn't seated correctly."

I flipped the switch to the 'off' position, took off my seat belt, and walked around the bulkhead that separated the cockpit from the cargo area.

When I stepped through the doorway into the back of the plane, I couldn't believe what I saw. When we took off this morning, each of the bladders held 300 gallons of fuel and was about 12 inches high. Now, the one with the hose hooked up to it was about three feet high. It was bulging and looked like an overfilled balloon that was about to burst.

I ran back into the cockpit and told Captain Ron about the bladder.

"Take the controls and let me go back there and see," he instructed.

He came back a few minutes later and sat back down in the pilot's seat.

"We watched as Ray tested those bladders at the Caicos Island airport," he said. "The only way this could happen is if the lines on the auxiliary fuel pump got reversed. That means someone deliberately sabotaged our plane."

"If that had happened before we left the Caicos Islands, I think that Charles, the tower operator, would have told you someone had messed with the plane," I mused. "He told you everything else, so he wouldn't have left out that important detail. That means it must have been in Great Inagua. Maybe that's why Tom seemed so nervous this morning . . . and that's why he was so late getting us to the airport. Maybe he didn't do it, but he knew it was being done."

"If he knew, why didn't he tell us?" Captain Ron asked.

"He was never alone with us today after he left for the airport. Remember, he sent Mikayla back to tell us we were being delayed. And, Mikayla is the one who came back to get us and take us to the airport. Mikayla was acting nervous but she didn't tell us, so someone must have threatened to hurt Tom if she did. And, if someone was watching Tom at the airport, then he couldn't tell us either," I reasoned. "What do we do now?"

"Well, since we're at the halfway point, we're as close to our destination as we are to Great Inagua," Captain Ron said. "If we turned around and went back to Great Inagua, whoever did this is probably still there. We can't land anywhere else with those illegal fuel bladders in the back or we'll get arrested. So, I believe our best course of action is to just keep going and land at the jungle strip."

"How about our range now since we don't have the extra fuel available?" I asked.

"It's going to be tight," Captain Ron said. "Not only do we not have the extra 900 gallons we thought we'd have, we must have pumped 300 out of the wing tank into that bladder. I didn't really count on needing the extra 900 gallons to get there, but losing that other 300 gallons means we won't have any reserve. I hope Santino can spot that strip quickly once we get there. We won't have time to do any sightseeing."

CHAPTER 95
The Promise

WE ENTERED COLOMBIAN AIR SPACE WEST of Barranquilla to avoid the more populated cities on the northern coast and we didn't want to fly over the Sierra Nevada de Santa Marta Mountains, which were east of Barranquilla, and almost 19,000 feet high.

As soon as we crossed the coast, we could see the Andes Mountains in front of us. There was snow on the higher peaks. The airstrip in the jungle was on the other side of the Andes, so we had to fly 300 miles over these mountains.

We planned to stay east of Bogota, which is at an altitude of almost 9,000 feet. The Andes in this area go up to 10,000 feet high. To provide a safety margin, we needed to climb to at least 11,000 feet, so we had to gain some altitude. That used more of our precious fuel.

We crossed the southeastern edge of the Andes and the mountains faded away behind us. We had just entered the Amazon Rainforest. The rainforest held some isolated savannahs called the llanos, but mostly it was just jungle . . . as far as we could see. The view below us was both beautiful and treacherous. But we didn't have time to sightsee. We still had 200 miles to go to get to that little airstrip on the 500-mile long Apaporis River . . . and we were running low on fuel.

Then the rain started.

"I'm going to start our descent so we'll be at an altitude of about 1,000 feet when we reach the Apaporis River," Captain Ron said. "We should be able to spot the strip at that altitude."

The sun was disappearing behind the horizon when we spotted the river. It was dusk. If that wasn't bad enough, the rain became a downpour. We couldn't make out any details on the ground. I could barely see the nose of the airplane.

I looked at our fuel gauges. They were on 'E'.

271

"It's raining so hard, I can't see anything," Captain Ron said. "We're going to have to get lower if we want to spot that strip."

He cut back the power to let the plane lose altitude.

I looked at the airspeed indicator. We were going 150 miles per hour.

When Captain Ron leveled out the plane, the altimeter showed we were only about 200 feet off the ground. Just barely above the trees.

The rain was pelting the windshield. We could see the river and the trees below us but not much of anything else.

We were in the area where the strip was supposed to be, but we couldn't find it. Santino's face was plastered up against a window so he could try and spot the strip or a familiar landmark. We cruised up the river for several miles and then the captain turned the plane around and we headed back down the river still searching for the elusive strip. Then I saw some lights.

"Look, over there," I said, as I pointed. "There are some lights. Maybe it's the guys on the strip trying to signal us."

The captain changed our heading and we headed towards the lights. As we flew over the lights, all we could see below us were trees. Then we saw some more lights. So, we headed for them. Again, there was nothing but jungle below us. We chased lights several more times. Every time, we got the same result. There was nothing but jungle around the lights.

"The strip wasn't at any of those lights. That must be villagers trying to signal to us not to land on top of their houses," Captain Ron said. "We need to stay over the river because the strip is supposed to be adjacent to it."

Just as Captain Ron turned back towards the river I watched the needle on tachometer number one fall to zero as the first engine quit and its propeller stopped turning.

Oh, God! We're out of fuel!

I panicked, but Captain Ron remained calm . . . like he had been through this a hundred times before.

"I've got to feather the prop to reduce drag," Captain Ron

said as he started flipping switches.

Then I saw the propeller on the second engine come to a halt. The third and fourth engines quickly followed suit and then none of the propellers were turning.

"We're going down," the Captain shouted. "I've got to push the nose down to keep the airspeed up so we'll have a controlled crash, otherwise we'll stall and fall like a rock. Check your seat belt and make sure it's tight."

* * *

In the few seconds before the crash time ceased to exist. My eyes became as big as saucers as I watched our fate unfold in front of us. I had always heard that your life flashes before your eyes in the seconds before your death. Now, I knew that was true. In an instant, everything I had ever done was played on a screen in my head . . . like a movie on fast-forward.

I remembered seeing my sons for the first time and holding them in my arms. I remembered the first word both of them spoke. Much to the chagrin of their mother, it was 'DaDa'. I remembered them letting loose of my hand and taking their first steps on their own.

I saw every time I had hurt someone's feelings . . . and right then, I felt their pain. I thought of the starving children from another country I had seen on TV and how I had done nothing to help feed them.

I felt every pain that I had ever caused anyone. And it hurt. The shame of my sins weighed on me and tears started flowing.

But the thought that foremost occupied my mind was that I was never going to see my sons again. I wasn't even going to be able to tell them goodbye. They would never know what happened to their dad. He would just disappear out of their lives. They would wonder if I left because of something they did. They would feel guilt for something that wasn't their fault. My death was going to cause them pain.

Then I did what everyone does as the last resort . . . when there is nothing else that can be done. I started praying. The prayer was in my head, but it was just as real as if I had shouted it from the rooftops.

Oh, God, I am so sorry I did this. You gave me life. You gave me sons. You made me for a reason. And I risked it all because I didn't trust You to provide for me and my family? Please don't make my sons grow up without their dad. They are Your children. You created them and You entrusted me to raise them. And I have failed You and them. Please let me go home to my sons. Please give me another chance. Please let me live through this and I will never do this again. I will put my trust in You in the future. I promise.

Then I turned to the Captain, "Don't hit the trees!" I screamed. "Don't hit the trees!" As if he had any choice. What else did I think could happen? We were in the middle of a jungle!

All I could see were leaves and branches thrashing the windshield as the plane plowed through the tops of the trees.

Then I saw the river in front of us. We were going to hit it crossways. It rushed up to the windshield as we hit it! Water went up and over the nose of the plane, and across the windshield with a thunderous splash.

I felt my body jolt forward against the seat harness as the plane came to an abrupt stop. I looked out the window on my side and saw the starboard wing, which had been torn from the plane, cartwheel through the air and land in the water hundreds of feet away.

* * *

The sparks created when the wing was torn from the airplane could have ignited the fumes that filled the fuel tanks causing them to explode. The plane could have cartwheeled when it hit the water, tearing it apart, and killing us. Tree branches could have plunged through the windshield and impaled us. The windshield could have broken and let water rush into the cockpit and drown us before we could escape. There are so many ways we could have been killed in that crash, but *God* was already answering my prayer.

* * *

The water was rising over the nose of the plane and up towards the windshield. The plane was sinking fast. And it was going down, nose first.

I looked down. I was still in my seat. I thrust my arms forward and looked at them. They were okay. I felt my face and looked at my hands. There was no blood. I was alive!

I looked over at Captain Ron. He was doing the same things. He was moving and he didn't seem to be hurt. He started unbuckling his seat harness. I unbuckled mine as well, and then I turned to check on Santino. His seat was empty! He was gone!

CHAPTER 96

The Rescue

CAPTAIN RON AND I CLIMBED OUT of our seats. The water was starting to come into the plane around the cockpit door. We were standing in ankle deep water. I spotted a metal box that was attached to the bulkhead wall. It was a grey box and had 'Life Raft' printed on it in bold white letters. I got the box off the wall and flipped open the latches. I raised the lid on the box and looked inside.

The box was empty.

We looked around to assess our situation. The plane was sinking in the river. Water was coming into the cockpit. Santino was missing. And we didn't have a life raft. When we crashed, the bladders broke loose from their tie downs and were thrown forward into the bulkhead wall. We could see two bladders protruding into the cabin through the bulkhead doorway. They were wedged in the doorway and were about halfway into the cabin.

"Where the heck is Santino?" I asked.

"The only place he could be is in the back of the plane," the Captain answered. "He must have ran into the back of the plane when he realized we were going to crash. The only way out of here for us is through the cockpit door. We have to open it now before it goes under water. Once it goes underwater, the water pressure will prevent us from opening it."

I looked at the bladders blocking the doorway to the cargo area of the plane. Santino was on the other side of those bladders. I felt along the top of the bladders. There was a small space between the top of the bladders and the top of the door. I thought I'd be able to squeeze through that space.

"I'm going back there and find Santino," I said. "There's no way I'm leaving him there to drown."

"Well, I'm going to open this cockpit door while I still can," Captain Ron said. "I'll go down the top of the plane and try to get the cargo doors open for you so you can get out."

With that, he opened the cabin door. Then the water really started rushing in. He climbed out the door and onto the top of the plane.

I scrambled up the bladders and squeezed through the gap. I climbed down the bladders on the other side. I was now in the cargo area of the plane. Two bladders were stuck in the bulkhead doorway and the overfilled one had burst open when it hit the bulkhead wall. So there was 600 gallons of Avgas floating on top of the water. The smell of gasoline was overpowering.

I could hardly see because it was so dark in the cargo area. Only a little twilight was coming in through the top half of the windows. The bottoms of the windows were already under water.

I could hear Santino moaning but I couldn't see him. I followed the sound and started feeling around in the dark until I found him. He was on his back. His legs were under the bladders that were wedged in the doorway and he was pinned to the floor. Water was already covering his chest. His head was barely out of the water.

I grabbed him under his armpits and pulled. He wouldn't budge. I pulled and pulled but he was stuck. The water kept getting higher and higher. I lifted his head up so he could still breathe and I kept trying to pull him free. Finally, the water was so deep that only his nose and eyebrows were still above the water. There were only seconds left before he would drown.

Once again, I turned to God as I screamed out loud, "DEAR GOD . . . HELP ME! IF YOU DON'T HELP ME, HE'S GOING TO DIE!"

Then, the bladders just rose up. Just like someone lifted them up.

* * *

Sure, you may think that since gasoline is lighter than water, the bladders just floated up when the water got deep enough. I guess that could have happened. But why did they rise up at just the instant when Santino only had seconds left to live? And why did they rise up just the instant I called on God to help? The timing was too critical for it to just be coincidence. There's no doubt in my mind that God intervened. Whether God lifted those bladders up, or He dispatched angels to do it, those bladders came up off of Santino just in time.

* * *

I pulled him free. He wasn't helping me. I had to drag him through the water. We got to the first window. It was an emergency exit and it was supposed to be able to be opened in case of an emergency. This definitely qualified. I turned the latch and pushed. The window wouldn't budge. It was under water and the water pressure wouldn't let me open it.

I dragged Santino to the next window. I tried to get it open, but it too was under water and wouldn't open. The water was now up to my waist. I realized our only chance was to get to the cargo doors at the rear of the plane before it sank. I couldn't understand why Santino wasn't helping me as I dragged him to the rear of the plane.

The cargo doors were wide open. The river was just reaching the bottom of the doors. I knew that when the river started pouring in through the doors, the plane was going to sink fast. I saw Captain Ron on top of the plane looking down at us through the doors

Without even thinking about it, I grabbed Santino around the waist and lifted him up into the air over my head so Captain Ron could grab him. I don't know how I did that. I'm not that strong. Santino weighed at least as much as me, or even more. So whether it was adrenaline, or God, or Angels I don't know. But I was able to lift him as if he weighed no more than a little child.

Captain Ron grabbed Santino's hands and pulled him onto the top of the plane.

Then I climbed up the door and was outside.

I sucked in my first breath of fresh air since I had climbed into the back of the plane. Oxygen rushed through my body. My head started spinning and I thought I was going to pass out. I hadn't realized that I had been breathing pure gasoline fumes inside that plane. I held on to the top of the doorway with one hand and the top of a door with the other as I pulled fresh air into my lungs.

Finally my head quit spinning and I looked up. Captain Ron was saying something to me. I couldn't make out what he was saying. It was like his voice was far away. His arm was stretching out towards me. Finally I understood.

"Grab my hand!" he was yelling.

I grabbed his hand and he pulled me onto the top of the plane. The water was now rushing into the plane through the wide-open cargo doors. We held onto the rudder and watched as the plane sank rapidly, nose first, into the dark water.

Huge air bubbles came bursting out of the water as the cargo doors disappeared under the water. Then the rapid sinking stopped. The air trapped in the tail of the plane must have been keeping the tail afloat. Smaller bubbles were trickling up around the rudder. That meant water was still filling the tail of the plane, but at a slower rate. We knew it was only a matter of time before the whole plane would disappear under the water.

I looked around to assess our situation. The only parts of the plane sticking out of the water were the tip of the left wing, the tip of one propeller, and the rudder we were holding onto. Captain Ron and I were standing up but Santino was lying down. Santino's screams drew my attention to him and I looked down at him.

My eyes got big as I took in what I saw. Santino's leg was badly broken and a bone was sticking out of the jeans over his thigh. No wonder he hadn't been able to help me get him out of the plane. He was in agonizing pain and he had to be in shock.

"Muerte . . . Muerte", Santino was screaming. He was no longer holding onto the plane and he was starting to slide off the plane into the water.

I didn't know much Spanish, but I knew that 'muerte' was the word for death.

"No muerte, Santino! No!" I yelled back. I grabbed his hand and wrapped his fingers around the front of the rudder. "Hold on, Santino, hold on."

I looked to see how far it was to the shore. I could barely see it because it was getting dark. It wasn't that far . . . maybe a hundred yards. I could swim that far. But I couldn't swim and pull Santino with me. If I swam away, I'd have to desert him to his fate. And I couldn't do that.

"Hold on, Santino, hold on," I pleaded again. I was having a hard enough time holding myself on as the swift current tried to pull us off the plane.

I looked up at the captain.

"Thanks, Captain," I said, "for opening the cargo doors."

He stared at me with a quizzical look.

"I didn't open those doors. I couldn't reach the handle. I saw them open up. I thought you opened them from inside the plane."

CHAPTER 97
Jungle Village

A FEW MINUTES LATER, WE HEARD the faint sound of a motor on the river. We listened quietly as the sound got louder. It was a motorboat and it was coming down the river toward us.

For a moment, the captain and I stared at each other. We didn't know if we should yell or keep quite. But we knew we weren't going to get out of here without help.

I decided to yell. "Help . . . help . . . we're over here!"

They must have heard us because we heard the boat start to come toward us.

I was expecting to see a motorboat pull up to the plane. But it wasn't. It was a dugout canoe! It was made from a single log that had been hollowed out. The front of the canoe was pointed and the back end was squared off. There was a Johnson outboard motor on the back of the boat.

There were two men wearing old worn out clothes in the boat. They were obviously natives from this area. I was never so glad to see someone. To me, they looked like angels.

They quickly took in our situation and the boat captain started speaking rapidly in Spanish and gesturing with his hands.

"No comprendo Espanol", I said. "Habla Ingles?" I asked, quickly using up most of the Spanish words I knew. "Do you speak English?"

"No. No hablo Ingles," he answered. Then he noticed Santino. He started speaking directly to Santino in Spanish, but Santino didn't respond.

I finally realized that he was asking if there was anyone else in the plane.

"No," I said, holding up three fingers and pointing to us. "Tres hombres . . . no mas."

He must have understood because he nodded his head. The other man used a paddle to maneuver the boat up against the plane and motioned for us to climb aboard. Captain Ron and I lowered Santino down first and the men in the boat grabbed him and got him down into the boat. Then they helped us as we climbed aboard.

With one last look at the plane, the driver revved up the Johnson outboard motor and we took off up the river. About ten minutes later, the boat pulled up to an embankment in front a small village.

* * *

The entire population, about 15 or 20 people, was standing on top of the bank watching us. One of the men in the boat yelled something and a couple of the men scrambled down the embankment to help get Santino out of the boat and up the bank.

The gasoline I had been wading in was really burning my skin now. My crotch felt like it was on fire. I jumped out of the boat and pulled my pants and underwear down around my ankles and started splashing water on my crotch.

"Do you have any soap?" I yelled as I looked up at the villagers standing on top of the embankment.

They all just stared at the gringo in the water with his pants pulled down. They didn't understand.

"Soap . . . Soap," I repeated, as I continued to scrub myself with the river water.

Finally, one man realized what I needed. "Ah . . . soap," he said, as he turned and ran off. He returned a moment later with a really old tattered box. He scrambled down the embankment and handed the box to me. The box looked like it had been out here in the jungle for years. The lettering and picture on the box were very faded but I could still make out 'Ivory Soap' printed on the box. I looked inside the box. There was a little soap in the bottom of box.

I poured the powered soap into my hands and started scrubbing again. When the soap was all gone, I splashed water on my crotch to rinse off. I watched as the lather got caught in the current and floated down stream.

I pulled my pants up and zipped them. Then I reached into my pocket where I had carried my passport. It was gone! It must have fallen out of my pocket and went down the river with the lather. There was nothing I could do about that now, so I climbed up the embankment and joined Captain Ron.

The boat captain was talking with Santino, and Santino was responding. All of the villagers were gathered around listening to the conversation. Santino must have been telling them what had happened because they would listen to Santino, look over at us, and then back to Santino. When Santino couldn't talk anymore, the villagers started talking amongst themselves and nodding their heads. Then they came over to where Captain Ron and I were standing and started patting us on the back and shaking our hands. Then they went back to trying to take care of Santino.

About 30 minutes later, we heard another boat coming down the river. It pulled up to the embankment beside the dugout canoe. This one was a regular boat and it too had a Johnson outboard motor on it. There were three men in the boat and they started questioning one of the villagers who was standing on top of the bank.

"Si, Si," the villager said.

The men in the boat got out and climbed up the bank. Two of them went over to Santino and the other one walked over to Captain Ron and me. In English, he said, "My name is Hernando. Tell me what happened."

Captain Ron told him that we couldn't find the strip, ran out of gas, and crashed into the river. We told him about the men in the dugout canoe who found us and brought us to this village.

"You passed over the airstrip three times," Hernando said. "We tried to signal you with our flashlights, but the plane just kept going. We could hear the plane going up and down the river and finally it got quiet. We assumed you had crashed since we didn't hear the engines any more. So, we got in our boat and started searching the river. We found the plane a couple of miles down the river. Only a little of the rudder is sticking out of the water. We didn't see anyone there and assumed you were all dead inside the plane. But, we started going to all the villages along the river just in case you were still alive or to see if anyone found your bodies floating in the river. Then we found you here."

One of the men who went to check on Santino joined us and started talking to Hernando in Spanish. They both stole glances at us as they talked.

"The villagers said Santino told them you saved his life," Hernando said. "Is this true?"

"We couldn't just leave him in the plane to drown," I said. "So, what do we do now?"

"For now, we'll take you back to our camp by the airstrip. In the morning, someone will take Santino downriver to the closest medical facility, which is about 50 miles away. We'll have to get on the radio and see what Mauricio wants us to do with you. By the way, thank you for saving Santino. He is a friend of ours. If you had left him on that plane to die, you would not have lived to see tomorrow."

They loaded Santino into their boat and then we got in. The ride to the camp at the airstrip was only about 15 minutes. As the boat pulled up to the bank, Hernando shouted out some orders. A couple of men ran down to the boat and lifted Santino out and carried him up to the camp. They covered him with a blanket, and put a pillow under his head. Then one of them made Santino take a couple sips of water.

Then everyone in the camp surrounded Hernando as he spoke to them in Spanish. They kept stealing glances at Captain Ron and me as Hernando told them what happened. When he finished talking, every one of them came over to Captain Ron and me and shook our hands.

Then a man handed us each a warm bottle of beer.

"Cerveza," he said. "Drink."

Even though the beer was warm, I don't think any beer has ever tasted as good as that one. I was probably just glad I was alive and could drink one. As soon as our bottles were empty, he handed us each another. We drank those and he tried to hand us each another.

"No. No mas Cerveza," I said, as I shook my hand in a negative motion.

"Si . . . drink . . . drink mas cerveza," he said as he pushed the beers into our hands.

He wouldn't take no for an answer until we each had drank at least six of the warm beers.

Then someone led us to a couple of hammocks where we would sleep for the night. There was mosquito netting over our hammocks. I noticed that none of the other hammocks had mosquito netting.

CHAPTER 98

The Cowboy

HERNANDO WOKE US IN THE MORNING.

"I spoke with Mauricio on the radio," he said. "He wants us to take you to a village about fifty miles upriver. You will be taken care of there until someone figures out how to get you home. Come and eat and then we will go."

They gave us tortillas filled with refried beans and cheese for breakfast. We ate as we stood around the campfire and drank strong black coffee. When we finished eating, Hernando handed us some old clothes and told us to change. The pants they gave me were dark green and very old with holes in the knees. The shirt was an old orange pullover shirt with a brown collar. The clothes were way too big for me, but I put them on. Then they put an old straw sombrero on my head. Captain Ron was dressed similarly.

"We want you to look like you belong here so you will be safe," Hernando said. "Sit in the bottom of the boat and keep your heads down so no one can see your faces."

The trip upriver took three or four hours. We passed a couple of other boats going the opposite way but they didn't pay any attention to us.

When we arrived at the village, we were taken to a small house. Hernando introduced us to Alberto, the man of the house.

"Alberto and his family will take care of you," Hernando said. "No one here speaks English, but you will be safe as long as you stay here. Do not wander about. If anyone comes around, Alberto will hide you until he knows it is safe. Someone will get in touch with you as soon as we know something." We watched as the only person here that could talk to us in English got back in the boat and left.

* * *

Alberto lived here with his wife and two teenage sons. They gave Captain Ron and me a small bedroom with two cots. This must have been the sons' bedroom because they moved out into the living room where they slept on some blankets on the floor. The house was made out of wood, but it had dirt floors. The windows had no glass, just shutters that you could close to keep out the rain. They didn't do much to keep out the mosquitos.

Alberto's wife cooked all the meals and we ate with the family. Breakfast was always tortillas, refried beans, pineapple or mango, and black coffee. Around noon, she would fix us a bowl of soup. Supper was tortillas, beans, white cheese, fruit, and usually a small piece of meat that I couldn't identify. I couldn't eat the meat. I was a semi-vegetarian at the time, although I did eat fish and chicken.

* * *

One afternoon, after we had been there several days, Captain Ron, Alberto, and I were sitting out in the yard under a mango tree when we saw a man walking up toward the house. He was tall and lanky and looked to be in his mid-twenties. He had a ruddy complexion and didn't look like he was a native from around here. His unkempt red hair was sticking out around the edges of the old, dirty, brown cowboy hat he was wearing. His jeans were worn and had holes in the knees. He was wearing a red and black, checkered, button up shirt that had seen its better days. And, he was barefoot.

Alberto quickly walked out to greet him. We watched as they shook hands and started talking. Alberto kept pointing at us as he was talking and the man kept stealing glances at us. After a few minutes, they walked over to where we were sitting.

"Hello, my name is Corey," the man said in English, as he reached out to shake our hands. "Alberto tells me you've been through quite an ordeal."

We both shook his hand.

"Wow. It's really great to meet someone who can speak English," I said. "But I don't know who you are or what you know about us."

"I know you came here in a plane to pick up some marijuana and the plane crashed about 50 miles downriver. Soldiers on patrol found your plane almost completely submerged in the river a couple of days ago. They assumed the pilots had been killed, but they couldn't find any bodies. Then they heard rumors that the pilots survived. They are searching the villages along the river looking for you. They are even offering a reward to anyone who will give them information leading to your capture."

"Why are you telling us this?" I asked. "Are you going to turn us in?"

"No," Corey said. "And so far, no one else along the river is offering them any help either because you risked your own lives to pull Santino out of that plane. But it is only a matter of time before someone tells them where you are. If the soldiers find you, it won't be good. They will put you in prison until someone pays a lot of money for your release. If no one pays, you could spend the rest of your lives there."

"Are you involved with the people who were selling us the marijuana?" I asked.

"No. My family has been ranchers here for 20 years, so I know everyone around here. Hernando got word to me that you were here and asked if I would be willing to take you to my ranch so the soldiers will not be able to find you. My ranch is about 20 miles from here. I raise cattle there to provide jobs for the people around here so they won't get involved in the drug trade. You will be safe there until Hernando can get you out of here."

"Then let's go," I said.

We followed Corey down to the river where he had a small boat tied up. Of course, it had a Johnson outboard motor on the back. We climbed in and Corey took us up river a few miles before he turned the boat onto a creek. The creek was narrow and was only big enough for a small boat. It snaked through the jungle for miles and tropical plants lined the banks on both sides. Some looked like the ornamental elephant ear plants I had seen back home, except these were huge. These plants were taller than a house and their leaves were six feet wide. Vines crossed the creek in many places and we had to duck to get under them. I expected to hear lions roaring in the jungle, but the only sounds I heard were the purring of the Johnson outboard motor and the incessant buzzing of the mosquitos around my ears.

CHAPTER 99

Jungle Adventures

THERE WERE TWO BUILDINGS THAT FORMED an 'L' shape in the middle of the ranch. Each building was about 12 feet wide and 30 feet long. The buildings were made out of rough-cut lumber. The windows had no glass, just wooden shutters that could be closed to keep out the rain. The roofs were made of thatch. There was no electricity. I was surprised to see that the floors were concrete instead of dirt.

One of the buildings was a barn that was used for storage and it was filled with tools, saddles, ropes, and feed. The front of the barn had a roof overhang about 8 feet wide. There were kerosene lanterns hanging on nails under the overhang. There were several stumps along the wall that were used as chairs. There were swinging hammocks strung out under the overhang to provide everyone with a place to sleep.

Corey had one of his men hang mosquito netting over two of the hammocks for the captain and me. Either he was paying us an honor, or he didn't want us to get malaria from a mosquito bite. We'd be harder to take care of if we were sick.

The other building was used as a kitchen and mess hall. There was a stack of firewood piled by the stove in the kitchen. A bucket of water sat on the counter beside a washbasin for cleaning the dishes. The dirty dishwater was simply thrown out the open window. A hand powered water pump sat right outside the kitchen.

The cook was the wife of one of the farmhands. Since they were married, they didn't have to stay at the farmhouse at night. They had a small one-room house on the ranch about a quarter mile away from the farmhouse.

The mess hall had one long table made out rough-cut lumber. It had built in benches on both sides and looked like a picnic table. Not only did everyone eat together at this table, it was also used to clean fish, beef, or any other edible animals that were killed on the ranch. Someone would cut up some meat on the table and then scrub off the blood with a bucket of water and a brush. Then we'd all sit down at the same table to eat a little while later.

The cook was not real imaginative. Breakfast was always refried beans, tortillas, some fresh fruit, and black coffee. Right after breakfast, the cook would start making soup. We had soup every day for lunch and dinner. The soup had whatever ingredients were available that day. Yucca must have been available all the time because there was always yucca in the soup. Sometimes there were carrots, potatoes, pieces of beef or fish, and some rice. I'd pick out any pieces of meat and put them on Captain Ron's plate before I started eating. The ranch hands got a kick out of watching me do this and they'd laugh.

There was a young boy on the ranch named Pepito who was about 12 years old and was an orphan. Corey had taken Pepito in when he was about six years old. Corey had assigned Pepito the job of taking care of Captain Ron and me. So when Corey and the ranch hands took off in the mornings on horseback to take care of the cattle, Pepito stayed behind with us. I tried teaching Pepito some English words and he tried teaching me some Spanish.

One day, just before lunch, Pepito found a huge dead spider and picked it up to show it to me. I hate spiders . . . alive or dead. When Pepito saw I was afraid of the dead spider, he threw it on me and started laughing. I chased him until I caught him and put him over my knee and spanked him. The other farmhands started laughing and that embarrassed Pepito. He got so mad, he wouldn't talk to me the rest of the day.

That afternoon, I told Corey I was tired of eating soup and asked if I could make us all some fried potatoes to go with our soup for dinner. He said something to the cook and I think she got offended because she took off her apron, threw it on the counter, and took off across the pasture towards her little house. Great . . . I had pissed off two people here in one day. Two people that I needed to help me survive.

I sliced up the 5-pound bag of potatoes I found in the pantry and fried them up in a huge skillet on the wood fired stove. None of the farmhands had ever had fried potatoes and they just stared at them. But the smell was awesome and Corey and I dug in. One of the farmhands finally picked up a small piece and put it in his mouth. He said something in Spanish and piled some on his plate. Then they all dug in. Everyone, that is, except Pepito who was still sulking. He was standing outside watching us through the open window. Finally he couldn't stand it anymore and came in to get some of the fried potatoes that the farm hands were obviously enjoying. But he was too late. They were all gone. All he had to eat was some leftover soup from lunch. Now he was mad all over again.

He got over it the next day.

* * *

As we were having coffee the next morning, we heard a motorboat coming up the creek. Corey had Pepito take Captain Ron and me out into the jungle to hide us until he knew if it was safe. Pepito showed us where to hide and took off back to the ranch. He came back a little later and took us back up to the ranch house.

"The soldiers that are looking for you are asking questions in the villages along the river," Corey said. "They could come here. We are going to have to hide you out in the jungle until they are gone."

So, we went on a safari into the jungle. Corey and his men used machetes to hack a path through the vegetation as we followed. They took us a mile or more back into the thick jungle and then they cleared out a place big enough for a tent.

"You will have to stay here until it is safe," Corey said. "Pepito will bring you food and coffee every day. He will whistle when he comes and gets close to the tent so you will know it is him. If you hear someone coming and they don't whistle, you need to run and hide."

Later that day, we heard someone coming and then we heard a whistle. It was Pepito. He was bringing us some soup and some coffee. He stayed with us while we ate then he took the dishes and left. Then it started raining. It rained all day and all night. We had to just stay in the tent and listen to the sounds of the jungle and the rain. The only protection we had were two machetes they had left for us. But that didn't keep the mosquitos away. They ate us up.

The next morning Pepito brought us some coffee and beans and tortillas for breakfast. Later that afternoon, Corey sent him out to get us and bring us back to the ranch. The soldiers had left the area and continued up the river. No one had told them that they had seen us.

Hernando came out to the ranch the next day with a short wave radio. He told Corey that Bryan would have someone in Florida on a certain frequency every night at 10 pm to talk with Captain Ron and me as long as we were here.

That night, we tuned the radio to that frequency and listened.

At 10 pm, we heard a distinctive whistling tune on the radio and then a man's voice, "Hey, captain, captain, captain, are you there?"

"Yes, I'm here," Captain Ron said into the microphone.

"Good. Good. Bryan sends his greetings," the man's voice said. "He wants to know if you and your friend are both ok?"

"Yes, yes. We are both fine," the captain said into the radio.

"Good. He wants you to enjoy your vacation for a few days more. He has arranged for another bus for you to drive home in," the man on the radio said. "Someone will come get you in a couple days. They will take you to the new bus with its cargo. You'll drive it to the same place you were going to before. OK?"

"OK," Captain Ron said. "We'll be waiting."

* * *

The next night, we tuned in again. We listened for a while and then we heard the same whistling tune and the same man's voice, "Captain, captain, captain, are you there?"

"Yes," the captain responded. "I'm here."

"Someone is coming for you in the morning. Do not . . . I repeat . . . do not, under any circumstances, go with him. Do

293

you understand?"

"I hear you but I don't understand," the Captain responded. "You don't want us to go with the man tomorrow?"

"That is correct. Do not go. Stay there."

"OK," Captain Ron said. "We'll wait for further instructions."

* * *

Corey went into the village two days later to pick up some supplies. He brought back some news as well. Hernando had set up another load of 20,000 pounds of marijuana at the same airstrip 50 miles downriver and had hired a FARC troop of 12 guerrillas to protect the marijuana.

* * *

FARC is the largest left wing guerrilla army in Colombia and is officially known as the Revolutionary Armed Forces of Colombia. They are considered terrorists and their main source of income is from drug trafficking.

* * *

Corey also heard that a pilot had flown a DC-6 up from Venezuela and landed it at the river airstrip where it was to be loaded with the marijuana and flown to the states by two American pilots.

However, the two American pilots never showed up, but the army did. The army commander in the area had heard that a plane was to be loaded at the strip and he sent a platoon of 20 men to stop the shipment. When they heard the DC-6 landing, they stormed the airstrip. The FARC opened fire on the army soldiers and a gun battle ensued. All 12 of the FARC guerrillas were killed along with 2 army soldiers and a couple of natives that made up the loading crew. Hernando and the pilot from Venezuela were arrested.

* * *

"We have a small air strip here on the ranch," Corey said. "My brother, Ricky, is a jungle pilot and he lands here to bring us supplies. See if Bryan can get someone to pick you up in San Martin if Ricky will fly you there. San Martin is a town about

150 miles west of here. There is an airport there and a road from San Martin to Bogota. A bus travels between San Martin and Bogota, but taking that bus trip could be dangerous for two gringos."

That night, we were back on the radio.

At 10 pm, we heard the familiar whistling tune. Captain Ron told the guy that we could get to San Martin if Bryan could arrange to get us transportation from there.

I asked Captain Ron to let me speak to the guy on the radio, and he handed me the microphone.

"Tell Bryan we will have to pay for a flight out of here and to cover our expenses with our guests here. Tell him that whoever comes to pick us up in San Martin will have to bring $5,000 to settle our debts."

Two days later, we got the go ahead. Get to San Martin and someone would meet us there with the money.

A couple days later, we heard a small airplane approaching. Then we saw a small plane circling the farmhouse. It was Corey's brother, Ricky. Corey waved at him to let him know it was okay to land. Ricky headed for the airstrip which was just a flat spot in a field with the weeds cut short.

Corey, Pepito, and all of the farm hands escorted us out to the waiting plane. It was a Cessna 172. One of the farmhands had killed a Lapa and he was holding it by the tail. The Lapa was the size of a small dog. It was red with white spots. He tried handing it to me.

"Why is he trying to give me this dead animal?" I asked Corey.

"Lapa is the gourmet of meats in the jungle," Corey explained. "He is honoring you with this gift. You must take it or you will offend him."

I accepted the Lapa and held it up by its tail as I smiled and nodded my head in approval of his gift. He smiled back. He was obviously pleased.

"Corey, please thank him profusely for this honor. And then explain that I'll have no way to prepare and eat it and it would be an insult to him if I took it and let it go to waste.

Please tell him I'd like to return the honor and let the cook fix it for everyone's dinner tonight as a way of thanking them for taking care of us."

Corey told the farmhand what I said and I handed the Lapa back to the farmhand. He took it, shook my hand, and nodded his head in approval.

I shook hands all around, but when I got to Pepito, there were tears in his eyes . . . and in mine. He gave me a big hug and I hugged him back.

"Adios, mi amigo, Pepito" I said. "I will miss you the most."

And then I climbed into the waiting plane.

CHAPTER 100

The Lawyer

THE FLIGHT TO SAN MARTIN ONLY took about an hour and a half. Ricky set the plane down at the small airport where he had left his car. We climbed into his car and made the ten-minute trip across town to his home.

His family was expecting us and had prepared a lunch for us. Just as we were finishing lunch, a black Cadillac pulled up outside with two men inside.

The man on the passenger side exited the Cadillac and came to the door. He was wearing a suit. He introduced himself as Vicente, a lawyer from Bogota, and said he was looking for Captain Ron and Ryan. Ricky invited him in and someone brought him a cup of coffee. While he sipped on the coffee, he reached into his suit coat and pulled out an envelope and handed it to Ricky.

"Here is a little something for your troubles," he said.

Ricky opened the envelope and looked at the money. It was $5,000 with two rubber bands wrapped around it.

Captain Ron and I said our thank-yous and goodbyes and got into the back seat of the Cadillac. Vicente got into the front passenger seat.

"We are going to my home in Bogota," Vicente said. "Sit back and enjoy your trip."

The trip to Bogota took about four hours. When the Cadillac pulled up to Vicente's house, I was impressed. The place looked like a mansion. There was a fountain in the center of the circular driveway, there were columns on either side of the enormous front door, and the landscaping was immaculate.

A servant opened the front door for us and greeted us.

"Show our guests to their rooms," Vicente instructed the servant. "Your rooms have their own bathrooms," Vicente told us, "and there are some clean clothes in the closet. You

297

should find something to fit you. You can bathe and rest. We'll have dinner in about an hour."

I checked out what I could see of the house on the way to my room. The thick plush carpet I was walking on was pure white. The door to my room was ornate. Inside the room was a white king size poster bed with matching furniture to go with it. The bathroom was white marble. It had two toilets, but one looked different. Of course, I used the one that looked different. When I pulled the handle to flush, a jet of water sprayed my behind and I jumped off the toilet and hit the wall. Now I know what a bidet is.

I showered and lay down on the bed. I must have fallen asleep because I was awakened a little later by a knock on the door. It was the servant.

"Dinner will be served in 15 minutes," he said.

I looked in the closet and found some clean clothes. There were several sizes and I found some to fit me. Then I made my way to the dining room.

The dining room was larger than my house back in the states. In the center was a beautifully carved wooden table that could seat 20 people. A huge crystal chandelier hung over the dining table. The table was already set for a formal dinner with fancy china and gold plated silverware.

Vicente and his family were already seated, as was Captain Ron. Vicente greeted me and told me to sit in the empty chair beside Captain Ron. Then servants wearing white gloves started bringing in food and wine. It was a feast. There was salad, fresh baked breads, several kinds of meats and fish, superbly prepared vegetables, and fresh fruits. As soon as your wine glass was half empty, a servant would rush over to refill it. When we couldn't eat any more, servants cleared away our dishes, and put dessert plates and coffee cups in front of us. Then a servant came around pouring us coffee while another pushed around a dessert cart filled with all sorts of desserts. Finally, I just couldn't eat another bite.

"If you have had enough to eat," Vicente said, "you can retire to your rooms for a good night's rest," Vicente said to

Captain Ron and me. "In the morning, after breakfast, we are going to take a trip to Barranquilla."

After eating all that food, it didn't take me long to fall asleep. I was awakened in the morning with another knock on my door.

"Breakfast will be served in 15 minutes," the servant said.

Breakfast was scrambled eggs, fresh fruits, assorted Danish pastries, coffee, and juice.

"You have a few minutes to freshen up, and then we'll go," Vicente said. "I'll meet you outside in 15 minutes."

We got in the back seat of the Cadillac and Vicente sat up front with the driver.

"We are going to the airport," Vicente said, "where we will take a commercial flight to Barranquilla."

The driver dropped us off in front of the airport and we went in.

"Sit here in the coffee shop," Vicente said, "while I go get our tickets." He gave the attendant some money for our coffees and left.

About 30 minutes later, we saw Vicente returning. There was an armed airport security officer with him.

I looked over at Captain Ron.

"Looks like we are being arrested," I said.

"Come with us," Vicente said when they reached our table.

There was nothing else we could do, so we got up and went with them. As we walked through the airport, we saw several other armed security guards. Every one of them came up to us and greeted Vicente. Vicente shook each one of their hands as he greeted them like old friends. Then he'd discreetly reach into his pocket and pull out a $100 bill and put it in their hand. As he moved the flap of his suit jacket out of the way so he could reach the hundred dollar bills in his pants pocket, I noticed he had a pistol stuck in his waistband.

There was a line of people standing at the security screening station with their luggage on the conveyor belt in front of the x-ray machine. The security guard with us escorted us right around them.

There was no security screening for Vicente and his guests.

Our guard escorted us all the way to the plane. By the time we reached the plane, Vicente must have passed out ten $100 bills. When we entered the plane, we were seated in first class.

* * *

When our flight landed in Barranquilla, a security guard was waiting for us. He escorted us through the airport to the front door where a limo was waiting for us. Vicente rewarded each of the guards we passed in this airport with one hundred dollar bills as well.

"I am taking you to one of my apartments here in Barranquilla," Vicente told us. "You will be safe there. Here is some money so you can buy food at the restaurant below the apartment. Don't go anywhere else. Since you don't have your passport, any policeman who stops you will arrest you. So eat at the restaurant and stay in the apartment. I will get back with you as soon as arrangements are made for your return home."

CHAPTER 101
Escape To Cartagena

THE APARTMENT WAS ON THE SECOND floor. It had two bedrooms and it was sparsely furnished. There was a cheap bed in each of the bedrooms and an old couch in the living room. There was a refrigerator in the kitchen, but it was empty. There was no television, no magazines, no nothing. It was really boring to stay in the apartment. I slept a lot to pass the time and did exercises when I was awake. I really looked forward to going down to the restaurant to eat three times a day. With no passport, I didn't want to wander around.

The days passed slowly.

I spent a lot of time thinking; wondering if Judy and my sons were OK, wondering if they knew I was still alive.

Finally, I couldn't stand it anymore. Cabin fever was getting to me. We had been here in the apartment for two weeks and hadn't heard from anyone. I put my face in my pillow that night so Captain Ron wouldn't hear me crying.

The next morning, after Captain Ron and I came back upstairs after breakfast, there was a knock on our door.

"Who is it?" I asked.

"My name is Carlos," he said. "Bryan sent me. Let me in."

I opened the door and Carlos came in.

"Bryan sent me to come get you," he said. "Gather your belongings and come quickly."

"How do I know Bryan sent you?" I asked.

"I know that your name is Ryan, and he is Captain Ron. Bryan said to tell you that Judy is okay and wants you to come home. He also said it is dangerous for you to stay here any longer. He wants me to take you to Cartagena where you will be able to leave Colombia and go home. But, you must come with me now before Vicente or one of his men show up . . . or you can stay. But I am leaving. You must make up your minds right now."

"Let's go," Captain Ron said. "He must be telling the truth. There's no other way he would have known your wife's name."

"Ok," I said. "Let's go."

We followed Carlos down the stairs and hopped into a new, shiny, black Chevrolet Suburban he had parked at the curb. He took one look around to make sure no one was watching and then we took off.

"When we get to Cartagena," Carlos said, "my boss will explain everything."

The trip to Cartagena took about three hours.

When we got there, Carlos parked the Suburban beside an identical one in the parking lot of a huge, really nice looking hotel. We followed him inside and took an elevator to the top floor. Carlos led us down the hall and knocked on the door at the end of the hall.

"It's me. And I have our guests," Carlos said.

The door opened and we went inside. The room was a corner suite with windows on two walls overlooking the city. There were six men in the room and they all had pistols tucked into their waistbands. Carlos introduced us only to his boss, Eduardo.

"I hear you have had quite an adventure," Eduardo said. "We have been waiting for you so we can all go out to dinner. Then I want to hear your story. Vamonos", he said, as he drained his drink and stood up.

Eduardo and three of his men got into one of the Suburbans. Captain Ron and I, and one other man, joined Carlos in the other. Carlos followed Eduardo across town to an expensive looking restaurant. Even though the restaurant was crowded, we were escorted immediately to a table. Eduardo said something to the waiter and rum and cokes were brought to our table.

"I ordered steaks for you," Eduardo said, looking at Captain Ron and me. "While we wait on our food, tell us what has happened to you."

They listened as we told them about the crash, our stay in

the jungle, and our time with Vicente.

"Vicente is a very rich and powerful man," Eduardo said. "His friends are some of the most powerful politicians in our country. Many of the cartels pay him millions of dollars every year that he shares with those politicians so they will not interfere with their drug business. Vicente can never have enough money. He owns many businesses and he makes money in other ways as well. He was not going to let you go until he collected as much money as he thought he could extort from Bryan. He was holding you for ransom."

"That explains why were at that apartment for two weeks." I said. "He knew that since we were in the country illegally, we would have to stay there or risk getting arrested."

"That is correct," Eduardo said. "I am sure that he had someone checking on you everyday to make sure you were still there. It could have been the owner of the restaurant below the apartment where he told you to eat. Bryan contacted me through a mutual friend. He wants me to help you get home. The best way to do that is for you to fly a planeload of pot back to the states. But not out of the jungle where you were headed before. Whoever made the decision for you to fly there made a very stupid decision. That is an extra 800 miles south of here and it is across the Andes Mountains. If your pickup had been on the Guajira Peninsula, you would not have needed extra fuel bladders, and you would have been home a month ago. Almost all of the Colombian pot that is flown to the states leaves out of the Guajira Peninsula. The Guajira is on the northern coast of Colombia about 200 miles east of here. All of the police there get paid to leave the planes alone so there is absolutely no risk to fly out of there. We can have a DC-6 flown up from Venezuela to the Guajira and you can fly it to the states from there. I can have the pot staged there within a week or so."

"I'm in," Captain Ron said and he looked over to me.

I ignored Captain Ron and looked at Eduardo as I remembered the promise I made if God would spare my life when the DC-6 crashed.

"Is there a way for me to catch a commercial flight to Miami?" I asked.

"I can make that happen," Eduardo said to me. "Captain Ron can fly the pot home in the DC-6 and he will make a paycheck so his time will not have been wasted. You, on the other hand will go home with empty pockets. Carlos can take you to the police station tomorrow to get a document saying your passport was stolen. Here, we call that a Denuncia. With that you can get a ticket out of here. You should be back in the states by tomorrow evening."

I felt a burden lift off my shoulders. After all this time, I was finally going home.

CHAPTER 102

A Lifetime Ago

THE DENUNCIA WAS A COUPLE OF typewritten pages with a picture of me stapled on the front. The police officer had placed his official stamp on the second page beside his signature. Carlos handed the officer a $100 bill, shook his hand, and we left.

I tried to read it when we got in the SUV but it was written in Spanish.

"I can't read this. What does it say?" I asked Carlos.

"It says your wallet and passport were in your man-bag," he said. "You were at a restaurant and left it on the table when you went to the restroom. While you were gone, someone stole it."

"The airport is not far," Carlos said. "It is only ten miles from here. It is a brand new airport that only opened last year in 1981. It is called the Ernesto Cortissoz International Airport and it was built to replace the old airport because it could not handle the big jets that land here now. Ah, there it is up ahead. We will go to the Avianca counter. Eduardo gave me the money for your ticket."

When we got to the Avianca counter, I told the agent that I needed a ticket to Miami. When she asked for my passport, I handed her the Denuncia.

"I lost my passport," I said. "I have this instead."

She looked at my picture and then at me. Then she read it.

"I have never seen one of these before," she said. "Let me call my supervisor."

Her supervisor read it and compared the picture to me.

"Bueno," he said. "Give the man a ticket."

"The flight from Cartagena to Miami has a change of planes in Jamaica," she said as she handed me my ticket and told me the gate number.

Carlos paid for the ticket and pointed to where I should head for the gate. I thanked him for all of his help. He shook my hand, wished me luck, and left.

* * *

I got a window seat on the right side of the plane. I was deep in thought as I watched the blue waters of the Caribbean Sea pass below me. It seemed like a lifetime ago when I last crossed this sea going in the other direction.

In fact it was.

I had learned a lot and my life would never be the same.

CHAPTER 103
Home Again

WHEN THE PLANE LANDED IN MIAMI, I didn't have to go to baggage claim. Everything I had I was carrying in a gym bag. There were a dozen lines for US citizens to check in through customs. The one I was in was moving fairly quickly. I watched how the agent I would soon be in front of did his job.

It was the same for everyone in the line in front of me. The agent was courteous and would only ask for the traveler's passport after he welcomed them back home to the States. He'd look at their passport to compare their face with the picture inside, enter their name into a computer, and stamp their passport.

He welcomed me back to the States as well before he asked for my passport.

"My passport was stolen," I said as I handed him the Denuncia. That's when I discovered that customs agents tend to get suspicious when you are entering the country after being overseas and you don't have a passport.

He looked at me like I was in the wrong line as he took the paperwork.

"Where is the rest of your luggage?" he asked as he glanced at the gym bag.

"It was stolen, too," I said. "This is all I have left."

He must have been bi-lingual because he read the Denuncia without any problem before he entered my name into his computer. Then he did a double take. His eyes got wide as he stared at the computer screen. I looked over to the screen to see what got his attention.

In big, bold, dark letters was a message. It read:

SUSPECTED SMUGGLER

He looked at me differently now as he picked up the phone in front of him and made a call. In seconds, two other agents joined us and invited me to come with them. One of them even carried my bag for me. They led me to a little room off to the side where we could have a private little chat.

While one started in with all the usual questions, the other dumped the contents of my bag onto a table and started a meticulous search of the meager contents. He picked up my half empty tube of toothpaste, took the cap off, and squeezed half of the toothpaste out onto a paper towel. After a visual inspection, and a smell test, he put the lid back on the tube and laid it aside. Evidently the toothpaste still looked and smelled like Crest.

He picked up the bag of 100% Arabica coffee that I had bought in the airport before I boarded the plane in Colombia. He pushed a 12-inch needle through the bag in several places to make sure there was nothing but coffee in the bag. Then it joined the toothpaste on the table. My dirty clothes didn't get stabbed or sniffed, but they did get a thorough inspection with his gloved hands. When he was satisfied that the coffee, toothpaste, and dirty clothes contained no contraband, he asked for my shoes.

"My shoes?" I asked.

"Yes, your shoes," he responded. "Is there anything in them you want to tell me about before I run them through an x-ray machine?"

After removing my shoes, I lifted up the liner inside the right one.

"Only a couple of $100 bills I hid in this one in case of an emergency," I said.

I showed him the bills before sticking them in my pocket and then handed him my shoes.

Satisfied that I wasn't smuggling any bales of pot inside my shoes, bag of coffee, or tube of toothpaste, they returned my belongings and let me go.

Using the two $100 bills, I rented a car and headed home.

* * *

Home was not the same as it was when I left three months ago. Keith was now living with his mother and Judy had moved out and filed for a divorce. The house was empty.

I was devastated, confused, and alone.

CHAPTER 104

The Sentence

AFTER TAKING A YEAR TO START emotional healing, I sold the house so I could move nearer to my sons and return to college once again. The last thing I carried out of the house was a box I was mailing to Pepito. It would be the first mail he had ever received. Inside the box was a Spanish-to-English dictionary, a small hand-held solar powered video game, a hand-crank powered flashlight, a picture of me with my sons, and a bag of Tootsie Rolls.

* * *

I almost graduated the following spring, but one month before I was to receive my diploma, marijuana, for the second time, kept me from getting my degree.

In the spring of 1983, a federal grand jury indicted twenty-one people involved in Operation Lemon Lot. On Friday the 13th in May 1983, in an organized effort involving police departments around the county, nineteen of those people were arrested.

Marcos Aguilara was sentenced to 60 years in prison and is still incarcerated.

Daryl Kirby was sentenced to 20 years but was released early.

John Taylor was sentenced to 30 years but was also released early.

Captain Ron was sentenced to 5 years and died of cancer before he was released.

Bryan and Striker eluded capture and successfully smuggled millions of dollars of marijuana into the States until they were finally arrested in 1986. Neither ever served any prison time.

I never heard what happened to DEA Agent Scott Jones or to Zeke. But unless they had some life-changing event, Jones probably couldn't wait to start his next Black Ops

Investigation, and Zeke probably went on being a thief.

* * *

Due to the enormous amount of evidence the government had against me, I pled guilty and threw myself at the mercy of the court in hopes of a more lenient sentence.

Before the judge sentenced me, he asked if I had anything to say.

"Your Honor," I began, "what I did was wrong. I could have died in that plane crash, but I promised God that if He let me live, I'd turn my life around. So when I got home, I quit the organization, got a full time job, went back to college, and started spending as much time as possible with my sons. God gave me another chance, and I guess today, I am asking you for one as well."

The judge looked at me, thought for a moment, and held up a huge stack of letters.

"I have never received so many letters on behalf of a defendant," he said. "These are all requests for leniency from your family, friends, pastors, supervisors, co-workers, and even your ex-wives. I could sentence you up to 15 years in prison, however, for some reason, I feel inclined to show you mercy. Don't make me regret my decision. You are hereby sentenced to two years in prison . . . *suspended*, 200 hours of community service, and two years of probation."

It took a few seconds for what he said to sink in. *Suspended?* I wasn't going to prison!

Relief flooded over me and tears of joy started to flow.

I jumped up and spun around in the air, raised a victory fist, and yelled, "YES!" before I regained my composure and turned to face the Judge once again. "Thank you, Your Honor, for your mercy today. You will not regret your decision."

* * *

I wrote several letters to the judge over the years letting him know when I finally got that elusive college degree, became a grandfather, got remarried to a wonderful Christian woman, and started going on mission trips. I wanted him to know he didn't have to regret his decision that day and hoped that my successful rehabilitation would encourage him to give some other defendant another chance.

EPILOGUE

PEOPLE HAVE ASKED ME WHY I wanted to share this story.

The answer is simply because I felt compelled to in hopes it might help someone out there know that they, too, can have a second chance . . . or a third . . . or a fourth . . . or as many as they need, because God will never give up on them.

If that someone is you, ask for His help. Life doesn't have to feel like a sentence. It can be an exciting adventure.

I *promise.*

NOTES

1) Prologue, Picture of DC-6, DC-6 Operation Manual, Figure 1-Exterior View, (March 15, 1948), Douglas Aircraft Co., Inc., Santa Monica, Calif., USA.

2) Chapter 52, Breffort, D. (2006). Lockheed Constellation: From Excalibur to Starliner Civilian and Military Variants. Paris: Histoire and Collections.

3) Chapter 68, Wikipedia. (2013, December 5). Pilot Licensing and Certification. Retrieved January 25,2014, from Wikipedia: http://en.wikipedia.org/wiki/Pilot_licensing_and_certification..

4) Chapter 68, Wikipedia. (2014, January 13). Airline Transport Pilot License. Retrieved January 25, 2014, from Wikipedia: http://en.wikipedia.org/wiki/Airline_Transport_Pilot_Licence..

5) Chapter 72, Wikipedia. (2013, November 24). Michael Manley. Retrieved January 25, 2014, from Wikipedia: http://en.wikipedia.org/wiki/Michael Manley.

6) Chapter 80, Picture, (August 3, 2015), ZS-MUL-IMG_3436(grey).jpg, Malcolm Reid, Used by permission.

7) Chapter 80, Picture, DC-6 Operation Manual, Figure 24 – Main Instrument Panel, (March 21, 1947), Douglas Aircraft Co., Inc., Santa Monica, Calif, USA.

8) Chapter 80, DC-6 Operation Manual, Section V, Recommended Operating Procedures, (March 21, 1947), Douglas Aircraft Co., Inc., Santa Monica, Calif, USA.

9) Chapter 99, United Nations Regional Information Centre for Western Europe. (June 7, 2015). The Guerrilla Groups in Colombia. Retrieved June 7, 2015, from http://www.unric.org.

10) Map, Central Intelligence Agency, (2002), Retrieved June 17, 2015, from Library of Congress Geography and Map Division, http://hdl.loc.gov/loc.gmd/g4800.ct002224.

###

ACKNOWLEDGMENTS

There are many friends and family members who encouraged me during the two years it took me to write this book, and helped proofread it when I thought I was done. It would be impossible to name them all, but to not acknowledge these would be unfair.

Thanks, Ron, for your suggestions on the order of events in the book, and for knowing that the Florida Gators don't play the Georgia Bulldogs in Gainesville. Any of their fans reading the book would have called me out on that error.

Thanks, Cheryl, for all the effort you put into finding missing words, typos, and especially for catching the problem with the secret phone code. My ignorance would have been blatant if that error had remained for my readers to find.

I also owe a big Thank You to Angela Blackman, Beth, Bill Bell, Bridgett Hargrave, Bryan Morgan, Darius Lewis, Daryl Kirby, John Taylor, Judy Foster, Ray Foley, Renee Thompson, Ron White, Sandi, Scott Jones, and Tom Cleveland who volunteered the use of their names for some of the characters in the book.

And a great big thanks to my editor, Chris, who I am now privileged to also call my friend. With his knowledge, help and guidance, this book not only became a reality, it came alive.

Thanks to all of you for helping me achieve one of my lifetime goals.

ABOUT THE AUTHOR

Rufus Hylton lives in Florida where he enjoys writing, fishing, exploring, photography, and spending time with family and friends. The Smuggler's Promise is his first book, but definitely not his last. Follow him on Facebook, Twitter and his website, www.RufusHylton.com